PRAISE FOR RIVERBEND AND *BAGHDAD BURNING*

"Riverbend is a thoughtful writer whose articulate, even poetic, prose packs an emotional punch while exhibiting an eye for detail."
—New York Times

"The importance of Riverbend's breathless, unedited, electronic first draft of history is clear: She is more of an expert on what it's like to be young, female and Iraqi than the best journalist could ever hope to be." **—The Washington Post**

"Passionate, frustrated, sarcastic, and sometimes hopeful. . . . Riverbend is most compelling when she gives cultural object lessons on everything from the changing status of Iraqi women to Ramadan, the Iraqi educational system, the significance of date palms and the details of morning rituals. The blog . . . offers quick takes on events from a perspective too often overlooked, ignored, or suppressed."
—Publishers Weekly

"In a voice that grips with drama and cuts to core with humor, Riverbend reports the personal side of war as no other account I know of does. Anyone who cares about the war in Iraq must read this book."
—Susan Sarandon

"I've learned more about the occupation of Iraq from Riverbend's blog than from just about any other news source. This 24-year-old Baghdad woman writes about everything from her house-proud neighbor, 'the Martha Stewart of Iraq,' to the rising toll of kidnappings, murders, and attacks on unveiled women by the religious fanatics whose empowerment is one of the many unintended consequences of the American invasion. With spiritedness and even humor, she writes about daily life under siege and families under incredible stress. Every American should read this book." **—Katha Pollitt**

"Her commanding gift for observation, her intelligence and her extraordinary language skills make her account of the life of an ordinary Iraqi family, which has been published in book form as Baghdad Burning, one of the most uniquely critical documents of life in this abused country under the conditions of the war and the US military occupation."
—from the Citation for the Lettre Ulysses Award for the Art of Reportage 2005

"[Riverbend] comments on everything from the financing of reconstruction and the shenanigans at Halliburton to the feasibility of a Kurdish state and the impact of Islamic Shari'a law on women. She also charts an ordinary life—ordinary, that is, in decidedly unordinary circumstances. . . . Feisty and learned: first rate reading for any American who suspects that Fox News may not be telling the whole story."

—*Kirkus Reviews*

"[T]he blog attains its highest value as a unique voice that reveals to us the thoughts, reflections, personal life, politics and history of Iraq. . . . What you get from [Riverbend] are candid, but cogently written, thoughts that come from her experience. She is not a theorist; she is a person trapped in a country that became a pawn in a geo-political power grab. Like most of us, she is an individual who is powerless to change the course of history, but she can trenchantly observe its passage."

—**BUZZFLASH** Reviews

"Her writing makes you feel at home in her world: you feel outraged when she describes the farcical "reconstruction efforts," you fret when her cousin goes missing, you worry when she hasn't posted in a while. . . . This document should be preserved as a part of history and shared with the less Internet-savvy. I wish it were required reading for every American."

—*BUST* Magazine

"Her descriptions of normal life in Iraq, including holiday customs and even recipes, extended families, and city neighborhoods, add a dimension to the war coverage that Western journalists have largely missed."

—*Library Journal* (starred review)

"In English that would put many Americans to shame, she chronicles daily life under the occupation, writing about water and electricity shortages with humor and exasperation, writing about violence with deep feeling. . . . Riverbend's take on politics is so perceptive that readers may wonder if she is actually a Beltway antiwar activist—although such readers should also question their assumption that an Iraqi couldn't write this well or be so well informed. But the greatest accomplishment of this intriguing book lies in its essential ordinariness. Riverbend is bright and opinionated, true, but like all voices of dissent worth remembering, she provides an urgent reminder that, whichever governments we struggle under, we are all the same."

—*Booklist* (featured review)

"All is shrouded in the fog of war, and Riverbend's need to make sense of the unrelenting savagery of life in harm's way is poignant, touching, and universally compelling."—*World Literature in Review*

"A cross between an underground manifesto and a polished cultural history. . . . A highly educated bilingual Muslim woman with a deep hunger for media and plenty of time to engage with it, Riverbend infuses her writing with sophisticated analysis. . . . With its blend if first-person mouthing off and spirited documentary style, Baghdad Burning offers fair and balanced coverage from inside one of the most rapidly changing—and poorly understood—regions in the world."   —*Time Out New York*

"Wedged between cynical rants . . . are posts that calmly enrich our understanding of what the war was like for Iraqis, both during and after."
—*San Francisco Chronicle*

< BAGHDAD BURNING II
MORE GIRL BLOG FROM IRAQ >

BY RIVERBEND

Introduction by
James Ridgeway and Jean Casella

The Feminist Press
at the City University of New York
New York

Published by the Feminist Press at the City University of New York
The Graduate Center
365 Fifth Avenue
New York, NY 10016
www.feministpress.org

First Feminist Press edition, 2006.
09 08 07 06   9 8 7 6 5 4 3 2 1

The Library of Congress has cataloged the first volume as follows:

Riverbend.
    Baghdad burning : girl blog from Iraq / by Riverbend ; foreword by Ahdaf Souief ; introduction by James Ridgeway.— 1st Feminist Press ed.
        p. cm.
    ISBN 1-55861-489-3 (pbk. : alk. paper)
    1. Iraq War, 2003—Weblogs. 2. Iraq War, 2003—Personal narratives, Iraqi. 3. Insurgency—Iraq—Weblogs. 4. Riverbend—Weblogs. 5. Riverbend—Diaries. I. Title.
    DS79.76.R587 2005
    956.7044'3'092—dc22
                                    2005000928

ISBN-13: 978-1-55861-529-8 (pbk.)
ISBN-10: 1-55861-529-6 (pbk.)

Text design and composition by Lisa Force
Printed in Canada by Transcontinental Printing

Introduction

When Riverbend began writing her blog, "Baghdad Burning," in August 2003, she introduced herself to her readers in just a few words: "A little bit about myself: I'm female, Iraqi, and 24. I survived the war. That's all you need to know. It's all that matters these days anyway." From later postings, readers would learn that she belonged to a middle-class Baghdad family that was about half Shia and half Sunni; that she was a practicing Muslim; that she had been educated, in part, abroad; that she was a computer programmer ("yes, yes . . . a geek") who had lost her job after the war began.

In that first posting, she also wrote, "I never thought I'd start my own weblog . . . All I could think, every time I wanted to start one was 'but who will read it?'" Just under three years later, Riverbend has her answer: Tens of thousands of people in countries around the world regularly read her "Girl Blog from Iraq." Thousands more have read the first year of her postings in book form, in the volume compiled and published in the spring of 2004 by the Feminist Press. A British edition from Marion Boyars helped to make the book available throughout the English-speaking world, and translations have been published or undertaken in Estonia, Austria, Greece, Italy, Japan, Norway, the Netherlands, and Spain, with several more likely in the future. Riverbend's blog has also formed the basis of dramatic productions in New York City and Portland, Maine, and at the Edinburgh Fringe Festival; German and Spanish theater pieces are planned as well. In the fall of 2005, the book *Baghdad Burning* received third prize from the international Lettre Ulysses Award for the Art of Reportage. In the spring of 2006, it was shortlisted for a Freedom of Expression Award from the Index on Censorship, and longlisted for the Samuel Johnson Prize—the UK's most prestigious and lucrative nonfiction book award—along with works by such renowned British writers as Alan Bennett, Tony Judt, and A.N. Wilson.

Anyone who has read Riverbend's work will understand why it has received such widespread attention. This young Iraqi woman is not only intelligent and remarkably well-informed about events in her own country and around the world; she is also astute at separating rhetoric from reality, and relentless in speaking truth to power. Whether she is parsing a speech by Donald Rumsfeld or deconstructing the new Iraqi constitution, nothing gets past Riverbend.

Riverbend's readers have come to rely upon her to provide discerning analysis of ever-changing events in Iraq. But even more, they turn to her as a rare source of information and insight on how these events affect the civilian population. Riverbend makes it impossible to forget that behind the headlines—the political posturing, the daily reports of chaos and violence, and even the disturbing stories of Westerners killed or kidnapped—are millions of ordinary Iraqi families, struggling simply to live their lives (and sometimes losing them). It is impossible for Riverbend to describe all of these lives. But over nearly three years, she has vividly described her own life and the lives of others in her neighborhood, her city, and elsewhere in her brutalized country. Readers may think of her as they read the dispassionate news accounts and numbing statistics. For many, she has become the human face of the war and occupation.

Although she is consistently modest in estimating her own significance, Riverbend understands that she and other Iraqi bloggers fill an essential gap left by other media. In an online interview with Al-Jazeera in April 2006, she explains her reasons for writing.

While I began blogging as a way to vent frustrations and fears about the instability and insecurity, I continue to blog because

I feel that the media covers the situation in my country in a very general way. Many articles or reports don't even begin to touch the daily reality Iraqis face. . . . Real Iraqis, the people currently suffering under a lack of security and a shortage of the most basic necessities like electricity and water, seem to have faded to the background.[1]

Detailed coverage has only grown more and more rare in the years since the occupation began. Even those journalists who resist the tendency to ignore or devalue Iraqi lives have found their work increasingly difficult and dangerous to carry out. According to the Committee to Protect Journalists, 72 journalists had been killed in Iraq by May of 2006—half of them intentionally murdered. An additional 34 had been kidnapped.[2] The majority of the journalists who lost their lives, as well as nearly all of the two-dozen support workers killed, were Iraqis, many of them working for foreign news organizations. (Riverbend memorializes one of these support workers, the translator for kidnapped American journalist Jill Carroll, in her posting on January 12, 2006.)

Many foreign journalists working in Iraq today have spoken of a "bunker mentality": Concerns for personal safety, they say, keep them inside secure compounds or embedded with Coalition forces, more distant than ever from opportunities to talk with Iraqi civilians. In a September 2004 email that was widely circulated on the web, *Wall Street Journal* correspondent Farnaz Fassihi describes working conditions in Iraq.

Being a foreign correspondent in Baghdad these days is like being under virtual house arrest. . . . I avoid going to people's homes and never walk in the streets. I can't go grocery shopping any more, can't eat in restaurants, can't strike a conversation with strangers, can't look for stories, can't drive in anything but a full armored car, can't go to scenes of breaking news, can't be stuck in traffic, can't speak English outside, can't take a road trip, can't say I'm an American, can't linger at checkpoints, can't be curious about what people are saying, doing, feeling. And can't and can't.[3]

The lack of media attention to the lives of ordinary Iraqis has far-reaching consequences, as the exiled Iraqi novelist Najem Wali describes in "Iraq Stories" (published in the excellent online magazine *Words Without Borders*).

> Journalists who visit Iraq hear many stories, yet they are prevent-ed from recording the majority of them because they must chase after the hot story, the quick journalistic news piece. . . . It is not strange therefore that people in the world today, especially in the United States, know only the "hot" stories in the daily news. And so today, when Iraqi people show up in the news, it is not as human beings who think and love and hate and expe-rience joy and sadness like the rest of humanity.[4]

Dehumanization of the "enemy" is a prerequisite for war—just as it is for terrorism and for torture—and Riverbend's work stands as a vital antidote to dehumanization. Writing from her own home, she brings the war into homes around the world. As one reads Riverbend, the distance between Baghdad and New York or Washington—or Omaha, or Denver, or London, or Rome—diminishes. When George W. Bush declares in a speech, "We either deal with terrorism and this extremism abroad, or we deal with it when it comes to us," Riverbend responds, "Don't Americans realize that 'abroad' is a country full of people—men, women and children who are dying hourly? 'Abroad' is home for millions of us. It's the place we were raised and the place we hope to raise our chil-dren—your field of war and terror" (July 1, 2005).

Riverbend provides a human perspective not only to the war and the occupation in general, but on specific events and developments in Iraq. The bloody offensive against Fallujah in November 2004 was depicted by the U.S. government as an operation to root out insurgents and "foreign fighters" (including those purportedly holed up at a local hospital, which was one of the first sites to be attacked). Some media outlets disputed these official accounts by reporting large numbers of civilian deaths, but they did so largely in terms of facts and figures. In contrast, Riverbend recounts the wrenching story of a young mother, Umm Ahmed, who had fled the approaching offensive, leaving her husband and eldest son behind. She wonders how the traumatized young woman will spend "the next couple of agonizing days, waiting for word from her son and husband." Riverbend has herself experienced such worry and fear, the "feeling of restlessness that gnaws away inside of you, leaving you feeling exhausted and agitated all at once. It's a thousand pessimistic voices whispering stories of death and destruction in your head" (November 1, 2004).

A gifted writer as well as a natural storyteller, Riverbend enriches her firsthand experiences with an exquisite sense of irony and a consummate appreciation of the absurdities of war in general, and the current situation in Iraq in particular. A month before the first round of much-touted Iraqi elections, she provides an entertaining account of a thirteen-hour wait to fill the family car with gasoline (half of which is subsequently siphoned out to power the neighborhood generator). "People are wondering," she remarks, "how America and gang (i.e. Iyad Allawi, etc.) are going to implement democracy in all of this chaos when they can't seem to get the gasoline flowing in a country that virtually swims in oil" (December 12, 2004).

In addition to her own stories and commentary, Riverbend provides dispatches from the Iraqi "street," where people often turn to word-of-mouth rumors or inventive theories in an effort to make sense of their disordered lives. In her own neighborhood, a prime source of information is the local grocer. "I feel like I have my finger on the throbbing pulse of the Iraqi political situation every time I visit Abu Ammar," she writes. "You can often tell just how things are going in the country from the produce available at his stand." A lack of tomatoes, for example, means the roads to Basra are closed, while an absence of citrus fruits signals trouble in Diyala province (February 18, 2005).

Riverbend's writing is often darkly comic. Her 2004 Christmas list includes "running water, landmine detectors, blast-proof windows"—and also "scented candles" because "it shows you care—but you're also practical." But neither her humor nor her toughness and self-possession can entirely obscure her own personal suffering. Only 26 years old (a fact that is easy to forget), this young woman mourns the destruction of her country, her people, and her own life. At times, this grief spills out, unmediated, in her writing. And along with the grief, there is anger. When the U.S. government announced that it had finally given up its search for weapons of mass destruction in Iraq, Riverbend writes:

"It's like having a loved one sentenced to death for a crime they didn't commit—having your country burned and bombed beyond recognition, almost. Then, after two years of grieving for the lost people, and mourning the lost sovereignty, we're told we were innocent of harboring those weapons. We were never a threat to America." She ends her entry by declaring, "Congratulations Bush—we are a threat now" (January 15, 2005). Even for a resilient and worldly young woman, the past three years have brought with them a growing sense of exhaustion and frustration. Yet her blog itself—her determination to continue speaking to the wide world outside her besieged city—testifies to her endurance and defiance.

BLOGGING THE WAR

The rare balance that Riverbend maintains between personal emotions and experiences, on one side, and objective observations and analysis, on the other, adds strength and immediacy to her writing. In her interview with Al-Jazeera, she remarks that this combination is intrinsic to blogging itself.

> Bloggers are not exactly journalists, which is a mistake many people make. They expect us to be dispassionate and unemotional about topics such as occupation and war, etc. That objective lack of emotion is impossible because a blog in itself stems from passion—the need to sit hours at one's computer, slouched over the keyboard, trying to communicate ideas, thoughts, fears and frustrations to the world.[5]

Though few bloggers have communicated their ideas and feelings as fluently and effectively as Riverbend, blogs in general have become an increasingly important source of firsthand information from Iraq. As of May 2006, the web site Iraq Blog Count lists 203 blogs by Iraqis (including some émigrés), with new blogs appearing every month. (Blogs by foreign soldiers in Iraq, listed separately on the site, number more than twenty.)[6]

"Baghdad Burning" is by most estimates the fifth Iraqi blog to be launched. The first, the mother of all Iraqi blogs, was "Where is Raed?"

by Salam Pax, who began blogging before the U.S. invasion in late 2002. Riverbend credits Salam Pax with helping her get started by having her "guest blog" on his site. As Salam Pax's blog became internationally known, many on the Internet suggested that he was in fact a Western shill and his blog a hoax—until he was tracked down by the *Guardian*, for whom he began writing a column.[7] Riverbend, who for her own safety remains anonymous to all but her family and close friends, continues to face similar accusations. The sources of such denunciations seem more political than empirical. Riverbend, along with the majority of Iraqi bloggers, firmly opposes the U.S. occupation. As these bloggers become a media force to be reckoned with—a source of alternative news and perspectives for more and more readers around the world—efforts to attack and "debunk" them have increased as well. Riverbend responded to these attacks in her recent interview with Al-Jazeera. Her interviewer asked: "Some of your detractors online have said you are unabashedly biased and anti-American and that you lament the ousting of the previous government. Is that true?" Riverbend replied:

> Unabashedly biased towards what? Iraq? One thing that bothers me is that many people equate being anti-occupation with anti-American. I am not anti-American—I know many wonderful Americans and correspond and communicate with them regularly. I am, however, anti-occupation. I don't wish for the "days of Saddam," if that's what you're asking. I am, however, completely against the presence of foreign troops in Iraq.[8]

Some of Riverbend's critics have even sought to "expose" her, speculating about her identity in a quest to attack her credibility. For all Iraqi bloggers, writing is an act of courage that involves some personal risk. Since Riverbend has one of the highest profiles of any Iraqi blogger today, her success makes her a target. She also faces risks not only as a critic of the occupation and of successive "puppet" governments, but as an outspoken young woman in a nation increasingly ruled by the dictates of Islamist fundamentalism, which she does not hesitate to attack.

In her book *On Shifting Ground: Muslim Women in the Global Era* (The Feminist Press), Fereshteh Nouraie-Simone explores the special significance blogging holds for young women in oppressive patriarchal societies. Nouraie-Simone is writing about the explosion of female bloggers in contemporary Iran—a country that, in terms of social restrictions, Iraq is increasingly coming to resemble.

> For educated young Iranian women, cyberspace is a liberating territory of one's own—a place to resist a traditionally imposed subordinate identity while providing a break from pervasive Islamic restrictions in public physical space. . . . The absence of the physical body in electronic space and the anonymity this offers have a liberating effect. . . . Iranian female bloggers share personal experiences, discuss issues, express feelings of outrage and frustration, and reflect on what is not allowed or tolerated in controlled Islamic physical space. They have claimed cyberspace for their expressions of individuality and desire for freedom.[9]

WOMEN IN THE NEW IRAQ

While the lives of all Iraqis have been transformed by the conflict, the lives of educated and politically secular women like Riverbend face particular constraints. Before the war began, Riverbend worked beside male colleagues and earned the same pay. "It was tedious," she says in one of her first posts, "it was back-breaking, it was geeky and it was . . . wonderful." In June 2003, after the war officially ended, she returned to the half-destroyed office where she had once worked (accompanied, as was now necessary, by two male relatives), only to be told "that females weren't welcome right now—especially females who 'couldn't be protected.'" She writes: "I cried bitterly all the way home—cried for my job, cried for my future and cried for the torn streets, damaged buildings and crumbling people." Riverbend tells her readers, "The story of how I lost my job isn't unique. It has actually become very common—despondently, depressingly, unbearably common"—and only destined, she predicts, to become more common still.

By the time the postings in this volume begin, Riverbend's fears have proven well-founded, with Islamist fundamentalism exerting a growing influence on women's daily lives. She describes a visit to a government ministry, where she is warned to "dress appropriately next time you come here." She writes, "No one could talk that way before the war and if they did, you didn't have to listen. You could answer back. Now, you only answer back and make it an issue if you have some sort of death wish or just really, really like trouble" (February 12, 2005).

The final draft of Iraq's new Constitution, approved in the fall of 2005, states clearly that "Islam is the official religion of the state and is a basic source of legislation," and that "No law can be passed that contradicts the undisputed rules of Islam."[10] As Riverbend points out, in her detailed analysis of the Constitution, "the problem is with the dozens of interpretations of Islamic rules and principles. . . . Who will decide which religious rules and principles are the ones that shouldn't be contradicted by the constitution?" (September 17, 2005).

Various Muslim feminists, including 2003 Nobel Peace Prize winner Shirin Ebadi, have argued convincingly that Islamic law can be deemed to support rather than undermine women's rights; it is all a matter of interpretation. But the process of creating the Iraqi Constitution itself suggested that women's rights were not likely to fare well in the new Iraq. According to an account in *Foreign Affairs*, women—and especially secular women—were excluded from the drafting process: Of the 55 members of the constitutional committee, only eight were women, and five of these were religious Shia. The committee "spent months arguing over whether Islam would be *the* source of legislation for the country (as the religious parties wanted) or *a* source (a compromise sought by the Kurds and other secularists)." When conservative Shia leaders threatened a walkout, the U.S. ambassador intervened, and "to gain concessions in other areas, he supported provisions that strengthened Islam's influence."[11] While the final draft of the Constitution did set aside 25 percent of the seats in the National Assembly for women, many of these women would represent the religious parties that held a legislative majority.

By most accounts, including Riverbend's own, conditions for women in postwar Iraq have rapidly grown quite grim. Less than six months after the invasion, Human Rights Watch released a report documenting a sharp rise in violence against women. According to the report, "Women and girls in Baghdad told Human Rights Watch that the insecurity and fear of sexual violence or abduction is keeping them in their homes, out of schools, and away from work and looking for employment." The report found that neither Iraqi police nor Coalition forces reacted effectively to this violence, "The insecurity plaguing Baghdad and other Iraqi cities has a distinct and debilitating impact on the daily lives of women and girls, preventing them from participating in public life at a crucial time in their country's history."[12]

A year and a half later, in its summary of conditions in Iraq during 2004, Amnesty International stated: "Women and girls continued to be harassed, injured and killed by armed groups and individuals, relatives, and members of the US-led forces. Many women lived under constant fear of being beaten, abducted, raped or murdered. . . . Several women political leaders were targeted in politically motivated attacks, and campaigners for women's rights were threatened."[13] The international women's human rights organization MADRE concurred with this assessment, and also cited a sharp rise in so-called honor killings, in which "rape survivors and women who violate conservative social mores are murdered by male family members to restore the family's 'honor.'" MADRE reported collaborating with an Iraqi women's group to create an "underground railroad" for women targeted for honor killings. MADRE's analysis concludes, "Caught in the social void created by the overthrow of the Ba'ath regime, many Iraqi women are fighting simultaneously against the US occupation and the rising tide of Islamic fundamentalism."[14]

Yanar Mohammed, of the Iraqi Organization of Women's Freedom, paints a personal and vivid picture of the situation on the ground:

The change happened overnight after the sudden invasion of Iraq. The US occupation authorities ousted the regime and dismantled all former security and defense institutions. Consequently, the system fell apart with no substitution, which gave rise to looting and women being abducted and trafficked to surrounding countries, where the borders were open for travelers with no serious inspection. . . . Until this very day, the streets are insecure, although some new elements have been added. Militias of religious fundamentalist parties roam around the city streets harassing women who do not wear the veil and Islamic dress. There were many killings of women professors and officials by these mobs, part of whom are in the government now. In the southern cities, pro-Iran Islamist groups have full control on the political scene. This has changed the streets into no-women zones where even the Christians do not dare to walk unveiled. Because of the failure of the public sector, most women lost their jobs and stayed without income for two years, which made them revert to a tribal scene where they were economically protected. Unemployment among women is still at a high rate of 90% and no social insurance programs have been put in place. . . . [The situation] has forced women to quit work and keep their daughters home, away from school. This concern also includes the misogynist attacks on women by the new Islamist fundamentalist resistance, which has brought Taliban-like methods in dealing with women.[15]

Riverbend herself reports that, amid the chaos and violence of present-day Iraq, women's rights have ceased to be a "primary concern," even for those who once supported them: "People actually laugh when someone brings up the topic. 'Let's keep Iraq united first . . . ' is often the response when I comment about the prospect of Iranian-style Sharia. Rights and freedoms have become minor concerns compared to the possibility of civil war, the reality of ethnic displacement and cleansing, and the daily certainty of bloodshed and death" (October 3, 2005).

GUN-BARREL DEMOCRACY

In nearly three years of postings, Riverbend's blog traces the road leading to the "daily certainty of bloodshed and death" that characterizes life in present-day Iraq. She began writing her blog just three months after George W. Bush declared the "mission accomplished" in Iraq. The war, he said, was over—though in fact, it had just begun. The first year of Riverbend's postings, collected in the first *Baghdad Burning* book, bore witness to the destruction the war had wrought on an already devastated nation.

Although Iraq, prior to the U.S. invasion, stood as one of the most modern, secular, and "Westernized" states in the Arab world, the Iraqi population had suffered under Saddam Hussein's brutally repressive regime for nearly 24 years. In the 1980s, an eight-year war with Iran (in which the United States provided support to Saddam) claimed a million lives and bankrupted both countries. The 1991 Persian Gulf War left much of Iraq's infrastructure in ruins, and that war and subsequent sanctions, combined with Saddam's corruption and intransigence, led to the deaths of hundreds of thousands of civilians—including, by reliable estimate, as many as 500,000 children under the age of five.[16]

After the first 18 months of the current conflict—through the fall of 2004, when the first volume of *Baghdad Burning* ends—estimates of civilian deaths ran as low as 15,000 and as high as 100,000.[17] Iraq's infrastructure remained badly damaged, with the electrical grid still operating at below pre-war levels, sewage treatment and safe drinking water still lacking in many parts of the country, schools and hospitals severely compromised, and oil production at a fraction of its full capacity. "Rebuilding" efforts were from the start slow and inadequate, and often profited U.S. companies more than they did Iraqis.

A September 2004 report from the Open Society Institute's Iraq Revenue Watch project assessed the performance of the Coalition Provisional Authority (CPA), which had assumed power in Iraq immediately after the war, under the leadership of Paul Bremer. The report found that the CPA had "failed to stop the misuse and waste of money that belonged to the Iraqi people and American taxpayers." Audits showed that "of $1.5 billion in contracts, the CPA awarded U.S. firms 74 percent of the value of all contracts paid for with Iraqi funds. Together with its British allies, U.S. and U.K. companies received 85 percent of the value of all such contracts. Iraqi firms, by contrast, received just 2 percent of the value of contracts paid for with Iraqi funds." The report also found that "60 percent of the value of all contracts paid with Iraqi funds went to Halliburton subsidiary Kellogg, Brown & Root (KBR)—the same company that Pentagon auditors in December 2003 found had overcharged the U.S. government as much as $61 million for fuel imports into Iraq."[18]

Riverbend's first volume of postings witnessed the official handover of Iraqi "sovereignty" in June 2004 to the Coalition-backed Iraqi Interim Government, which was still in power at the start of this second volume. Referred to by Riverbend as the "Vichy government," the Interim Government had chosen as its prime minister Iyad Allawi, a secular Shia and a former Ba'athist who had long lived in the West, and was widely known to have been an asset for both the CIA and British intelligence. His main advantage, according to the BBC, was "being equally mistrusted by everyone in Iraq's multifarious population."[19] Allawi, who from the start declared his determination to crush the Iraqi insurgency, quickly stirred controversy by creating a domestic spying agency, giving himself the power to declare martial law, and restricting press freedoms, which included shutting down Al-Jazeera. In November 2004, Riverbend writes about life under Allawi's declared State of Emergency: "So what does an 'Emergency State' signify for Iraqis? Basically, it means we are now *officially* more prone to being detained, raided, and just generally abused by our new Iraqi forces and American ones." The 10 p.m. curfew, she says, "hasn't really made an impact because people have stopped leaving their houses after dark anyway" (November 10, 2004).

The Iraqi Interim Government was replaced by the Iraqi Transitional Government after the first round of Iraqi legislative elections, held in January 2005. In the run-up to the elections, Riverbend reports that most people she knows have decided not to take part, out of fear for their safety and "a sense that nothing is going to be achieved anyway."

> The lists are more or less composed of people affiliated with the very same political parties whose leaders rode in on American tanks. Then you have a handful of tribal sheikhs. Yes— tribal sheikhs. Our country is going to be led by members of religious parties and tribal sheikhs—can anyone say Afghanistan? . . . So basically, this war helped us make a transition from a secular country being run by a dictator to a chaotic country being run by a group of religious clerics. (December 12, 2004)

The legitimacy of the elections was undermined by the vast disparities in voter turnout: Sunni leaders had called for a postponement and then a boycott, and high levels of insurgent violence at polling places were reported in Sunni areas. The largest Sunni party won only 2 percent of the vote—vastly disproportionate to the approximately 20 percent of Sunnis in the Iraqi population. The clear winner, the United Iraqi Alliance (UIA), won 140 of the 275 seats in the new National Assembly. The UIA is a coalition of several religious Shia parties, including the two largest, the Supreme Council for the Islamic Revolution in Iraq (SCIRI) and the Da'awa Party. Riverbend refers to these groups as "Iranian inclined," and while the extent of their direct ties to Iran is subject to debate, they share a religious and political vision with the Islamic Republic. The UIA had the tacit support of Grand Ayatollah Ali al-Sistani, the Iranian-born cleric who as a young man had moved to Najaf, Iraq, a prime Shia holy site. He is the senior religious leader of Shia Islam, widely considered the most politically powerful figure in postwar Iraq.

Riverbend's clear aversion to Sistani and to the religious Shia political parties has less to do with any sectarian (or, as some have charged, Ba'athist) loyalties than with her well-grounded fears of what it will mean to live in a nation effectively "run by a group of religious clerics." She also objects to the fact that, in their enthusiasm to overthrow Saddam and assume power in Iraq, these parties supported the invasion by Coalition forces—thus her assertion that their "leaders rode in on American tanks."

Riverbend and other secular Iraqis face a difficult reality: About 60 percent of Iraq's population is made up of Shia, many of them quite religious. Thus, even truly democratic elections are bound to lead to a Shia-dominated government, and also likely, a religious state. But as Riverbend—and many others—argue, real democracy cannot be practiced under occupation. The dangerous and chaotic situation in Iraq only foments sectariansim and religioius extremism, leaving moderate Iraqis of all religious persuasions voiceless—if they remain in Iraq at all. After a half-dozen college professors are murdered, presumably by religious extremists, Riverbend writes: "Whoever is behind the assassinations, Iraq is quickly losing its educated people. More and more doctors and professors are moving to leave the country. The problem with this situation is not just major brain drain—it's the fact that this diminishing educated class is also Iraq's secular class" (November 25, 2005).

After a long and contentious process, the Iraqi Transitional Government produced the new Iraqi Constitution, approved by referendum in October 2005. A second round of Iraqi parliamentary elections, in December 2005, produced what is meant to be a permanent government. Riverbend predicted correctly that more people would participate this time around, "not because Iraqis suddenly believe in American-imposed democracy under occupation, but because the situation this last year has been intolerable" (December 15, 2005). Turnout was indeed high, about 70 percent, and included many more Sunnis than the January elections, though a group of Sunni and secular parties alleged that fraud, intimidation, and violence were far more widespread than reported. Two new Sunni parties won, between them, 55 seats in parliament. The UIA was once again the overall winner, with 128 seats. Due to internal disputes, it would take the newly elected assembly months to form a government and choose a new prime minister and cabinet, and even longer to fill key cabinet posts. Within months of the elections, violence in Iraq exploded to new levels, disposing of the Bush Administration's contention that elections would bring peace and stability to Iraq.

THE BALKANIZATION OF IRAQ

In the course of writing her blog, Riverbend repeatedly decries her country's loss of sovereignty to a foreign occupation and its "puppets," and laments its transformation into a religious state. By the fall of 2005, she also worries that it may soon cease to be a country at all. In her analysis of the new Iraqi Constitution, she is troubled by the inclusion of what she calls a "Roadmap to Divide Iraq"—provisions for the transfer of power from the central, national government to largely autonomous regional governments (like the one already established in Kurdistan) if the regions' residents so choose. She writes: "So here's a riddle: what do you call a region with its own constitution, its own government, its own regional guard and possibly its own language? It's quite simple—you call it a country."

What is described as "decentralization" or "federalism" would, in practice, lead inevitably to divisions along sectarian lines, with separate Shia, Sunni, and Kurdish areas. Considering this possibility, Riverbend writes, "Federalism is ok when a country is stable. . . . In present-day Iraq it promises to be catastrophic. It will literally divide the country and increase instability. This is especially true with the kind of federalism they want to practice in Iraq. Federalism based on geography is acceptable, but federalism based on ethnicity and sect? Why not simply declare civil war and get it over with?" (September 23, 2005).

Some critics have pointed out that such a breakup of centralized power stood to help Western oil companies recover control over Iraq's valuable oil and gas resources— lost decades earlier due to the rise of the Organization of Petroleum Exporting Countries (OPEC) and Saddam's nationalization of the petroleum industry. Regional governments would likely turn to U.S. and British companies as partners in rebuilding and operating the industry. The lucrative oil fields of the south, as well as critical access to the Persian Gulf, moreover, lie in Shia-dominated areas.[20]

By the spring of 2006, a number of Western leaders were talking openly of a "three-state solution" to the problem of "intercommunal violence."[21] Riverbend takes a very different position, insisting that the violence between various religious and ethnic groups in Iraq is spurred and sustained by the occupation.[22] Most Iraqis, she said, did not want to see their nation divided. An ABC News poll of Iraqi civilians in the fall of 2005 seemed to support her views: Two-thirds opposed the continuing presence of Coalition troops in their country; and a majority of both Sunnis and Shia still favored a unified country.[23] Riverbend repeatedly asserts that, under the occupation, Iraqis were being forced to choose sides, and to identify themselves on sectarian grounds even if they had no wish to do so. These divisions, in turn, often served outside interests. She summarizes her views brilliantly—and poignantly—in one fall 2005 posting:

Iraq has been the land of dreams for everyone except Iraqis—the Persian dream of a Shia-controlled Islamic state modeled upon Iran and inclusive of the holy shrines in Najaf, the pan-Arab nationalist dream of a united Arab region with Iraq acting as its protective eastern border, the American dream of controlling the region by installing permanent bases and a Puppet government in one of its wealthiest countries, the Kurdish dream of an independent Kurdish state financed by the oil wealth in Kirkuk . . . The Puppets the Americans empowered are advocates of every dream except the Iraqi one: The dream of Iraqi Muslims, Christians, Arabs, Kurds and Turkmen . . . the dream of a united, stable, prosperous Iraq which has, over the last two years, gone up in the smoke of car bombs, military raids and a foreign occupation. (November 6, 2005)

By the time Riverbend made the last of the blog entries collected in this book, such dreams indeed seemed dead, as the interrelated forces of occupation and religious and ethnic factionalism brought new levels of bloodshed to Iraq. Although the Bush Administration tended to exaggerate their importance, foreign fighters contributed to the increase in violence. The United States claimed to be making progress in crushing former Saddam supporters in the insurgency—but these were quickly replaced by highly motivated religious extremists, whose tactics, including suicide bombings, killed more and more civilians. On the rise, at the same time, were Shia militias, including Muqtada al-Sadr's Mahdi Army, the SCIRI-linked Badr Corps, and the notorious Wolf Brigade. Although the United States officially opposed "unsanctioned" militias, these groups at times received government funding, and even fought beside Coalition forces, sharing the goal of crushing Sunni insurgents.[24]

These armed groups were fiercely fighting against one another as well as against the occupation. Attacks by Sunni insurgents increasingly targeted Shia civilians, or anyone seen as collaborating with the occupation. After the destruction of the Al Askari Mosque, one of Shia Islam's most sacred sites, the Mahdi Army and other Shia militias became full-fledged urban death squads, murdering Sunni civilians and clerics despite calls for calm from religious leaders. By the end of February, even Riverbend, who still believes most Iraqis do not want civil war, writes: "I'm sitting here wondering if this is actually what civil war is like. Has it become a reality? Will we look back at this in one year, two years . . . ten . . . and say, 'It began in February 2006 . . .'?" She wonders whether this is happening "like a nightmare in that you don't realize it's a nightmare while having it—only later, after waking up with your heart throbbing, and your eyes searching the dark for a pinpoint of light, do you realize it was a nightmare . . . " (February 27, 2006).

One of the most frightening developments of all, for Iraqi civilians, was the growing evidence of death squads operating within the Iraqi police force, carrying out "extrajudicial killings" under the guise of nightly security raids. Riverbend relates the terrifying story of one such raid, at her aunt's house. She asks, "Who do you call to protect you from the New Iraq's security forces?" (February 11, 2006).

By March 2006, where this volume ends, the UN human rights envoy to Iraq told the Washington Post that "executions—many of them following torture—now account for up to three-fourths of the hundreds of corpses coming into Baghdad's main morgue each week."[25] The final entry in the volume, in fact, is set outside the Baghdad morgue, where Riverbend and her brother wait while their cousin searches for a missing relative. She describes the cars with "simple, narrow wooden coffins on top of them, in anticipation of the son or daughter or brother," the scenes of grief and despair, and writes, "although it was surprisingly warm that day, I pulled at my sleeves, trying to cover my suddenly cold fingers" (March 28, 2006). Readers, too, may feel a chill, especially if they are from one of the countries that invaded and occupies Riverbend's.

THE POLITICS OF OCCUPATION

In both volumes of her blog entries, Riverbend shows herself to be a keen observer and interpreter of the political scene not only in her own country, but in the United States as well. Anticipating complaints that U.S. politics are none of her business, she declares, early in this volume, "Americans, you made it my business when you occupied my country last year" (October 25, 2004).

As this volume of Riverbend's postings begins, Americans were preparing to vote in the 2004 presidential election, with both candidates seeking to use the war in Iraq to their own advantage. Kerry, who had voted to authorize the war, made a halfhearted effort to back away from his former support, at the same time citing his record in Vietnam as proof of his superior experience; Bush exploited the emotions still lingering from the 9/11 attacks and played on voters' fears, citing the war on terror and continuing, albeit with less enthusiasm, to reference Iraq's weapons of mass destruction.

Riverbend makes it clear that she dreads the prospect of Bush's reelection, which, she believes, "will say that this catastrophe in Iraq was worth its price in American and Iraqi lives. His reassignment to the White House will sanction all the bloodshed and terror we've been living with for the last year and a half" (October 25, 2004). And she is bitter about the election results. To the voters in the "red states" that went for Bush, she says that red is "the color of the blood of thousands of Iraqis and by the time this four-year catastrophe in the White House is over, thousands of Americans, likely" (November 4, 2005).

Throughout the 18 months covered in this volume, the American body count indeed continued to mount, while the number of Iraqi civilian casualties grew exponentially. More evidence of abuse emerged from Abu Ghraib, with little response from the administration other than an effort to suppress the photographs. A story appeared in the *Washington Post* about a system of secret prisons in Europe, resulting not in reform or abandonment of the alleged torture practices, but the launch of a White House investigation into the source of the leak. When Arizona Senator John McCain sponsored legislation banning torture, Vice President Dick Cheney led opposition to the measure. The legislation eventually passed the Congress, but before signing it, Bush attached stipulations that would provide him with handy loopholes for the future. The image of the United States was further damaged by revelations of likely atrocities against Iraqi civilians by U.S. troops at Haditha and elsewhere.

Riverbend responds fiercely and bluntly to such developments, addressing her U.S. readers directly: "Americans, the name of your country which once stood for 'freedom and justice' is tarnished worldwide. . . . You were deceived repetitively and duped into two wars. Your sons and daughters are dying, and killing, in foreign lands. Your embassies are in danger all over the world. 'America' has become synonymous with 'empire,' 'hegemony,' and 'warfare'" (October 25, 2004).

As Bush's second term progressed, the administration continued to shun any admission of problems or errors. Time and again the president appeared in public to announce a "turning point" in the war that would result in victory. Both Bush and Rumsfeld insisted that the insurgency in Iraq was on the decline, even as it grew and diversified. But as the number of Americans killed in Iraq grew daily, and the divisions and deaths among Iraqis continued to accelerate, approval ratings for both the president and the war began to slip.

Several retired U.S. military leaders publicly announced their opposition to the war, declaring it ill conceived, dishonestly justified, botched, and unwinnable. Even previously docile members of Congress began to speak up, perhaps emboldened by Pennsylvania representative John Murtha, a former Marine colonel and a longtime supporter of the military, who demanded immediate troop withdrawal. In the spring of

2006, Congress voted to prohibit military funds from being spent to build permanent bases in Iraq. "Permanent" is, however, a relative term, and there were continuing indications that the United States was digging in for the long haul.

In doing so, the United States seemed increasingly likely to stand alone. By the spring of 2006, several U.S. allies in the always largely symbolic "Coalition of the Willing" had withdrawn—or promised to withdraw—their own troops from Iraq. Spain and Italy had both voted out pro-war governments, and South Korea had voted to draw down its troops. In Britain, where public opposition to the war had always run high, Prime Minister Tony Blair remained steadfast, despite dissension in his own party and despite growing violence in the Shia-dominated area around Basra, in the south, where most British troops were stationed. In May 2006, nine British soldiers were killed, of a total of 113 since the war had begun. Yet at the end of the month, on a visit to Washington, Blair joined Bush in declaring that Iraq was on the road to peace and democracy, and the war and occupation had been worthwhile.

On May 1, 2003, President Bush had declared, "Major combat operations have ended. In the battle of Iraq, the United States and our allies have prevailed." On that date, the cost of the war to U.S. taxpayers was $19 billion. In 2006 that figure had risen to $320 billion. On May 1, 2003, 139 U.S. troops had been killed. Three years later, on May 1, 2006, the total was 2,477. Total wounded then numbered 542; three years later they numbered 17,869. Back then there were about 5,000 insurgents; three years later there were between 15,000 and 20,000 in the insurgency, and countless more in the armed militias that were killing both occupation forces and civilians. Iraqi civilian deaths had increased four-fold in the three years, to 40,000 or more.

As Riverbend writes in one of her final entries, reflecting on the third anniversary of the war, "God protect us from the fourth year."

James Ridgeway and Jean Casella
Memorial Day, May 2006

NOTES

1. Firas Al-Atraqchi, "Iraqi Blogger Documents History," Al-Jazeera (online), April 6, 2006: http://english.aljazeera.net/NR/exeres/4C5B8EE6-F99C-4AB9-84B6-40F7F8F9B656.htm.

2. Committee to Protect Journalists, "Iraq: Journalists in Danger": http://www.cpj.org/Briefings/Iraq/Iraq_danger.html.

3. "Subject: From Baghdad" (email originally written to friends), available at: http://www.poynter.org/column.asp?id=45&aid=72659.

4. Najem Wali, "Iraq Stories," translated from the Arabic by Jennifer Kaplan, Words Without Borders: The Online Magazine for International Literature: http://www.wordswithoutborders.org/article.php?lab=IraqStories.

5. Al-Atraqchi, op. cit.

6. See Iraq Blog Count at http://iraqblogcount.blogspot.com. One Iraqi blogger, An Average Iraqi, has attempted to compile a chronological history of Iraqi blogging, found at http://aviraqi.blogspot.com/2005/10/iraqi-bloggers-from-pax-to-sanyora.html.

7. Salam Pax's posts begin at http://dear_raed.blogspot.com and continue at http://justzipit.blogspot.com; also see "Salam's Story" in the *Guardian*, May 30, 2003, at http://www.guardian.co.uk/g2/story/0,3604,966768,00.html. His was also the first of the Iraqi blogs to be published in book form; see *Salam Pax: The Clandestine Diary of an Ordinary Iraqi* (New York: Grove Press, 2003).

8. Al-Atraqchi, op. cit.

9. Fereshteh Nouraie-Simone, "Wings of Freedom: Iranian Women, Identity, and Cyberspace," in *On Shifting Ground: Muslim Women in the Global Era*, ed. Fereshteh Nouraie-Simone (New York: Feminist Press, 2005).

10. The full text of the Iraqi Constitution can be found at http://www.epic-usa.org/Portals/1/finalconstitutionenglish.pdf.

11. Isobel Coleman, "Women, Islam, and the New Iraq," *Foreign Affairs*, January/February 2006.

12. Human Rights Watch, *Climate of Fear: Sexual Violence and Abduction of Women and Girls in Baghdad* (HRW report E1508), July 16, 2003: http://hrw.org/reports/2003/iraq0703.

13. Amnesty International, *Amnesty International Report 2005*, May 25, 2005: http://web.amnesty.org/report2005/index-eng.

14. MADRE, "Iraq: Country Overview": http://www.madre.org/countries/Iraq.html.

15. Ana Elena Obando, Interview with Yanar Mohammed, WHRnet (Women's Human Rights Net), February 2006: http://www.whrnet.org/docs/interview-yanar-0603.html.

16. David Cortright, "A Hard Look at Iraqi Sanctions," *The Nation*, December 3, 2001, http://www.thenation.com/doc/20011203/cortright.

17. The low estimate comes from the site Iraq Body Count, which compiles

day-by-day casualty counts from verified sources and is generally considered conservative; see http://www.iraqbodycount.org. The high estimate is based on a sample-based survey by public health researchers published in the British medical journal *The Lancet*; see "Study Puts Iraq Toll at 100,000," CNN.com, October 29, 2004: http://www.cnn.com/2004/WORLD/meast/10/29/iraq.deaths.

18. Iraq Revenue Watch/OSI, "Disorder, Negligence and Mismanagement: How the CPA Handled Iraq Reconstruction Funds," Report No. 7, September 2004: http://www.iraqrevenuewatch.org/reports/092404.shtml.

19. BBC News (online), "Who's Who in Iraq: Iyad Allawi," May 28, 2004: http://news.bbc.co.uk/2/hi/middle_east/3757923.stm.

20. Iraq is, by most estimates, second only to Saudi Arabia in the size of its proven oil and gas reserves. The exploitation of oil in what was then called Mesopotamia was begun by the British in the late nineteenth century. Over time, Iraqi oil was divided up among the members of the international oil cartel, the so-called Seven Sisters, dominated by five U.S. companies—Exxon, Mobil, Chevron, Gulf, and Texaco—along with British Petroleum and Royal Dutch Shell. They controlled the business through World War II and up to the creation of OPEC, the organization of mostly Middle Eastern nations that formed a cartel of its own and demonstrated its newfound power during the energy crisis of the early 1970s. A comprehensive source on the Iraqi oil industry, past, present, and future, is the NGO World Policy Forum's "Oil in Iraq" web page: http://www.globalpolicy.org/security/oil/irqindx.htm.

21. For example, a much-discussed *New York Times* op-ed by Joseph R. Biden, ranking Democrat on the Senate Foreign Relations Committee, and Leslie H. Gelb, former president of the Council on Foreign Relations, called "Unity Through Autonomy in Iraq." The piece proposes, as a model for Iraq's future, the 1995 Dayton Accords on Bosnia, which "kept the country whole by, paradoxically, dividing it into ethnic federations." Biden and Gelb base their position, in large part, on their belief that "intercommunal violence has surpassed the insurgency as the main security threat." *New York Times*, May 1, 2006.

22. Scholarly support for this argument is provided by Gareth Porter in the journal of the Middle East Policy Council. The Bush administration, Porter writes, has depicted the challenge in Iraq "as one of defeating a threat to a democratic regime from an antidemocratic insurgency composed of Saddam loyalists and foreign Islamic terrorists," and has "refused to recognize that the Sunni insurgency was not organized against an existing democratic state but against a foreign occupation." He points out that, while the insurgency was initially launched by Saddam's security services, it "almost immediately swelled to much larger proportions because of a combination of Sunni anger at the tactics used by the U.S. occupation forces in the Sunni region and a fear of marginalization and revenge at the hands of the Shiites." The ranks of insurgents were further increased through the arrival of the so-called foreign fighters, some of whom believed they were defending an Arab nation both against a Western occupation and a perceived Persian threat

from Iran. "The Third Option in Iraq," Middle East Policy Council Journal 12:3 (Fall 2005): http://www.mepc.org/journal_vol12/0509_porter.asp.

23. Will Lester, "Poll: Most Iraqis Oppose Troops' Presence," ABC News (online), December 12, 2005: http://abcnews.go.com/International/wireStory?id=1397064. Also see the summary of results of various polls of Iraqi civilians, compiled by the Voters for Peace Education Project: http://www.votersforpeace.org/content/view/16/33.

24. For more on the complicated web of militia groups active in present-day Iraq, see Lionel Beehner, "Iraq: Militia Groups" (Backgrounder), Council on Foreign Relations, June 9, 2005: http://www.cfr.org/publication/8175/iraq.html#1.

25. Ellen Knickmeyer, "Execution Victims Spike at Baghdad Morgue," Washington Post, March 3, 2006: http://www.washingtonpost.com/wp-dyn/content/article/2006/03/02/AR2006030201902.html. Also see Solomon Moore, "Killings Linked to Shiite Squads in Iraqi Police Force," Los Angeles Times, November 29, 2005: http://www.latimes.com/news/nationworld/world/la-fg-death29nov29,0,3364 549,full.story?coll=la-home-headlines.

> ## Editor's Note

Based on Riverbend's most frequent spellings, cities' and politicians'
names have been standardized throughout this book. Words that are
spelled using a mix of numerals and letters, for instance *burgu3* (burqa)
are intentional and transliterate Arabic terms using standard computer
keystrokes. Select material to which the blog hyperlinks is included here
to illustrate Riverbend's commentary and appears set off in boxes.

October Through December 2004

A year and a half after George W. Bush declares the war over and "mission accomplished," the casualty counts in Iraq, both civilians and military, are rising.

As October begins, Coalition and Iraqi soldiers launch a "pacification drive"—a major offensive—on the city of Samarra, north of Baghdad in the so-called Sunni Triangle. U.S. officials say that insurgents and "foreign fighters" have seized control in the city. Some suggest that the attack has been timed to precede the U.S. presidential election. More than 100 insurgents are killed in the offensive. Meanwhile, in Fallujah the running siege continues.

It will be a bloody month in Baghdad, as well. On September 30, explosions kill more than 40 people, most of them children. On October 4, the supposedly secure American-controlled "Green Zone" is hit; six are killed, including four American civilians. The attack is attributed to the network of Jordanian extremist Abu Mussab Al-Zarqawi, which has recently renamed itself Al-Qaeda in Iraq.

What is broadly referred to as the "insurgency," initially composed mostly of former Ba'athists, has become larger and more complicated in its composition, as various factions take action against the U.S. occupation. These include "foreign fighters" with international terrorist ties, like Al-Zarqawi, as well as homegrown groups like the Badr Corps (also known as "Badir's Brigade" or "Faylaq Badir"), the Shiite militia associated with the Supreme Council for Islamic Revolution in Iraq, which formed decades earlier to oppose Saddam.

There are also car bomb attacks on one of the capital's main streets and on an elementary school in Mosul; 21 die, and 90 are injured. Two days later, 16 are killed in a car bomb attack on a National Guard building in what heretofore had been a relatively calm area near the Syrian border. On October 14, insurgents again breach the Green Zone, setting off bombs in a market and café. There are more car bombings, with 13 people killed in Baghdad and Mosul.

British hostage Kenneth Bigley is confirmed dead, the third in a group of three beheaded, reportedly by Al-Zarqawi's group, which had demanded the release of Iraqi woman prisoners. On October 19, the humanitarian agency CARE announces that Margaret Hassan, the group's highly respected head of Iraq operations, has been kidnapped. She is shown on TV pleading for her life. Four weeks later, CARE says that on the basis of a video, they believe Hassan to be dead.

On October 20, 2004, Staff Sgt. Ivan Frederick is sentenced to eight years in prison for his role in the abuse and torture of prisoners at Abu Ghraib. He admits to having taken part in a faked threat of execution, in which a prisoner had wires attached to his hands and was told that he would be electrocuted if he stepped or fell off the box he was forced to stand on. Other charges include hitting prisoners, making a group of nude prisoners form a human pyramid, and forcing prisoners to masturbate and simulate oral sex. Although Frederick is among the enlisted soldiers who say they received orders from higher up, no commanding officers are ever court-martialed.

On October 25, Al-Zarqawi's group takes credit for killing 50 National Guardsmen in the east of the country.

In the final month before the U.S. presidential election, proof that Saddam Hussein possessed WMDs remains elusive. The Bush Administration had hoped it could convince people they were for real when it found some suspicious-looking trailers, and promptly presented them as evidence that Saddam was making biological weapons. But on inspection, the Iraq Survey Group reports that the trailers were not "part of any BW [biological weapons] program."

Even though Bush's rationale for going to war looks less and less plausible, the president's reelection campaign is managing to convince many voters that Saddam's military program posed real danger. Although there is absolutely no evidence of any link between Saddam and Al-Qaeda and no evidence at all connecting Iraq to the 9/11 attacks, many American voters still believe the campaign rhetoric. A national Harris poll shows 63 percent of those polled "believe that Iraq, under Saddam Hussein, was a serious threat to U.S. security," and 38 percent say that Iraq had WMDs at the time of the U.S. invasion. A surprising 62 percent think Saddam Hussein "had strong links to Al-Qaeda," and 41 percent say that Saddam "helped plan and support" the 9/11 hijackers' attack.

Some voters, especially among right-wing Christians, are determined to stick with Bush because of his position on domestic social issues, especially his opposition to giving gay people the right to marry. But many others are convinced that he is the man who will keep the nation more secure. To achieve this image, the Bush campaign manages to overcome not only the harsh truths about the war in Iraq, but also the realities of the administration's conduct before and during the 9/11 attacks. (Having ignored growing warnings of an attack, the president is shuffled around the country on Air Force One while the nation is left in the hands of Vice President Dick Cheney, who, secreted with political aides in the bunker beneath the White House, calls in strikes against aircraft that have already crashed.)

The Bush campaign also profits from a vicious smear campaign against John Kerry, in which the Vietnam veteran is pictured as a coward and wishy-washy liberal. It is aided by Kerry's own unwillingness to take strong positions on the war and other key issues.

On November 2, 2004, George W. Bush defeats John Kerry. Six days after Bush gets his "mandate" for a second term, the United States opens an all-out assault on Fallujah in the biggest military action since the invasion. Much of the city is badly damaged, and an estimated one-third of the population flees before or during the fighting. A U.S. Marine corporal is caught on video shooting a wounded, unarmed Iraqi inside a mosque. He says he thought the man was pretending to be dead and was concealing a weapon; the military will conclude that the soldier was acting in self-defense.

November turns into the worst month so far for U.S. casualties, with 137 troops killed. As of December 7, 1,275 U.S. military personnel have been killed, and 9,765 have been wounded. Deaths of Iraqi police and

security forces number over 2,000. More than 50 Iraqis serving as inter-
preters for U.S. forces have been killed. Iraqi civilian deaths, by the
cross-verified (and generally conservative) numbers at Iraq Body Count
(http://www.iraqbodycount.net/) run between 14,000 and 17,000; other
estimates are much higher.

On December 8, Secretary of Defense Donald Rumsfeld speaks to
troops in Kuwait. He cites Franklin Roosevelt's speech on the day after
Pearl Harbor, and speaks of making "certain this form of treachery shall
never again endanger us"—presumably suggesting that the "preemp-
tive" war in Iraq may have prevented another attack like Pearl Harbor.

The gathering is called a "Kuwait town meeting," and soldiers are
given permission to question Rumsfeld. One receives applause when
he asks Rumsfeld, "We've had troops in Iraq for coming up on three
years and we've always staged here out of Kuwait. Now why do we soldiers have to dig through local landfills for pieces of scrap metal and
compromised ballistic glass to up-armor our vehicles and why don't we
have those resources readily available to us?"

After asking him to repeat the question, Rumsfeld replies that the
Army is working to produce armor as fast as it can. He tells the forces,
"As you know, you go to war with the Army you have. They're not the
Army you might want or wish to have at a later time. Since the Iraq conflict began, the Army has been pressing ahead to produce the armor necessary at a rate that they believe—it's a greatly expanded rate from what
existed previously, but a rate that they believe is the rate that is all that
can be accomplished at this moment."

In mid-December, at least 60 Iraqis are killed in bombings in the
Shia holy cities of Najaf and Karbala. Bush blandly states he expects
"hundreds of innocent" civilians will be killed as the country prepares
for elections. The violence continues as the month goes on, and the
largest Sunni political party pulls out of the approaching elections, saying the country is too unsafe for there to be a fair vote.

On December 21, insurgents set off a bomb in a crowded mess tent,
killing 19 soldiers and injuring scores more. On Christmas Eve, Rumsfeld turns up in Baghdad, and assures the troops the insurgency can be
put down.

—James Ridgeway

SAMARRA BURNING . . .

The last few days have been tense and stressful. Watching the military attacks on Samarra and hearing the stories from displaced families or people from around the area is like reliving the frustration and anger of the war. It's like a nightmare within a nightmare, seeing the corpses pile up and watching people drag their loved ones from under the bricks and steel of what was once a home.

To top it off, we have to watch American military spokespersons and our new Iraqi politicians justify the attacks and talk about "insurgents" and "terrorists" like they actually believe what they are saying . . . like hundreds of civilians aren't being massacred on a daily basis by the world's most advanced military technology.

As if Allawi's gloating and Bush's inane debates aren't enough, we have to listen to people like Powell and Rumsfeld talk about "precision attacks." What exactly are precision attacks?! How can you be precise in a city like Samarra or in the slums of Sadir City on the outskirts of Baghdad? Many of the areas under attack are small, heavily populated, with shabby homes several decades old. In Sadir City, many of the houses are close together and the streets are narrow. Just how precise can you be with missiles and tanks? We got a first-hand view of America's "smart weapons." They were smart enough to kill over 10,000 Iraqis in the first few months of the occupation.

The explosions in Baghdad aren't any better. A few days ago, some 40 children were blown to pieces while they were gathering candy from American soldiers at the opening of a sewage treatment plant. (Side note: That's how bad things have gotten—we have to celebrate the reconstruction of our sewage treatment plants.) I don't know who to be more angry with—the idiots and PR people who thought it would be a good idea to have children running around during a celebration involving troops or the parents for letting their children attend. I hope the people who arranged the explosions burn within the far reaches of hell.

One wonders who is behind the explosions and the car bombs. Bin Laden? Zarqawi? Possibly . . . but it's just too easy. It's too perfect. Bin Laden hit the WTC and Afghanistan was attacked. Iraq was occupied. At first, any explosion or attack on troops was quickly blamed on "loyalists" and "Ba'athists" and EVERYTHING was being coordinated by Saddam. As soon as he was caught, it became the work of "Islamic extremists" and Al-Qaeda and Zarqawi suddenly made his debut. One wonders who it will be after it is discovered that Zarqawi has been dead for several months or that he never even existed. Whoever it is, you can bet his name will be three syllables or less because that is Bush's limit.

A week ago, four men were caught by Iraqi security in the area of A'adhamiya in Baghdad. No one covered this on television or on the Internet, as far as I know—we heard it from a friend involved in the whole thing. The four men were caught trying to set up some explosives in a residential area by some of the residents themselves. One of the four men got away, one of them was killed on the spot and two were detained and interrogated. They turned out to be a part of Badir's Brigade (Faylaq Badir) [more widely known as the Badr Corps], the militia belonging to the Supreme Council of the Islamic Revolution in Iraq. Should the culprits never have been caught, and should the explosives have gone off, would Zarqawi have been blamed? Of course.

I'm very relieved the Italian hostages have been set free . . . and I hope the other innocent people are also freed. Thousands of Iraqis are being abducted and some are killed, while others are returned . . . but it is distressing to see so many foreigners being abducted. It's like having a guest attacked in your own home by the neighbor's pit bull—you feel a sense of responsibility even though you know there was no way you could have prevented it.

I wasn't very sympathetic though, when that Islamic group came down from London to negotiate releasing Kenneth Bigley. I do hope he is returned alive, but where are all these Islamic groups while Fallujah, Samarra, Sadir City and other places are being bombed? Why are they so concerned with a single British citizen when hundreds of Iraqis are dying by the month? Why is it "terrorism" when foreigners set off bombs in London or Washington or New York and it's a "liberation" or "operation" when foreigners bomb whole cities in Iraq? Are we that much less important?

Wednesday, October 13, 2004

VALIUM . . .

Apparently, some topic that came up during a recent *Oprah* show has caught a lot of attention. Before I continue, let me first say—yes—we do know who Oprah is. MBC Channel 2 has been showing *Oprah* for the last few months—but the shows are a few weeks old. It's a popular show in Iraq because Iraqis find it amusing to watch some of the more absurd problems being discussed on the show—like how to find a good plastic surgeon, or what to purchase on a shopping spree on Fifth Avenue, etc. I'm not a huge fan of *Oprah*, but I used to watch the show when there was an interesting topic being discussed. I more or less stopped watching after she brought on Condi Rice and tried to make a compassionate hero out of her—that was disgusting, to be quite frank.

Anyway, I got an email from "Will" (and I answered it, Will, but it bounced right back at me). Will was asking me whether it was true or not that people in Iraq were becoming addicted to valium and whether valium was easily available over the counter. (See http://www.dailykos .com/story/2004/10/6/17810/0170.)

Valium has always been available over the counter. Iraq is one of those countries where you can get almost any medication "over the counter." It actually depends on the pharmacy, but generally speaking, everything from sedatives to antibiotics are sold over the counter. Medication is also really cheap here. I mean *really* cheap. We had, prior to the blockade, one of the best pharmaceutical companies in the region—"Samarra Drugs," which made everything from amoxicillin to flu medicine.

Will asked if valium had become addictive after the war. Of course it has. Valium is a staple during wars. I remember when we were preparing for the war, we would make list after list of "necessities." One list was for pharmaceutical necessities. It included such basics as cotton, Band-Aids, alcohol, gauze and an ordinary painkiller. It also included medicines such as ampicloxine, codeine and valium. No one in the family takes valium, but it was one of those "just in case" medications— the kind you buy and hope you never have to use.

We had to use it during the first week of April [2003], as the tanks started rolling into Baghdad. We had an older aunt staying at our house (she had been evacuated from her area) and along with my cousin, his wife, his two daughters, and an uncle, the house was crowded and—at bizarre moments—almost festive.

The bombing had gotten very heavy and our eating and sleeping schedules were thrown off balance. Everything seemed to revolve around the attack on Baghdad—we'd hastily cook and eat during the lulls in bombing and we'd get snatches of sleep in between the "shock and awe." There were a few nights where we didn't sleep at all—we'd just stay up and sit around, staring at each other in the dark, listening to the explosions and feeling the earth tremble beneath.

So imagine this. It's a chilly night in Baghdad and the black of the sky suddenly lights up with flashes of white—as if the stars were exploding in the distance. The bombing was so heavy, we could hear the windows rattling, the ground shaking and the whiz of missiles ominously close. We were all gathered in the windowless hallway—adults and children. My cousin's daughters were wrapped in blankets and they sat huddled up close to their mother. They were so silent, they might have been asleep—but I knew they weren't because I could vaguely see the whites of their eyes, open wide, across the lamp-lit hallway.

Now, during the more lively hours of a shock and awe bombing storm, there's no way you can have a normal conversation. You might be able to blurt out a few hasty sentences, but eventually, there's bound to be an explosion that makes you stop, duck your head and wonder how the house didn't fall down around you.

Throughout this, we sit around, mumbling silent prayers, reviewing our lives and making vague promises about what we'd do if we got out of this one alive. Sometimes, one of us would turn to the kids and crack some lame joke or ask how they were doing. Often, the answer would be in the form of a wan smile or silence.

So where does the valium fit in? Imagine through all of this commotion, an elderly aunt who is terrified of bombing. She was so afraid, she couldn't, and wouldn't, sit still. She stood pacing the hallway, cursing Bush, Blair, and anyone involved with the war—and that was during her calmer moments. When she was feeling especially terrified, the curses and rampage would turn into a storm of weeping and desolation (during which she imagines she can't breathe)—we were all going to die. They would have to remove us from the rubble of our home. We'd burn alive. And so on. And so forth.

During those fits of hysteria, my cousin would quietly, but firmly, hand her a valium and a glass of water. The aunt would accept both and in a matter of minutes, she'd grow calmer and a little bit more sane. This aunt wasn't addicted to valium, but it certainly came in handy during the more hectic moments of the war.

I guess it's happening a lot now after the war too. When the load gets too heavy, people turn to something to comfort them. Abroad, under normal circumstances, if you have a burden, you don't have to bear it alone. You can talk to a friend or relative or psychiatrist or SOMEONE. Here, everyone has their own set of problems—a death in the family, a detainee, a robbery, a kidnapping, an explosion, etc. So you have two choices—take a valium, or start a blog.

The other "drug" problem we're having is much more serious. Before the war and occupation, drugs (you know—cocaine, marijuana, etc.) weren't that big a problem in Iraq. Sure, we all heard of a certain person or certain area where you could get hashish or marijuana or something . . . but it wasn't that common. A big reason was because selling drugs was punishable by death. Now, you can find drugs in several areas in Baghdad and all sorts of pills have become quite common in the south. People living in Basrah and Najaf and other areas in the south complain that Iranians are smuggling them into the country and selling them. Iran has a large drug trade and now, we're getting some of their exports in Iraq.

There are certain areas in Baghdad that are well-known for their criminals and various crimes, ranging from rape to kidnapping to killing. Often the culprits are junkies who do what they do because they're high on something or another, or because they need the money.

One friend of E.'s was actually detained on one occasion by some Iraqi police because he had forgotten his car's registration papers. He was hauled off to the station along with his cousin and they were both locked up in a crowded cell. Half an hour into the detention, a police officer came along with some sort of pill and offered it to the prisoners for 250 Iraqi dinars a piece.

During my more thoughtful moments, I do think about the growing drug problem. I know that it is going to get bigger and there's nothing immediate that we can do to stop it. There seem to be such bigger problems out there that drugs seem to be the least of our worries. Schools have started again and parents worry that their kids will be abducted or blown to pieces. I think our growing drug problem hasn't gotten that much attention with the media because, while it's going to wreak havoc in the long run, drugs don't suddenly blow off an arm or a leg, and they don't explode inside of your car and they don't come falling out of a plane to burn homes and families . . . in other words, people don't perceive them as a very immediate threat.

It's like discovering you have cancer while you're fighting off a hungry alligator—you'll worry about the disease later. **posted by river @ 1:39 AM**

Monday, October 25, 2004

AMERICAN ELECTIONS 2004 . . .

Warning—the following post is an open letter of sorts to Americans.

So elections are being held in America. We're watching curiously here. Previously, Iraqis didn't really take a very active interest in elections. We knew when they were being held and quite a few Iraqis could give an opinion about either of the candidates. I think many of us realized long ago that American foreign policy really had nothing to do with this Democrat or that Republican.

It sometimes seems, from this part of the world, that democracy in America revolves around the presidential elections—not the major decisions. War and peace in America are in the average American's hands about as much as they are in mine. Sure, you can vote for this man or that one, but in the end, there's something bigger, more intricate and quite sinister behind the decisions. Like in that board game Monopoly, you can choose the game pieces—the little shoe, the car, the top hat . . . but you can't choose the way the game is played. The faces change but the intentions and the policy remain the same.

Many, many people have asked me about the elections and what we think of them. Before, I would have said that I really don't think much about it. Up until four years ago, I always thought the American elections were a pretty straightforward process: two white males up for the same position (face it people—it really is only two—Nader doesn't count), people voting and the person with more votes wins. After the debacle of four years ago, where Bush Jr. was *assigned* president, things are looking more complicated and a little bit more sordid.

I wouldn't normally involve myself in debates or arguments about who should be American president. All I know is that four years ago, we prayed it wouldn't be Bush. It was like people could foresee the calamity we're living now and he embodied it. (Then, there's that little issue of his being completely ridiculous . . .)

So now there are three different candidates—Bush, Kerry and Nader. We can safely take Nader out of the equation because, let's face it, he won't win. We have a saying in Iraq, "*Lo tetla'a nakhla ib rasseh*" (if a palm tree grows out of his head) . . . The real contest is between Bush and Kerry. Nader is a distraction that is only taking votes away from Kerry.

Who am I hoping will win? Definitely Kerry. There's no question about it. I want Bush out of the White House at all costs. (And yes—who is *in* the White House *is* my business—Americans, you made it my business when you occupied my country last year.) I'm too realistic to expect drastic change or anything phenomenal, but I don't want Bush reelected because his reelection (or shall I call it his "reassignment") will condone the wars on Afghanistan and Iraq. It will say that this catastrophe in Iraq was worth its price in American and Iraqi lives. His reassignment to the White House will sanction all the bloodshed and terror we've been living with for the last year and a half.

I've heard all the arguments. His supporters are a lot like him—they'll admit no mistakes. They'll admit no deceit, no idiocy, no manipulation, no squandering. It's useless. Republicans who *don't* support him, but feel obliged to vote for him, write long, apologetic emails that are meant, I assume, to salve their own conscience. They write telling me that he should be "reelected" because he is the only man for the job at this point. True, he made some mistakes and he told a few fibs, they tell me—but he really means well and he intends to fix things and, above all, he has a plan.

Let me assure you Americans—he has NO PLAN. There is no plan for the mess we're living in—unless he is cunningly using the Chaos Theory as a basis for his Iraq plan. Things in Iraq are a mess and there is the sense that the people in Washington don't know what they're doing, and their puppets in Iraq know even less. The name of the game now in Iraq is naked aggression—it hasn't been about hearts and minds since complete areas began to revolt. His Iraq plan may be summarized with the Iraqi colloquial saying, "*A'athreh ib dafra,*" which can be roughly translated to "a stumble and a kick." In other words, what will happen, will happen and hopefully—with a stumble and a kick—things will move in the right direction.

So is Kerry going to be much better? I don't know. I don't know if he's going to fix things or if he's going to pull out the troops, or bring more in. I have my doubts about how he will handle the current catastrophe in Iraq. I do know this: Nothing can be worse than Bush. No one can be worse than Bush. It will hardly be fair to any president after Bush in any case—it's like assigning a new captain to a drowning ship. All I know is that Bush made the hole and let the water in, I want him thrown overboard.

Someone once wrote to me, after a blog barrage against Bush, that I should tone down my insults against the president because I would lose readers who actually supported him. I lost those readers the moment I spoke out against the war and occupation because that is what Bush is all about. He's not about securing America or Iraq or "the region"—he's about covering up just how inadequate he is as a person and as a leader with war, nonexistent WMD, fabled terrorists and bogeymen.

I guess what I'm trying to say is this: Americans, the name of your country which once stood for "freedom and justice" is tarnished worldwide. Your latest president has proved that the great American image of democracy is just that—an image. You can protest, you can demonstrate, you can vote—but it ends there. The reins were out of your hands the moment Bush stepped into the White House. You were deceived repetitively and duped into two wars. Your sons and daughters are dying, and killing, in foreign lands. Your embassies are in danger all over the world. "America" has become synonymous with "empire," "hegemony," and "warfare." And why? All because you needed to be diverted away from the fact that your current president is a failure.

Some people associate the decision to go to war as a "strength." How strong do you need to be to commit thousands of your countrymen and women to death on foreign soil? Especially while you and your loved ones sit safely watching at home. How strong do you need to be to give orders to bomb cities to rubble and use the most advanced military technology available against a country with a weak army and crumbling infrastructure? You don't need to be strong—you need to be mad.

Americans—can things be worse for you? Can things be worse for us in Iraq? Of course they can . . . only imagine—four more years of Bush. **posted by river @ 10:35 PM**

Monday, November 01, 2004

SOME TERRORISTS . . .

The sky has been overcast these last few days. It's a smoggy, grayish combination of dust, smoke and humidity. I guess it has matched the general mood in many ways—somewhat dark and heavy.

I've been very worried about Fallujah. So worried, in fact, that I find it hard to sleep at night, wondering how the situation will unfold in that troubled area. Things are bad in Baghdad, but they are far worse in Fallujah. Refugees have been flowing out of the area for weeks now. They've been trying to find havens in Baghdad and the surrounding regions.

. . .

I met my first Fallujah refugees last week. One of my aunts was feeling a little bit under the weather and the phones in her area were down, so we decided to pay a brief visit after breaking the [Ramadan] fast in the evening. As we pulled our car into her driveway, I discerned strange, childish voices in the garden. Since my aunt has only an eight-year-old daughter, S., I assumed the neighbors' children were over to play.

S. tripped over to the car and helped open the door. She was jumping with excitement and pleasure at so many guests. I glanced towards the garden, expecting to see children but besides a big palm and a couple of rose bushes, I couldn't see anything. "Where are your friends?!" I asked, pulling out the Iraqi sweets we had brought for my aunt. She looked over her shoulder and smiled, pointing to the palm tree. I squinted at the tree in the dark garden and glimpsed a small head and a flashing pair of eyes, which quickly disappeared. I nodded sagely and called out, "Hello, palm tree!" S. giggled as the palm tree softly replied, "Hello."

"It's fine," S. called over her shoulder to the garden, "You can come out—it's only my cousin and her parents!" We walked towards the house and S. continued her prattling. "Mommy is feeling much better. We have guests today. Well, we had them from yesterday. They are my friends. They're daddy's relatives . . . they don't have to go to school but I do."

The living room was in commotion as we entered it. The television was turned on high to some soap opera and mixed with the shouts of an Egyptian soap star was an infant crying, a mother "shushing" it, and my aunt and her husband discussing the fate of a telephone line which had been dead for the last four days. The woman with the infant suddenly rose as we entered the room and made way for the door leading to the hallway.

After the initial greetings and salams, my aunt rushed out of the room and came back in with the very reluctant woman and her baby. "This is Umm Ahmed." She introduced us and firmly sat the woman back down on the couch. "She's from Fallujah . . ." my aunt explained. "She's my husband's relative—but we never met before this." She turned to give an encouraging smile to Umm Ahmed, who was looking somewhat like a deer caught in headlights.

The woman was tall and graceful. She was wearing a longish

traditional dishdasha (something like a heavy, embroidered nightgown) and her head was covered with a light, black shawl that kept slipping back to reveal dark brown hair streaked with strands of silver. I tried guessing her age but it was nearly impossible—she had a youthful look about her and I guessed she was probably around 33 or 34. Her face, however, was pinched with strain and worry, and that, combined with the silver in her hair, made her seem like she was forty. She nodded at us nervously and held the infant tighter.

"Umm Ahmed and her lovely children are here until things are better in Fallujah," my aunt declared. She turned to my little cousin with the words, "Go get Sama and Harith." I assumed Sama and Harith were the children hiding behind the palm tree. A moment later, Sama and Harith, led by S. entered the living room. Sama was a delicate girl of about ten, while Harith was a chubby little boy who looked to be six or seven. They avoided eye contact and quickly ran over to their mother.

"Say 'hello,'" Umm Ahmed urged quietly. Sama came forward to shake hands but Harith tried to hide behind his mother.

"What lovely children!" My mother smiled and pulled Sama in for a kiss. "How old are you, Sama?"

"Eleven," came the soft answer, as she went back to sit next to her mother.

"How is the situation in Fallujah?" My father asked. We all knew the answer. It was terrible in Fallujah and getting worse by the day. They were constantly being bombarded with missiles and bombs. The city was in ruins. Families were gathering what they could and leaving. Houses were being demolished by tanks and planes. But the question had to be asked.

Umm Ahmed swallowed nervously and her frown deepened. "It's quite bad. We left two days ago. The Americans are surrounding the city and they wouldn't let us out using the main road. We had to be smuggled out through another way . . ." The baby began to whine softly and she tried to rock it to sleep. "We had to leave . . ." she said apologetically, "I couldn't stay there with the children."

"Of course you couldn't," came my aunt's firm reply. "That's crazy. It's suicide—the bastards aren't leaving anyone alive."

"I hope everyone is ok . . ." I offered tentatively. Umm Ahmed focused for a moment on me and shook her head, "Well, last week we buried our neighbor Umm Najib and her two daughters. They were sleeping when a missile fell in the garden and the house collapsed."

"And my windows were broken . . ." Harith suddenly added, excitedly, then disappeared again behind his mother.

"The windows were broken and the front door was blown in. We were all ok because ever since the war we've all been sleeping in the living room," Umm Ahmed explained, automatically, like she had told the story a hundred times. As she spoke, the baby's fists went up into the air and it gave out a little cry. It was a welcome sound—the agonizing subject could be changed. "And is this Ahmed?" I asked, rising to look at the infant. My aunt was calling her "Umm Ahmed" which means, "The Mother of Ahmed." Usually, the name of the eldest child is used as an informal way to speak with the parents. "Abu Ahmed" is "The Father of Ahmed." I didn't understand why she wasn't Umm Harith or Umm Sama, but since this was the last child, it must be "Ahmed."

"No—this is Majid." Sama answered my question softly. The baby looked about four months old and had a shock of dark hair, covered with what seemed at first sight to be a little white cap. His eyes were the same hazel color as his mother's. I smiled down at Majid and noticed that the white thing on his head wasn't a cap—it was a white gauze bandage. "What's the bandage for?" I asked, hoping it was just to keep his head warm.

"When we were fleeing the city, we had to come in a pickup truck with two other families. His head got hit with something and there was a scratch. The doctor said that he has to keep the bandage on so that there won't be an infection." Her eyes filled as she looked down at the infant and rocked him a bit harder.

"Well, at least everyone is safe . . . you were very wise to come here." My mother offered. "Your children are fine—and that's what's important."

This phrase didn't have quite the effect we expected. Umm Ahmed's eyes suddenly flowed over and in a moment, she was crying freely. Sama frowned and gently took the baby from her mother's arms, rising to walk him around in the hallway. My aunt quickly poured a glass of water out for Umm Ahmed and handed it to her, explaining to us, "Ahmed, her fourteen-year-old son, is with his father, still in Fallujah."

"I didn't want to leave him . . ." The glass of water shook in her hands. "But he refused to leave without his father and we got separated last minute as the cars were leaving the city . . ." My aunt rushed to pat her back and hand her some tissues.

"Umm Ahmed's husband, God protect him, is working with one of the mosques to help get some of the families out." My aunt explained, sitting down next to Umm Ahmed and reaching to pull a teary Harith onto her lap. "I'm sure they'll both be fine—maybe they're already in Baghdad . . ." my aunt added with more confidence than any of us felt. Umm Ahmed nodded her head mechanically and stared vaguely at the rug on the floor. Harith rubbed at his eyes and clung to a corner of his mother's shawl. "I promised her," my aunt explained, "that if we don't hear from them in two more days, Abu S. will drive out to Fallujah, and he can look for them. We've already left word with that mosque where all the refugees go in Baghdad."

As I sat staring at the woman, the horror of the war came back to me—the days upon days of bombing and shooting—the tanks blasting away down the streets, and helicopters hovering above menacingly. I wondered how she would spend the next couple of agonizing days, waiting for word from her son and husband. The worst part of it is being separated from the people you care about and wondering about their fates. It's a feeling of restlessness that gnaws away inside of you, leaving you feeling exhausted and agitated all at once. It's a thousand pessimistic voices whispering stories of death and destruction in your head. It's a terrible feeling of helplessness in the face of such powerful devastation.

So Umm Ahmed is one of the terrorists who were driven from the city. Should her husband and son die, they will be leaders from Al-Qaeda or even relatives of Abu Mussab Al-Zarqawi himself . . . that's the way they tell the story in America.

It makes me crazy to see Bush and Allawi talking about the casualties in Fallujah like every single person there is a terrorist lurking not in a home, but in some sort of lair, making plans to annihilate America. Allawi was recently talking about how the "peace talks" weren't going very well and a major military operation was the only option available. That garbage and the rest about Abu Mussab Al-Zarqawi is for Americans, Brits and Iraqis living in comfortable exile.

Allawi is vile and the frightening thing is that he will *never* be safe in Iraq without American military support. As long as he is in power, there will be American tanks and bases all over the country. How does he expect to win any support by threatening to unleash the occupation forces against Fallujah? People are greeting refugees from Fallujah like heroes. They are emptying rooms in houses to accommodate them and donating food, money and first-aid supplies.

Everyone here knows Abu Mussab Al-Zarqawi isn't in Fallujah. He isn't anywhere, as far as anyone can tell. He's like the WMD: surrender your weapons or else we'll attack. Now that the damage is done, it is discovered that there were no weapons. It will be the same with Zarqawi. We laugh here when we hear one of our new politicians discuss him. He's even better than the WMD—he has legs. As soon as the debacle in Fallujah is over, Zarqawi will just move conveniently to Iran, Syria or even North Korea.

As for the "peace talks" with Fallujah—they never existed. They've been bombing Fallujah for several weeks now. They usually do the bombing during the night, and no one is there to cover the damage and all the deaths. It's only later we hear about complete families being buried alive or shot to death by snipers on the street.

By the way, Americans—100,000 deaths in a year and a half, and the number is rising. Keep Bush another four years and we just might hit the half-million mark . . . **posted by river @ 9:57 PM**

HELP SOMEONE . . .

The Jarrars have started a fantastic campaign to collect money and, working along with some of the few remaining NGOs in Baghdad, purchase first-aid supplies, food and other necessities to send along to Iraqi cities in dire need of this stuff. You can read more about it on Raed's blog.

To all those wonderful, amazing people out there who have written to me over the last year: You offered me so much—whatever I needed—as some have written. Those of you who really do want to help or contribute anything to Iraq, donate what you can. The smallest amount really does make a difference (God, I'm sounding like a tv evangelist). I do mean it though—your contribution will help some child or family.

For more questions, you can contact any one of the Jarrars—especially Raed or Khalid to get more information.

Raed's Blog: Raed in the Middle [http://raedinthemiddle.blogspot.com]
Khalid's Blog: Secrets in Baghdad [http://secretsinbaghdad.blogspot.com]

A link—Guerrilla News Network [http://gnn.tv] is showing Eminem's
Mosh music video, a politically inspired video about the elections. I'm trying to view it but with my link it's impossible. **posted by river @ 10:01 PM**

Thursday, November 04, 2004

DISAPPOINTMENT . . .

Well, what is there to say? Disappointment doesn't even begin to
describe it . . .

To the red states (and those who voted for Bush): You deserve no
better—I couldn't wish worse on you if I tried. He represents you perfectly . . . and red really is your color. It's the color of the blood of thousands of Iraqis and by the time this four-year catastrophe in the White
House is over, thousands of Americans, likely.

To the blue states (and those who were thinking when they voted):
Condolences. Good luck—you'll need it.

I'm thinking of offering up the idea of "Election Condolences" to
Hallmark or Yahoo Greetings. The cards can have those silly little
poems inside of them, like:

Condolences and heartfelt tears—
You get Bush for four more years!

or

Sympathies in advance
For when they reinstate the draft!
We hope (insert_name_here) stays as safe as he/she can
And writes frequently while in Iran

or

Bush and Cheney—what a pair!
Who said life isn't fair?
While Iraq gets tanks and occupation—
You have idiots to run your nation!

or

Cheer up . . .
Your son was too young for Afghanistan.
And it's still a bit early for Iran—
But there's plenty of time for Syria . . .
And he'll definitely serve in North Korea!

I guess justice was too much to ask for. **posted by river @ 11:45 PM**

Wednesday, November 10, 2004

RULE OF IRAQ ASSASSINS MUST END . . .

I'm not feeling well—it's a combination of the change of weather and the decline in the situation. Eid is less than a week away but no one is feeling at all festive. We're all worried about the situation in Fallujah and surrounding regions. We've ceased worrying about the explosions in Baghdad and are now concerned with the people who have left their homes and valuables and are living off of the charity of others.

Allawi declared a "State of Emergency" a couple of days ago . . . A state of emergency *now* —because previous to this week, we Iraqis were living in an American-made Utopia, as the world is well aware. So what does an "Emergency State" signify for Iraqis? Basically, it means we are now *officially* more prone to being detained, raided, and just generally abused by our new Iraqi forces and American ones. Today they declared a curfew on Baghdad after 10 p.m. but it hasn't really made an impact because people have stopped leaving their houses after dark anyway.

The last few days have been tense and heart-rending. Most of us are really worried about Fallujah. Really worried about Fallujah and all the innocents dying and dead in that city. There were several explosions in Baghdad these last few days and hardly any of them were covered by the press. All this chaos has somehow become uncomfortably normal. Two years ago I never would have dreamed of living like this—now this lifestyle has become the norm and I can barely remember having lived any other way.

My cousin kept the kids home from school, which is happening quite often. One of the explosions today was so close, the house rocked with the impact and my cousin's wife paled, "Can you imagine if the girls had been at school when that happened—I would have died."

Dozens of civilians have died these last few days in Ramadi, Fallujah, and Samarra. We are hearing about complete families being killed under the rain of bombs being dropped by American forces. The phone lines in those areas seem to be cut off. We've been trying to call some relatives in Ramadi for the last two days, but it's next to impossible. We keep getting that dreadful busy tone and there's just no real way of knowing what is going on in there. There is talk of the use of cluster bombs and other forbidden weaponry.

We're hearing various stories about the situation. The latest is that 36 American troops have been taken prisoner along with dozens of Iraqi troops. How do people feel about the Iraqi troops? There's a certain rage. It's difficult to sympathize with a fellow-countryman while he's killing one of his own. People generally call them "Dogs of Occupation" here because instead of guarding our borders or securing areas, they are used to secure American forces. They drive out in front of American cars in order to clear the roads and possibly detonate some of those road mines at a decent distance from the American tanks. At the end of the day, most of them are the remnants of militias and that's the way they act.

And now they are being used in Fallujah against other Iraqis. The whole situation is making me sick and there's a fury building up. The families in Fallujah have been relegated to living in strange homes and mosques outside of the city . . . many of them are setting up their families inside of emptied schools and municipal buildings in Samarra and neighboring areas. Every time I see Allawi on tv talking about his regrets about "having to attack Fallujah" I get so angry I could scream. He's talking to the outside world, not to us. Iraqis don't buy his crap for an instant. We watch him talk and feel furious and frustrated with our new tyrant.

I was watching CNN this morning and I couldn't get the image of the hospital in Fallujah being stormed by Iraqi and American troops out of my head—the Iraqis being made to lay face-down on the ground, hands behind their backs. Young men and old men . . . and then the pictures of Abu Ghraib replay themselves in my mind. I think people would rather die than be taken prisoner by the Americans.

The borders with Syria and Jordan are also closed and many of the highways leading to the borders have been blocked. There are rumors that there are currently 100 cars ready to detonate in Mosul, being driven by suicide bombers looking for American convoys. So what happens when Mosul turns into another Fallujah? Will they also bomb it to the ground? I heard a report where they mentioned that Zarqawi "had probably escaped from Fallujah" . . . so where is he now? Mosul?

Meanwhile, Rumsfeld is making his asinine remarks again,

"There aren't going to be large numbers of civilians killed and certainly not by U.S. forces." [Press Briefing, November 8, 2004, http://www.defenselink.mil/transcripts/2004/tr20041108-secdef1541.html]

No—there are only an "estimated" 100,000 civilians in Fallujah (and these are American estimations). So far, boys and men between the ages of 16 and 60 aren't being counted as "civilians" in Fallujah. They are being rounded up and taken away. And, *of course* the U.S. forces aren't going to be doing the killing: The bombs being dropped on Fallujah don't contain explosives, depleted uranium or anything harmful—they contain laughing gas—that would, of course, explain Rumsfeld's idiotic optimism about not killing civilians in Fallujah. Also, being a "civilian" is a relative thing in a country occupied by Americans. You're only a civilian if you're on their side. If you translate for them, or serve them food in the Green Zone, or wipe their floors—you're an innocent civilian. Everyone else is an insurgent, unless they can get a job as a "civilian."

So this is how Bush kicks off his second term. More bloodshed.

"Innocent civilians in that city have all the guidance they need as to how they can avoid getting into trouble."

How do they do that Rumsfeld? While tons of explosives are being dropped upon your neighborhood, how do you do that? Do you stay inside the house and try to avoid the thousands of shards of glass that shoot out at you from shattering windows? Or do you hide under a table and hope that it's sturdy enough to keep the ceiling from crushing you? Or do you flee your house and pray to God you don't come face to face with an Apache or tank or that you aren't in the line of fire of a sniper? How do you avoid the cluster bombs and all the other horror being dealt out to the people of Fallujah?

There are a couple of things I agree with. The first is the following:

"Over time you'll find that the process of tipping will take place, that more and more of the Iraqis will be angry about the fact that their innocent people are being killed . . ."

He's right. It is going to have a decisive affect on Iraqi opinion— but just not the way he thinks. There was a time when pro-occupation Iraqis were able to say, "Let's give them a chance . . ." That time is over. Whenever someone says that lately, at best, they get a lot of nasty looks . . . often it's worse. A fight breaks out and a lot of yelling ensues . . . how can one condone occupation? How can one condone genocide? What about the mass graves of Fallujah? Leaving Islam aside, how does one agree to allow the murder of fellow-Iraqis by the strongest military in the world?

The second thing Rumsfeld said made me think he was reading my mind:

"Rule of Iraq assassins must end . . ."

I couldn't agree more: Get out, Americans. **posted by river @ 1:02 AM**

ONE OF THOSE WEEKS . . .

These last few days have been explosive—literally.

The sounds seem to be coming from everywhere. I've gotten tired of running upstairs and out on to the roof to find out where it's coming from. It feels like the first days of the war sometimes—planes, explosions, bullets, smoke . . . roads cut off.

We haven't attempted to leave the house but an uncle who was supposed to visit called to say he wouldn't be able to come because so many roads were blocked. Many people were told not to go to work and students stopped going to college yesterday. It's one of those weeks. Some areas in Baghdad seem to be cut off by armed gangs.

Eid is in a couple of days and that means there's Eid cleaning to do. The water was cut off all day today and the electricity was gone too. This seems to be happening all over Baghdad—we heard about the same situation in several areas. Can someone say "collective punishment"?! WE didn't kidnap your relatives, Allawi . . . it was Zarqawi, remember?!

Fallujah is still being destroyed and the stories we hear are mixed. It's difficult to tell what's true and what isn't. All we know is that there are dozens of civilians being killed. They also say 18 Americans have died and over a hundred are wounded.

Mosul is also a mess. They are saying there isn't a tank or patrol car in sight in that city.

Read more about the situation at Juan Cole [http://juancole.com]—would love to say more but the generator is going to be turned off in a couple of minutes.

Informed Comment, http://www.juancole.com, November 10, 2004

Associated Press surveys developments on Tuesday, including the deaths of 10 US troops in the fighting at Fallujah along with 2 Iraqi National Guardsmen. 11 troops had been killed on Monday, though the military spokesman did not give details.

The US continued to bombard the city heavily, destroying buildings and the Abbasi Restaurant. A US military spokesman estimated the

> number of guerrillas dead as a result of the bombing and of artillery fire at 90. Fallujah hospital said that 12 civilians had been killed and 17 wounded.
>
> CNN was reporting on Tuesday afternoon that the US troops had taken about 1/3 of Fallujah, which suggests that they are meeting very heavy resistance. The fighting is much harder here than it was at Baghdad during the war! Al-Hayat Wednesday morning was saying via AFP that US troops had reached the center of the city.
>
> Al-Hayat reports that in Baqubah, guerrillas attacked two police stations, killing 25 policemen, with 4 guerrillas killed; many persons were wounded.
>
> In Mosul, guerrillas fired mortar rounds at a US base, killing two US troops.
>
> A curfew was maintained in Baghdad. In some Sunni Arab cities, government offices closed altogether.
>
> AP says "A group of Iraqi Sunni clerics called for a boycott of the election. The vote is being held "over the corpses of those killed in Fallujah," said Harith al-Dhari, director of the Association of Muslim Clerics. A major Sunni political party quit the interim Iraqi government in protest over the U.S. assault."

posted by river @ 1:57 AM

Saturday, November 13, 2004

MURDER . . .

People in Fallujah are being murdered. The stories coming back are horrifying. People being shot in cold blood in the streets and being buried under tons of concrete and iron . . . where is the world? Bury Arafat and hurry up and pay attention to what's happening in Iraq.

They say the people have nothing to eat. No produce is going into the city and the water has been cut off for days and days. Do you know what it's like to have no clean water??? People are drinking contaminated water and coming down with diarrhoea and other diseases. There are corpses in the street because no one can risk leaving their home to bury people. Families are burying children and parents in the gardens of their homes. WHERE IS EVERYONE???

Furthermore, where is Sistani? Why isn't he saying anything about the situation? When the South was being attacked, Sunni clerics everywhere decried the attacks. Where is Sistani now, when people are looking to him for some reaction? The silence is deafening.

We're not leaving the house lately. There was a total of 8 hours of electricity today and we've been using the generator sparingly because there is a mysterious fuel shortage . . . several explosions were heard in different places.

Things are deteriorating swiftly.

More on Fallujah crisis here:

BBC News, http://news.bbc.co.uk. November 11, 2004
Eyewitness: Smoke and Corpses . . .

US troops, backed by Iraqi forces, are locked in a fierce fight to wrest the city of Falluja [Fallujah] from rebel control. The BBC News website spoke by phone to Fadhil Badrani, an Iraqi journalist and resident of Falluja who reports regularly for Reuters and the BBC World Service in Arabic. We are publishing his and other eyewitness accounts from the city in order to provide the fullest possible range of perspectives from those who are there:

A row of palm trees used to run along the street outside my house—now only the trunks are left.

The upper half of each tree has vanished, blown away by mortar fire.

From my window, I can also make out that the minarets of several mosques have been toppled.

There are more and more dead bodies on the streets and the stench is unbearable.

Smoke is everywhere. . . .

A house some doors from mine was hit during the bombardment on Wednesday night. A 13-year-old boy was killed. His name was Ghazi.

I tried to flee the city last night but I could not get very far. It was too dangerous.

I am getting used to the bombardment. I have learnt to sleep

> *through the noise—the smaller bombs no longer bother me. . . .*
>
> *It is hard to know how much people outside Falluja are aware of what is going on here.*
>
> *I want them to know about conditions inside this city—there are dead women and children lying on the streets.*
>
> *People are getting weaker from hunger. Many are dying from their injuries because there is no medical help left in the city whatsoever.*
>
> *Some families have started burying their dead in their gardens. . . .*

Iraqis will never forgive this—never. It's outrageous—it's genocide and America, with the help and support of Allawi, is responsible. May whoever contributes to this see the sorrow, terror and misery of the people suffering in Fallujah. **posted by river @ 1:30 AM**

Tuesday, November 16, 2004

AMERICAN HEROES . . .

I'm feeling sick—literally. I can't get the video Al-Jazeera played out of my head [http://www.aljazeera.com/me.asp?service_ID=5716]:

The mosque strewn with bodies of Iraqis—not still with prayer or meditation, but prostrate with death—Some seemingly bloated . . . an old man with a younger one leaning upon him . . . legs, feet, hands, blood everywhere . . . The dusty sun filtering in through the windows . . . the stillness of the horrid place. Then the stillness is broken—in walk some Marines, guns pointed at the bodies . . . the mosque resonates with harsh American voices arguing over a body—was he dead, was he alive? I watched, tense, wondering what they would do—I expected the usual Marine treatment—that a heavy, booted foot would kick the man perhaps to see if he groaned. But it didn't work that way—the crack of gunfire suddenly explodes in the mosque as the Marine fires at the seemingly dead man and then come the words, "He's dead now."

"He's dead now." He said it calmly, matter-of-factly, in a sort of sing-song voice that made my blood run cold . . . and the Marines around him didn't care. They just roamed around the mosque and began to drag around the corpses because, apparently, this was nothing to them. This was probably a commonplace incident.

We sat, horrified, stunned with the horror of the scene that unfolded in front of our eyes. It's the third day of Eid and we were finally able to gather as a family—a cousin, his wife and their two daughters, two aunts, and an elderly uncle. E. and my cousin had been standing in line for two days to get fuel so we could go visit the elderly uncle on the final day of a very desolate Eid. The room was silent at the end of the scene, with only the voice of the news anchor and the sobs of my aunt. My little cousin flinched and dropped her spoon, face frozen with shock, eyes wide with disbelief, glued to the television screen, "Is he dead? Did they kill him?" I swallowed hard, trying to gulp away the lump lodged in my throat and watched as my cousin buried his face in his hands, ashamed to look at his daughter.

"What was I supposed to tell them?" He asked, an hour later, after we had sent his two daughters to help their grandmother in the kitchen. "What am I supposed to tell them—'Yes darling, they killed him—the Americans killed a wounded man; they are occupying our country, killing people and we are sitting here eating, drinking and watching tv'?" He shook his head, "How much more do they have to see? What is left for them to see?"

They killed a wounded man. It's hard to believe. They killed a man who was completely helpless—like he was some sort of diseased animal. I had read the articles and heard the stories of this happening before—wounded civilians being thrown on the side of the road or shot in cold blood—but to see it happening on television is something else—it makes me crazy with anger.

And what will happen now? A criminal investigation against a single Marine who did the shooting? Just like what happened with the Abu Ghraib atrocities? A couple of people will be blamed and the whole thing will be buried under the rubble of idiotic military psychologists, defense analysts, Pentagon officials and spokespeople and it will be forgotten. In the end, all anyone will remember is that a single Marine shot and killed a single Iraqi "insurgent" and it won't matter anymore.

It's typical American technique—every single atrocity is lost and covered up by blaming a specific person and getting it over with. What people don't understand is that the whole military is infested with these psychopaths. In this last year we've seen murderers, torturers and xenophobes running around in tanks with guns. I don't care what does it: I don't care if it's the tension, the fear, the "enemy" . . . it's murder. We are occupied by murderers. We're under the same pressure, as Iraqis, except that we weren't trained for this situation, and yet we're all expected to be benevolent and understanding and, above all, grateful. I'm feeling sick, depressed, and frightened. I don't know what to say any- more . . . they aren't humans and they don't deserve any compassion.

So why is the world so obsessed with beheadings? How is this so very different? The difference is that the people who are doing the beheadings are extremists . . . the people slaughtering Iraqis—tortur- ing in prisons and shooting wounded prisoners—are "American Heroes." Congratulations, you must be so proud of yourselves today.

Mykeru.com has pictures [http://www.mykeru.com/weekly/2004_ 1114_1120.html#111604].

Excuse me please, I'm going to go be sick for a little while. **posted by river @ 9:37 PM**

Sunday, December 12, 2004

FUEL SHORTAGE . . .

It has been a sad few weeks.

The situation seems to be deteriorating daily. To brief you on a few things: Electricity is lousy. Many areas are on the damned 2 hours by 4 hours schedule and there are other areas that are completely in the dark—like A'adhamiya. The problem is that we're not getting much generator electricity because fuel has become such a big problem. People have to wait in line overnight now to fill up the car. It's a mys- tery. It really is. There was never such a gasoline crisis as the one we're facing now. We're an oil country and yet there isn't enough gasoline to go around . . .

Oh don't get me wrong—the governmental people have gasoline (they have special gas stations where there aren't all these annoying peo- ple, rubbing their hands with cold and cursing the Americans to the skies) . . . The Americans have gasoline. The militias get gasoline. It's the people who don't have it. We can sometimes get black-market gasoline but the liter costs around 1,250 Iraqi dinars which is almost $1—compare this to the old price of around 5 cents. It costs almost 50,000 Iraqi dinars to fill up the generator so that it works for a few hours and then the cost isn't so much the problem as just getting decent gasoline is. So we have to do without electricity most of the day.

Cooking gas has also become a problem. The guy who sells us the gas cylinders isn't coming around because apparently he can't get the used cylinders exchanged for full ones. People are saying that it costs around 10,000 Iraqi dinars to buy one on the street and then, as usual, you risk getting one that might explode in the kitchen or be full of water. We're trying to do more and more of our "cooking" on the kerosene heater. The faucet water is cold, cold, cold. We can't turn on the water heater because there just isn't enough electricity. We installed a kerosene water heater some time last year but that has also been off because there's a kerosene shortage and we need that for the heaters.

I took my turn at "gasoline duty" a couple of weeks ago. E. and my cousin were going to go wait for gasoline so I decided I'd join them and keep them company. We left the house at around 5 a.m. and it was dark and extremely cold. I thought for sure we'd be the first at the station but I discovered the line was about a kilometer long with dozens and dozens of cars lined up around the block. My heart sank at the discouraging sight but E. and the cousin looked optimistic, "We just might be able to fill up before evening this time!" E. smiled.

I spent the first hour jabbering away and trying to determine whether or not gasoline was actually being sold at the station. E. and the cousin were silent—they had set up a routine. One of them would doze while the other watched in case a miracle occurred and the line actually started moving. The second hour I spent trying to sleep with my neck at an uncomfortable angle on the back head rest. The third hour I enthusiastically tried to get up a game of "memorize the license plate." The fourth hour I fiddled with the radio and tried to sing along to every song being played on air. (It should be mentioned that at this point E. and the cousin threatened to throw Riverbend out of the car.)

All in all, it took E. and the cousin 13 hours to fill the car. I say E. and the cousin because I demanded to be taken home in a taxi after the first six hours and E. agreed to escort me with the condition that I would make sandwiches for him to take back to the cousin. In the end, half of the tank of gasoline was kept inside of the car (for emergencies) and the other half was sucked out for the neighborhood generator.

People are wondering how America and gang (i.e., Iyad Allawi, etc.) are going to implement democracy in all of this chaos when they can't seem to get the gasoline flowing in a country that virtually swims in oil. There's a rumor that this gasoline crisis has been concocted on purpose in order to keep a minimum of cars on the streets. Others claim that this whole situation is a form of collective punishment because things are really out of control in so many areas in Baghdad—especially the sub-urbs. The third theory is that this is being done purposely so that the Iraq government can amazingly bring the electricity, gasoline, kerosene and cooking gas back in January before the elections and make them-selves look like heroes.

We're also watching the election lists closely. Most people I've talked to aren't going to go to elections. It's simply too dangerous and there's a sense that nothing is going to be achieved anyway. The lists are more or less composed of people affiliated with the very same political parties whose leaders rode in on American tanks. Then you have a handful of tribal sheikhs. Yes—tribal sheikhs. Our country is going to be led by members of religious parties and tribal sheikhs—can anyone say Afghanistan? What's even more irritating is that election lists have to be checked and confirmed by none other than Sistani!! Sistani—the Iranian religious cleric. So basically, this war helped us make a transi-tion from a secular country being run by a dictator to a chaotic coun-try being run by a group of religious clerics. Now, can anyone say "theocracy in sheep's clothing"?

Ahmed Chalabi is at the head of one of those lists—who would join a list with Ahmed Chalabi at its head?

The borders are in an interesting state. Now this is something even Saddam didn't do: Iraqi men under the age of 50 aren't being let into the country. A friend of ours who was coming to visit was turned back at the Iraqi border. It was useless for him to try to explain that he had been outside of the country for 10 years and was coming back to visit his family. He was 47 and that meant he, in his expensive busi-ness suit, shining leather shoes, and impressive Samsonite baggage, might be a "Jihadist." Silly Iraqis—Iraqi men under 50 are a sure threat to the security of their country. American men with guns and tanks are, on the other hand, necessary to the welfare of the country. Lebanese, Kuwaitis and men of other nationalities being hired as mercenaries are vital to the security of said country. Iranian men coming to visit the shrines in the south are all welcome . . . but Iraqi men? Maybe they should head for Afghanistan.

The assault on Fallujah and other areas is continuing. There are rumors of awful weapons being used in Fallujah. The city has literally been burnt and bombed to the ground. Many of the people displaced from the city are asking to be let back in, in spite of everything. I can't even begin to imagine how difficult it must be for the refugees. It's like we've turned into another Palestine—occupation, bombings, refugees, death. Sometimes I'll be watching the news and the volume will be really low. The scene will be of a man, woman or child, wailing in front of the camera; crying at the fate of a body lying bloodily, stiffly on the ground—a demolished building in the background and it will take me a few moments to decide the location of this tragedy—Fallujah? Gaza? Baghdad? **posted by river @ 8:37 PM**

Saturday, December 18, 2004

CHRISTMAS WISHLIST . . .

I have to make this fast.

No electricity for three days in a row (well, unless you count that glorious hour we got 3 days ago . . .). Generators on gasoline are hardly working at all. Generators on diesel fuel aren't faring much better—most will only work for 3 or 4 straight hours; then they have to be turned off to rest.

Ok—what is the typical Iraqi Christmas wishlist (I won't list "peace," "security" and "freedom"—Christmas miracles are exclusive to Charles Dickens), let's see:

1. 20 liters of gasoline
2. A cylinder of gas for cooking

3. Kerosene for the heaters

4. Those expensive blast-proof windows

5. Landmine detectors

6. Running water

7. Thuraya satellite phones (the mobile phone services are really, really bad of late)

8. Portable diesel generators (for the whole family to enjoy!)

9. Coleman rechargeable flashlight with extra batteries (you can never go wrong with a fancy flashlight)

10. Scented candles (it shows you care—but you're also practical)

When Santa delivers please make sure he is wearing a bullet-proof vest and helmet. He should also politely ring the doorbell or knock, as a more subtle entry might bring him face to face with an AK-47. With the current fuel shortage, reindeer and a sleigh are highly practical— but Rudolph should be left behind as the flashing red nose might create a bomb scare (we're all a little jumpy lately).

By the way, until further notice, please send any emails to river-bend_baghdad@yahoo.com as I'm having some minor problems with the other accounts. **posted by river @ 3:57 PM**

January Through March 2005

In January, the Iraq Survey Group announces that it has ended its search for WMD in Iraq. They have concluded that two years earlier, when the United States invaded Iraq, Saddam Hussein had no WMD stockpiles, nor had he started any programs to produce them.

The Bush Administration promptly launches a new public relations campaign, announcing that the president has set up an independent commission "to find out what went wrong" with prewar intelligence on WMDs "and to correct those flaws." While the Commission's report, issued a year later, will not be entirely to the president's liking, critics of the administration nonetheless suggest that its creation is another piece of clever political spin: In creating the "Commission on the Intelligence Capabilities of the United States Regarding Weapons of Mass Destruction," they keep the focus strictly on "intelligence failures." This approach ignores the fact that top administration officials, already intent upon going to war with Iraq, clearly pressured the CIA into reaching certain conclusions, ignored evidence to the contrary, and further distorted intelligence to serve its aims.

The administration also hastens to emphasize that none of this means the United States should not have invaded Iraq. White House spokesperson Scott McClellan explains, "We had a regime that had a history of using weapons of mass destruction and had a history of defying the international community and had a history of ties to terrorist organizations in Iraq. We had the attacks on September 11, that taught us we must confront threats before it's too late. That's what the the president's committed to doing. Because this is about making America more secure."

Whether America is indeed "more secure" is, of course, doubtful: one intelligence official tells CNN that "many of the military and intelligence personnel who had been assigned to the weapons search are now working on counterinsurgency matters." As Riverbend herself points out, though Iraq was not a threat to Americans before the invasion, thanks to the war and occupation, "Congratulations Bush, we are a threat now."

At the end of January, in the first elections since the war, more than 8 million Iraqis go to the polls to elect a transitional National Assembly. This 275-member body is supposed to write a new constitution for the country.

The Shia United Iraqi Alliance comes away the clear winner, with 48 percent of the vote and a majority of assembly seats. The leading Kurdish party is second, with 26 percent, and Iyad Allawi's slate gets about 14 percent.

Insurgent groups have promised to disrupt the elections. Security is heavy and the attacks are declared to have been less widespread than anticipated, although they kill more than 40 people. But a majority of Sunni Iraqis does not participate in the elections. Sunnis are between 20 and 30 percent of the population, but the largest Sunni party receives less the 2 percent of the vote. Sunnis leaders have declared that the elections cannot produce fair results, in part because the violence in concentrated in Sunni areas. They want the election postponed, and when their request is turned down, many advocate a boycott. Others simply refuse to participate in an election held under foreign occupation.

Kidnappings of both Iraqis and foreigners continue. After a month in captivity, kidnapped Italian journalist Giuliana Sgrena is recovered unharmed on March 4 by members of the Italian military secret service, but one of her rescuers is shot in the head by American forces on the road to the Baghdad airport. Subsequent American reports say that the car was speeding, that it did not respond to signals to stop, and that they had no idea the rescue had taken place; Italian reports disagree on all three points.

The war gets worse and worse. In a car bombing at Hilla, south of

Baghdad, 114 people are killed. For American troops, January is the third most deadly month since they entered Iraq, with 107 soldiers killed. In another month the total will have surpassed 1,500. At home, the Pentagon's recruiting drive takes a dive.

—James Ridgeway

NEW YEAR AND ELECTIONS . . .

We spent New Year at home (like last year). It was a very small family gathering and E. and I tried to make it as festive as possible, under the circumstances. We agreed, amongst ourselves in the area, to have the generator turned on from 10 p.m. until 2 a.m. so we could ride out 2004 on a wave of electricity.

The good part of the evening consisted of food. Food is such a central issue for an Iraqi occasion—be it happy or sad. We end up discussing the food before anything else. For us, it was just some traditional Iraqi food and some junk food like popcorn, corn chips, and lots of candy.

We sat watching celebrations from different parts of the world. Seeing the fireworks, lights, droves of laughing and singing people really emphasizes our current situation. It feels like we are kind of standing still while the world is passing us by. It really is difficult to believe that come April, two years will have passed on the war and occupation. On most days, an hour feels like ten and yet, at the same time, it becomes increasingly difficult to get a good sense of passing time. I guess that is because we measure time with development and since things seem to be deteriorating in many ways, it feels almost as if we're going backwards, not forwards.

. . .

On the other hand, the whole tsunami/earthquake crisis also had a dampening affect on celebrations this year. It is a tragedy that will haunt the area for decades. To lose so many people so swiftly and violently is horrific. Watching all that chaos and death kind of makes you feel that maybe Baghdad isn't the absolute worse place to be.

We had our own fireworks as we began the New Year countdown. At around 10 minutes to 2005, the house shook with three colossal explosions not too far away. It came as something of a surprise at that particular moment and my cousin's two young daughters, after the initial fright, started giggling uncontrollably. E. clapped his hands and began to yell, "Yeah—FIREWORKS!! Goodbye 2004!!" which was followed by a sort of impromptu dance by the kids.

The elections are set for the 29th. It's an interesting situation. The different sects and factions just can't seem to agree. Sunni Arabs are going to boycott elections. It's not about religion or fatwas or any of that so much as the principle of holding elections while you are under occupation. People don't really sense that this is the first stepping stone to democracy as the Western media is implying. Many people sense that this is just the final act of a really bad play. It's the tying of the ribbon on the "democracy parcel" we've been handed. It's being stuck with an occupation government that has been labeled "legitimate" through elections.

We're being bombarded with cute Iraqi commercials of happy Iraqi families preparing to vote. Signs and billboards remind us that the elections are getting closer . . .

Can you just imagine what our history books are going to look like 20 years from now?

"The first democratic elections were held in Iraq on January 29, 2005 under the ever-watchful collective eye of the occupation forces, headed by the United States of America. Troops in tanks watched as swarms of warm, fuzzy Iraqis headed for the ballot boxes to select one of the American-approved candidates . . ."

It won't look good.

There are several problems. The first is the fact that, technically, we don't know the candidates. We know the principal heads of the lists but we don't know who exactly will be running. It really is confusing. They aren't making the lists public because they are afraid the candidates will be assassinated.

Another problem is the selling of ballots. We're getting our ballots through the people who give out the food rations in the varying areas. The whole family is registered with this person(s) and the ages of the varying family members are known. Many, many, many people are not going to vote. Some of those people are selling their voting cards for up to $400. The word on the street is that these ballots are being bought by people coming in from Iran. They will purchase the ballots, make false IDs (which is ridiculously easy these days) and vote for SCIRI [Supreme Council for the Islamic Revolution in Iraq] or Da'awa candidates. Sunnis are receiving their ballots although they don't intend to vote, just so that they won't be sold.

Yet another issue is the fact that on all the voting cards, the gender of the voter, regardless of sex, is labeled "male." Now, call me insane, but I found this slightly disturbing. Why was that done? Was it some sort of a mistake? Why is the sex on the card anyway? What difference does it make? There are some theories about this. Some are saying that many of the more religiously inclined families won't want their womenfolk voting so it might be permissible for the head of the family to take the women's ID and her ballot and do the voting for her. Another theory is that this "mistake" will make things easier for people making fake IDs to vote in place of females.

All of this has given the coming elections a sort of sinister cloak. There is too much mystery involved and too little transparency. It is more than a little bit worrisome. American politicians seem to be very confident that Iraq is going to come out of these elections with a secular government. How is that going to happen when many Shia Iraqis are being driven to vote with various fatwas from Sistani and gang? Sistani and some others of Iranian inclination came out with fatwas claiming that nonvoters will burn in the hottest fires of the underworld for an eternity if they don't vote (I'm wondering—was this a fatwa borrowed from right-wing Bushies during the American elections?). So someone fuelled with a scorching fatwa like that one—how will they vote? Secular? Yeah, right. **posted by river @ 2:40 PM**

. . .

THE PHANTOM WEAPONS . . .

The phone hasn't been working for almost a week now. We just got the line back today. For the last six days, I'd pick up the phone and hear . . . silence. Nothing. This vast nothingness would be followed by a few futile "hellos" and a forceful punching of some random numbers with my index finger. It isn't always like this, of course. On some days, you can pick up the telephone and hear a bunch of other people screaming "Allooo? Allooo?" E. once struck up a conversation with a complete stranger over the phone because they were both waiting for a line. E. wanted to call our uncle and the woman was trying to call her grandson.

The dial-tone came about an hour ago (I've been checking since morning) and I'm taking advantage of it.

The electricity situation isn't very much better. We're getting two hours of electricity (almost continuous) and then eight hours of no electricity (continuous). We still can't get the generators going for very long because of the fuel shortage. Kerosene is really becoming a problem now. I guess we weren't taking it very seriously at first because it really is probably the first time Iraq has seen a kerosene shortage and it is still difficult to believe. They say in 1991 when there was a gasoline shortage which lasted for the duration of the war and some time after, kerosene was always plentiful. This isn't the situation now. We're buying it for obscene prices and it's really only useful for the lamps and the heaters.

It feels like just about everyone who can is going to leave the country before the elections. They say the borders between Syria and Jordan might be closed a week before elections so people are rushing to get packed and get out. Many families are simply waiting for their school-age children to finish mid-year finals or college exams so they can leave.

This was an interesting piece of news a couple of days ago:

The United States has ended its physical search for weapons of mass destruction (WMD) in Iraq, which was cited by the first administration of President George W Bush as the main reason for invading the country, the White House has said. [http://sify.com/news/fullstory.php?id=13647921]

Why does this not surprise me? Does it surprise anyone? I always had the feeling that the only people who actually believed this war was about weapons of mass destruction were either paranoid Americans or deluded expatriate Iraqis—or a combination of both. I wonder now, after hundreds and hundreds of Americans actually died on Iraqi soil and over a hundred-thousand Iraqis are dead, how Americans view the current situation. I have another question—the article mentions a "Duelfer Report" stating the weapons never existed and all the intelligence was wrong. This report was supposedly published in October 2004. The question is this: Was this report made public before the elections? Did Americans actually vote for Bush with this knowledge?

Over here, it's not really "news" in the sense that it's not new. We've been expecting a statement like this for the last two years. While we were aware the whole WMD farce was just a badly produced black comedy, it's still upsetting to hear Bush's declaration that he was wrong. It's upsetting because it just confirms the worst: Right-wing Americans don't care about justifying this war. They don't care about right or wrong or innocents dead and more to die. They were somewhat ahead of the game. When they saw their idiotic president wasn't going to find weapons anywhere in Iraq, they decided it would be about mass graves. It wasn't long before the very people who came to "liberate" a sovereign country soon began burying more Iraqis in mass graves. The smart weapons began to stupidly kill "possibly innocent" civilians (they are only "definitely innocent" if they are working with the current Iraqi security forces or American troops). It went once more from protecting poor Iraqis from themselves to protecting Americans from "terrorists." Zarqawi very conveniently entered the picture.

Zarqawi is so much better than WMD. He's small, compact and mobile. He can travel from Fallujah to Baghdad to Najaf to Mosul . . . whichever province or city really needs to be oppressed. Also, conveniently, he looks like the typical Iraqi male—dark hair, dark eyes, olive skin, medium build. I wonder how long it will take the average American to figure out that he's about as substantial as our previously alleged WMD.

. . .

Now we're being "officially" told that the weapons never existed. After Iraq has been devastated, we're told it's a mistake. You look around Baghdad and it is heart-breaking. The streets are ravaged, the sky is a bizarre grayish-bluish color—a combination of smoke from fires and weapons and smog from cars and generators. There is an endless wall that seems to suddenly emerge in certain areas to protect the Green Zoners . . . There is common look to the people on the streets—under the masks of fear, anger and suspicion, there's also a haunting look of uncertainty and indecision. Where is the country going? How long will it take for things to even have some vague semblance of normality? When will we ever feel safe?

A question poses itself at this point—why don't they let the scientists go if the weapons don't exist? Why do they have Iraqi scientists like Huda Ammash, Rihab Taha and Amir Al-Saadi still in prison? Perhaps they are waiting for those scientists to conveniently die in prison? That way—they won't be able to talk about the various torture techniques and interrogation tactics . . .

I hope Americans feel good about taking their war on terror to foreign soil. For bringing the terrorists to Iraq—Chalabi, Allawi, Zarqawi, the Hakeems . . . How is our current situation going to secure America? How is a complete generation that is growing up in fear and chaos going to view Americans ten years from now? Does anyone ask that? After September 11, because of what a few fanatics did, Americans decided to become infected with a collective case of xenophobia . . . Yet after all Iraqis have been through under the occupation, we're expected to be tolerant and grateful. Why? Because we get more wheat in our diets?

Terror isn't just worrying about a plane hitting a skyscraper . . . terrorism is being caught in traffic and hearing the crack of an AK-47 a few meters away because the National Guard want to let an American humvee or Iraqi official through. Terror is watching your house being raided and knowing that the silliest thing might get you dragged away to Abu Ghraib where soldiers can torture, beat and kill. Terror is that first moment after a series of machine-gun shots, when you lift your head frantically to make sure your loved ones are still in one piece. Terror is trying to pick the shards of glass resulting from a nearby explosion out of the living-room couch and trying not to imagine what would have happened if a person had been sitting there.

The weapons never existed. It's like having a loved one sentenced to death for a crime they didn't commit—having your country burned and bombed beyond recognition, almost. Then, after two years of grieving for the lost people, and mourning the lost sovereignty, we're told we were innocent of harboring those weapons. We were never a threat to America . . .

Congratulations Bush—we are a threat now. **posted by river @ 10:53 PM**

IMAD KHADDURI'S BLOG . . .

Remember Imad Khadduri? He's the Iraqi nuclear scientist who wrote the book *Iraq's Nuclear Mirage* [http://www.iraqsnuclearmirage.com/index_en.php], which is a must-read. He's finally blogging. Check out his site, "Free Iraq" [http://abutamam.blogspot.com]—"Free Iraq" being more of a command and not a description of the current state of the country . . .

He links a lot of interesting articles and always has commentary in English (plus some of the stuff he writes in Arabic). **posted by river @ 11:06 PM**

Saturday, January 22, 2005

BLEAK EID . . .

It's the third day of Eid. Eid is the Islamic holiday and usually it's a time for families to get together, eat, drink and celebrate. Not this Eid. This Eid is unbearable. We managed a feeble gathering on the first day and no one was in a celebratory mood. There have been several explosions—some far and some near but even those aren't as worrisome as the tension that seems to be growing on a daily basis.

There hasn't been a drop of water in the faucets for six days. Six days. Even at the beginning of the occupation, when the water would disappear in the summer, there was always a trickle that would come from one of the pipes in the garden. Now, even that is gone. We've been purchasing bottles of water (the price has gone up) to use for cooking and drinking. Forget about cleaning. It's really frustrating because everyone cleans house during Eid. It's like a part of the tradition. The days leading up to Eid are a frenzy of mops, brooms, dusting rags and disinfectant. The cleaning makes one feel like there's room for a fresh start. It's almost as if the house and its inhabitants are being reborn. Not this year. We're managing just enough water to rinse dishes with. To bathe, we have to try to make-do with a few liters of water heated in pots on kerosene heaters. Water is like peace—you never really know just how valuable it is until someone takes it away. It's maddening to walk up to the sink, turn one of the faucets and hear the pipes groan with nothing. The toilets don't function . . . the dishes sit piled up until two of us can manage to do them—one scrubbing and rinsing and the other pouring the water.

Why is this happening? Is it because of the electricity? If it is, we should at least be getting water a couple of hours a day—like before. Is it some sort of collective punishment leading up to the elections? It's unbelievable. At first, I thought it was just our area but I've been asking around and apparently, almost all of the areas (if not all) are suffering this drought.

I'm sure people outside of the country are shaking their heads at the words "collective punishment." "No, Riverbend," they are saying, "That's impossible." But anything is possible these days. People in many areas are being told that if they don't vote—Sunnis and Shia alike—the food and supply rations we are supposed to get monthly will be cut off. We've been getting these rations since the beginning of the nineties and for many families, it's their main source of sustenance. What sort of democracy is it when you FORCE people to go vote for someone or another they don't want?

Allawi's people were passing out pamphlets a few days ago. I went out to the garden to check the low faucet, hoping to find a trickle of water and instead, I found some paper crushed under the garden gate. Upon studying it, it turned out to be some sort of "Elect Allawi" pamphlet promising security and prosperity, amongst other things, for occupied Iraq. I'd say it was a completely useless pamphlet but that isn't completely true. It fit nicely on the bottom of the cage of E.'s newly acquired pet parakeet. They say the borders are closed with Jordan and possibly Syria. I also heard yesterday that people aren't being let into Baghdad. They have American check-points on the main roads leading into the city and they say that the cars are being turned back to wherever they came from. It's a bad situation and things are looking very bleak at this point.

It's amazing how as things get worse, you begin to require less and less. We have a saying for that in Iraq, "*Ili yishoof il mawt, yirdha bil iskhooneh*," which means, "If you see death, you settle for a fever." We've given up on democracy, security and even electricity. Just bring back the water. posted by river @ 4:19 PM

Thursday, January 27, 2005

WATER ANXIETY . . .

I have to make this fast. We have about two hours of electricity—hopefully. The water came back yesterday evening. It's just a little drizzle but it's certainly better than nothing.

E. was the first to hear it. We were sitting in the living room and he suddenly jumped up, alert, "Do you hear that?" He asked. I strained my ears for either the sound of a plane or helicopter or gun shots. Nothing . . . except, wait . . . something . . . like a small stream of . . . water? Could it be? Was it back? We both ran into the bathroom where we had the faucets turned on for the last eight days in anticipation of water. Sure enough, there it was—a little stream of water that kept coming and going as if undecided. E. and I did a little victory dance in front of the sink with some celebratory hoots and clapping.

This was followed by a lot of work. We spent the rest of the evening filling anything that was fillable—pots, pans, cups, bottles and buckets. The formerly empty area under the staircase is now filled with big pots of water covered with trays and mismatching pot covers to keep out stray bugs and dust.

I almost didn't sleep last night. I kept worrying the water would be cut off again. I actually crept downstairs at 4 a.m. to see if it was still there and found E. standing in the bathroom doorway doing the same. My mother is calling the syndrome "water anxiety." We were hoping the flow would grow stronger at night but apparently the water pressure is really low. E. and I rose early this morning because we decided last night that should the water continue to flow, we'd attempt to fill up the big water tank on the roof. The water from this tank goes directly to the electric water heater but since we haven't been using that for a while now, we decided to close up the tank and use it as a sort of secondary storage. We cannot get caught off-guard again. Drinking water rose to almost 1,000 dinars a liter this last week.

E. and I spent the day carrying up buckets of water. The water flow is so weak, it takes about 17 minutes to fill up a 10 liter plastic pail (I was timing it). We've carried up about 10 buckets now. The water still doesn't reach the kitchen faucets so we've managed to move the dirty dishes to the bathroom and are washing them there.

Unfortunately, the electricity situation has deteriorated. We're getting about four hours for every twenty hours in our area—I'm not quite sure what's going on in the other areas. It feels like we're almost cut off from each other.

Baghdad has been unstable these last few days. We had several explosions this last week and although the number of explosions wasn't surprising, the force of a couple of them had us wincing. There's a real fear of the coming elections and what they might bring. I don't like the idea that they've selected schools as election sites. School is out right now, but the security threat is obvious—elections sites are most likely going to be bombed. Schools are having a difficult time as it is getting things fixed and replaced, they don't need the added trauma of an explosion. It's just a bad idea.

The curfew begins at six from now on and there's also a "driving curfew" in addition to the ordinary one. I don't have the exact hours but I know that during several hours of the day, it's ok to be on foot but not ok to be in a car. I don't have the slightest idea how they're going to enforce that one.

Ghazi Al-Yawir, our alleged current president, was giving an interview on LBC yesterday. Apparently, he and Allawi aren't on the same election list anymore because they had a falling out as to who should head the list. Ghazi proposed the president should be the head of the list and Allawi claimed somebody Shia (Allawi himself) should head the list. Now, Allawi's group is 285 on the election ballot and Yawir's group is 288, I think.

My favorite question during the interview was when the reporter asked him what he thought of Chalabi possibly being arrested. Ghazi looked flustered and a little bit unsure (apparently he hasn't been watching CNN while abroad). He actually told her that the person who claimed Chalabi was wanted was probably speaking his own "personal" opinion and that it wasn't representative of the "government"—never mind the person in question was the Minister of Defense. To be perfectly fair, he didn't mention which government he was referring to—I couldn't tell if he was talking about the United States, the United Kingdom or the current group of Puppets. He claimed that for Chalabi to be arrested there needed to be "proof" he had actually done something wrong . . . the Interpol wanting him really wasn't enough.

It's a bit discouraging to watch the current government be so uncoordinated. It's like they don't even communicate with each other. It's also somewhat disturbing to know that they can't seem to decide who is a criminal and who isn't. Isn't there some "idiot's guide to being a good Vichy government"?

They say communications are going to be cut off very soon. Telephones are often cut off and the mobile network is sometimes inaccessible for days at a time but we heard there also might not be web access. Students have a mid-year vacation right now but no one is going anywhere. Almost everyone is trapped at home because the security situation is quite bad and no one wants to be caught in an area where an explosion might occur. If the bomb doesn't kill you, the Iraqi security forces or the Americans might and if no one kills you then you risk getting a bag over the head and a trip to Abu Ghraib.

There's an almost palpable anxiety in the air these last couple of weeks and it's beginning to wear on people—fuel shortages, water shortages and a lack of electricity. It's like the first days of the war all over again.

Juan Cole has "The Speech Bush SHOULD have Given" and it's quite good. In my opinion, during this year's inaugural Bush could have summed it up with the following: "Ha! I can't believe you people actually reelected me! Unbelievable! Some people just loooove the abuse!!!"

. . .

Informed Comment, http://www.juancole.com, January 26, 2005

This is the speech that I wish President Bush had given in fall, 2002, as he was trying to convince Congress to give him the authority to go to war against Iraq.

My fellow Americans:
I want us to go to war against Iraq. But I want us to have our eyes open and be completely realistic.

A war against Iraq will be expensive. It will cost you, the taxpayer, about $300 billion over five years. I know Wolfowitz is telling you Iraq's oil revenues will pay for it all, but that's ridiculous. Iraq only pumps about $10 billion a year worth of oil, and it's going to need that just to run the new government we're putting in. No, we're going to have to pay for it, ourselves. . . . The cost of the war is going to drive up my already massive budget deficits from about $370 billion to more like $450 billion a year. Just so you understand, I'm going to cut taxes on rich people at the same time that I fight this war. Then I'm going to borrow the money to fight it, and to pay for much of what the government does. And you and your children will be paying off that debt for decades. . . .

So I'm going to put you, your children, and your grandchildren deeply in hock to fight this war. I'm going to make it so there won't be a lot of new jobs created, and I'm going to use the excuse of the Federal red ink to cut way back on government services that you depend on. . . .

Then, this Iraq War that I want you to authorize as part of the War on Terror is going to be costly in American lives. By the time of my second inaugural, over 1,300 brave women and men of the US armed forces will be dead as a result of this Iraq war, and 10,371 will have been maimed and wounded, many of them for life. America's streets and homeless shelters will likely be flooded, down the line, with some of these wounded vets. They will have problems finding work, with one or two limbs gone and often significant psychological damage. They will have even more trouble keeping any jobs they find. They will be mentally traumatized the rest of their lives by the horror they are going to see, and sometimes commit, in Iraq. But, well we've got a saying in Texas. I think you've got in over in Arkansas, too. You can't make an omelette without . . . you gotta break some eggs to wrassle up some breakfast.

> *I know Dick Cheney and Condi Rice have gone around scaring your kids with wild talk of Iraqi nukes. I have to confess to you that my CIA director, George Tenet, tells me that the evidence for that kind of thing just doesn't exist. . . Iraq just doesn't pose any immediate threat to the United States and probably doesn't have anything useful left of their weapons programs of the 1980s.*
>
> *There also isn't any operational link between a secular Arab nationalist like Saddam and the religious loonies of al-Qaeda. They're scared of one another and hate each other more than each hates us. In fact, I have to be perfectly honest and admit that if we overthrow Saddam's secular Arab nationalist government, Iraq's Sunni Arabs will be disillusioned and full of despair. They are likely to turn to al-Qaeda as an alternative. So, folks, what I'm about to do could deliver 5 million Iraqis into the hands of people who are insisting they join some al-Qaeda offshoot immediately. Or else.*
>
> *So why do I want to go to war? Look, folks, I'm just not going to tell you. I don't have to tell you. There is little transparency about these things in the executive, because we're running a kind of rump empire out of the president's office. After 20 or 30 years it will all leak out. Until then, you'll just have to trust me.*

posted by river @ 4:29 PM

Saturday, February 12, 2005

AND LIFE GOES ON . . .

The elections have come and gone. The day of elections was a day of eerie silence punctuated by a few strong explosions and the hum of helicopters above. We remained at home and watched the situation on tv. E. left for about an hour to see what was happening at the local polling area, which was a secondary school nearby. He said there were maybe 50 people at the school and a lot of them looked like they were involved with the local electoral committee. The polling station near our house was actually being guarded by SCIRI people (Badir's Brigade).

It was like a voting marathon for all of the news channels—

everywhere you turned there was news of the elections. CNN, Euronews, BBC, Jazeera, Arabia, LBC . . . everyone was talking elections. The Arab news channels were focusing largely on voting abroad while CNN kept showing footage from the southern provinces and the northern ones.

I literally had chills going up and down my spine as I watched Abdul Aziz Al-Hakeem of Iranian-inclined SCIRI dropping his ballot into a box. Behind him, giving moral support and her vote, was what I can only guess to be his wife. She was shrouded literally from head to foot and only her eyes peeped out of the endless sea of black. She stuffed her ballot in the box with black-gloved hands and submissively followed a very confident Hakeem. E. turned to me with a smile and a wink, "That might be you in a couple of years . . ." I promptly threw a sofa cushion at him.

Most of our acquaintances (Sunni and Shia) didn't vote. My cousin, who is Shia, didn't vote because he felt he didn't really have "representation" on the lists, as he called it. I laughed when he said that, "But you have your pick of at least 40 different Shia parties!" I teased, winking at his wife. I understood what he meant though. He's a secular, educated, non-occupation Iraqi before he's Sunni or Shia—he's more concerned with having someone who wants to end the occupation than someone Shia.

We're hearing about various strange happenings at different voting areas. They say that several areas in northern Iraq (some Assyrian and some Christian areas) weren't allowed to vote. They also say that 300 different ballot boxes from all over the country were disqualified (mainly from Mosul) because a large number of the vote ballots had "Saddam" written on them. In other areas there's talk of Badir's Brigade people having bought the ballots to vote, and while the people of Fallujah weren't allowed to vote, people say that the identities of Fallujans were temporarily "borrowed" for voting purposes. The stories are endless.

In spite of that, we're all watching for the results carefully. When the "elected" government takes control, will they set a timetable for American withdrawal? That would be a shocker considering none of the current parties would be able to remain in power without being forcefully backed by America with tanks and troops. We hear American politicians repeatedly saying that America will not withdraw until Iraq can secure itself. When will that happen? Our current National Guard or *Haress il Watani* are fondly called *Haress il Wathani* or "Infidel Guard" by people in the streets. On top of it all, to be one of them is considered such a disgrace by the general population that they have to wear masks so that none of them can be identified by neighbors and friends.

The results won't really matter when so many people boycotted the elections. No matter what the numbers say, the reality of the situation is that there are millions of Iraqis who will refuse to submit to an occupation government. After almost two years of occupation, and miserable living conditions, we want our country back.

I do have my moments of weakness though, when I wonder who will be allowed to have power. Politicians are talking about a balance that might arise from a Shia-Kurdish alliance and it makes a lot of sense in theory. In theory, the Kurdish leaders are Sunni and secular and the Shia leaders are, well, they're not exactly secular. If they get along, things should work out evenly. That looks good on blogs and on paper. Reality is quite different. Reality is that the Kurdish leaders are more concerned about their own autonomy and as long as the Kurdish north remains secular, the rest of Iraq can go up in flames.

An example is the situation in Baghdad today. The parties that have power in colleges today are actually the Iranian inclined Shia parties like Da'awa and SCIRI. Student representatives in colleges and universities these days mainly come from the abovementioned parties. They harass Christian and Muslim girls about what they should and shouldn't wear. They invite students to attend *latmiyas* (mainly Shia religious festivities where the participants cry and beat themselves in sorrow over the killing of the Prophet's family) and bully the cafeteria or canteen guy into not playing music during Ramadhan and instead showing the aforementioned *latmiyas* and Shia religious lectures by Ayatollah So-and-So and *Sayid* Something-or-Another.

Last week my cousin needed to visit the current Ministry of Higher Education. After the ministry building was burned and looted, the employees had to be transferred to a much, much smaller building in another part of the city. My cousin's wife wanted to have her college degree legalized by the ministry and my cousin wasn't sure how to go about doing it. So I volunteered to go along with him because I had some questions of my own.

. . .

We headed for the building containing the ministry employees (but hardly ever containing the minister). It was small and cramped. Every eight employees were stuck in the same room. The air was tense and heavy. We were greeted in the reception area by a bearded man who scanned us disapprovingly. "Da'awachi," my cousin whispered under his breath, indicating the man was from the Da'awa Party. What could he do for us? Who did we want? We wanted to have some documents legalized by the ministry, I said loudly, trying to cover up my nervousness. He looked at me momentarily and then turned to the cousin pointedly. My cousin repeated why we were there and asked for directions. We were told to go to one of the rooms on the same floor and begin there.

"Please dress appropriately next time you come here." The man said to me. I looked down at what I was wearing—black pants, a beige high-necked sweater and a knee-length black coat. Huh? I blushed furiously. He meant my head should be covered and I should be wearing a skirt. I don't like being told what to wear and what not to wear by strange men. "I don't work here—I don't have to follow a dress code." I answered coldly. The cousin didn't like where the conversation was going. He angrily interceded, "We're only here for an hour and it really isn't your business."

"It is my business," came the answer. "She should have some respect for the people who work here." And the conversation ended. I looked around for the people I should be respecting. There were three or four women who were apparently ministry employees. Two of them were wearing long skirts, loose sweaters and headscarves and the third had gone all out and was wearing a complete *jubba* or robe-like garb topped with a black head scarf. My cousin and I turned to enter the room the receptionist had indicated and my eyes were stinging. No one could talk that way before the war and, if they did, you didn't have to listen. You could answer back. Now, you only answer back and make it an issue if you have some sort of death wish or just really, really like trouble.

Young females have the option of either just giving in to the pressure and dressing and acting "safely"—which means making everything longer and looser and preferably covering some of their head or constantly being defiant to what is becoming endemic in Iraq today. The problem with defiance is that it doesn't just involve you personally, it involves anyone with you at that moment—usually a male relative. It means that there might be an exchange of ugly words or a fight and probably, after that, a detention in Abu Ghraib.

If it's like this in Baghdad, I shudder to think what the other cities and provinces must be like. The Allawis and Pachichis of Iraq don't sense it—their families are safely tucked away in Dubai and Amman, and the Hakeems and Jaffaris of Iraq promote it.

At the end of the day, it's not about having a Sunni or Shia or Kurd or Arab in power. It's about having someone who has Iraq's best interests at heart—not America's, not Iran's, not Israel's . . . It's about needing someone who wants peace, prosperity, independence, and above and beyond all, unity. **posted by river @ 12:41 AM**

Friday, February 18, 2005

GROCERIES AND ELECTION RESULTS . . .

Yesterday, one of our neighbors stopped by the house. She was carrying a hot plate of some green beans in a tomato sauce. "Abu Ammar has some wonderful green beans," she confided. "But you have to tell him to give you some of the ones he hides under the table—the ones on display are a little bit chewy." I added green beans to the grocery list and headed off with E. to Abu Ammar.

Our local grocer, Abu Ammar has a vegetable and fruit stand set up about 400 meters away from our house, on the main street. He has been there for as long as anyone can remember and, although you would not know it to see him, Abu Ammar is quite the entrepreneur. He wears a traditional dishdasha all year round and, on cold days, a worn leather jacket and a black wool cap he pulls down over his ears.

We, and almost every house on the street, buy our groceries from him. He sets up his stand early in the morning and when you pass by it at just the right time, there's a myriad of colors: the even brown of potatoes, deep green of spinach, bright orange of citrus fruits and the glossy red of sweet Iraqi tomatoes . . . And Abu Ammar is almost always there—come rain or sun or war, sitting in the midst of his vegetables and fruits, going through a newspaper, a cigarette in his mouth, and crackling out of his little transistor radio are the warm tones of Fayrouz. On those rare occasions when Abu Ammar isn't there, you can tell something is very wrong.

Abu Ammar sat there in his usual place. I could tell he was doing a crossword today because he kept making marks on the newspaper. Abu Ammar rose to greet us and handed me a few plastic bags so I could pick and choose the vegetables I wanted. "I have some very good lemons today," he declared, tucking the newspaper under his arm and pointing to a pyramid of small greenish-yellow fruits. I wandered over to the lemons and inspected them critically.

I feel like I have my finger on the throbbing pulse of the Iraqi political situation every time I visit Abu Ammar. You can often tell just how things are going in the country from the produce available at his stand. For example, when he doesn't have any good tomatoes we know that the roads to Basra[h] are either closed or really bad and the tomatoes aren't getting through to Baghdad. When citrus fruit isn't available during the winter months, we know that the roads to Diyala are probably risky and oranges and lemons couldn't be delivered. He'll also give you the main news headlines he picks up from various radio stations and, if you feel so inclined, you can read the headlines from any one of the assorted newspapers lying in a pile near his feet. Plus, he has all of the neighborhood gossip.

"Did you know Abu Hamid's family is going to move?" He took a drag from the cigarette and pointed with his ballpoint pen towards a house about 100 meters away from his stand.

"Really?" I asked, turning my attention to the tomatoes, "How did you hear?" "I saw them showing the house to a couple last week and then I saw them showing it again this week . . . they're trying to sell it."

"Did you hear about the election results?" E. asked Abu Ammar. Abu Ammar shook his head in the affirmative and squashed his cigarette with a slippered foot. "Well, we were expecting it." He shrugged his shoulders and continued, "Most Shia voted for list 169. They were blaring it out at the *Husseiniya* near our house the night of the elections. I was there for evening prayer." A *Husseiniya* is a sort of mosque for Shia. We had heard that many of them were campaigning for list 169—the Sistani-backed list.

I shook my head and sighed. "So do you still think the Americans want to turn Iraq into another America? You said last year that if we gave them a chance, Baghdad would look like New York," I said in reference to a conversation we had last year. E. gave me a wary look and tried to draw my attention to some onions, "Oh hey—look at the onions—do we have onions?"

Abu Ammar shook his head and sighed, "Well if we're New York or we're Baghdad or we're hell, it's not going to make a difference to me. I'll still sell my vegetables here."

I nodded and handed over the bags to be weighed. "Well . . . they're going to turn us into another Iran. You know list 169 means we might turn into Iran." Abu Ammar pondered this a moment as he put the bags on the old brass scale and adjusted the weights.

"And is Iran so bad?" he finally asked. Well no, Abu Ammar, I wanted to answer, it's not bad for *you*—you're a man . . . if anything your right to several temporary marriages, a few permanent ones and the right to subdue females will increase. Why should it be so bad? Instead I was silent. It's not a good thing to criticize Iran these days. I numbly reached for the bags he handed me, trying to rise out of that sinking feeling that overwhelmed me when the results were first made public.

It's not about a Sunni government or a Shia government—it's about the possibility of an Iranian modeled Iraq. Many Shia are also appalled with the results of the elections. There's talk of Sunnis being marginalized by the elections but that isn't the situation. It's not just Sunnis—it's moderate Shia and secular people in general who have been marginalized.

The list is frightening—Da'awa, SCIRI, Chalabi, Hussein Shahristani and a whole collection of pro-Iran political figures and clerics. They are going to have a primary role in writing the new constitution. There's talk of Shari'a, or Islamic law, having a very primary role in the new constitution. The problem is, whose Shari'a? Shari'a for many Shia differs from that of Sunni Shari'a. And what about all the other religions? What about Christians and Mendiyeen?

Is anyone surprised that the same people who came along with the Americans—the same puppets who all had a go at the presidency last year—are the ones who came out on top in the elections? Jaffari, Talbani, Barazani, Hakim, Allawi, Chalabi . . . exiles, convicted criminals and war lords. Welcome to the new Iraq.

Ibraheim Al-Jaffari, the head of the pro-Iran Da'awa party gave an interview the other day. He tried very hard to pretend he was open-minded and that he wasn't going to turn the once-secular Iraq into a fundamentalist Shia state but the fact of the matter remains that he is the head of the Da'awa party. The same party that was responsible for some of the most infamous explosions and assassinations in Iraq during the last few decades. This is the same party that calls for an Islamic Republic modeled like Iran. Most of its members have spent a substantial amount of time in Iran.

Jaffari cannot separate himself from the ideology of his party.

Then there's Abdul Aziz Al-Hakeem, head of the Supreme Council for the Islamic Revolution in Iraq (SCIRI). He got to be puppet president for the month of December and what was the first thing he did? He decided overburdened, indebted Iraq owed Iran 100 billion dollars. What was the second thing he did? He tried to have the "personal status" laws that protect individuals (and especially women) eradicated.

They try to give impressive interviews to Western press but the situation is wholly different on the inside. Women feel it the most. There's an almost constant pressure in Baghdad from these parties for women to cover up what little they have showing. There's a pressure in many colleges for the segregation of males and females. There are the threats, and the printed and verbal warnings, and sometimes we hear of attacks or insults.

You feel it all around you. It begins slowly and almost insidiously. You stop wearing slacks or jeans or skirts that show any leg because you don't want to be stopped in the street and lectured by someone who doesn't approve. You stop wearing short sleeves and start preferring wider shirts with a collar that will cover up some of your neck. You stop letting your hair flow because you don't want to attract attention to it. On the days when you forget to pull it back into a ponytail, you want to kick yourself and you rummage around in your handbag trying to find a hair band . . . hell, a rubber band to pull back your hair and make sure you attract less attention from *them.*

We were seriously discussing this situation the other day with a friend. The subject of the veil and hijab came up and I confessed my fear that, while they might not make it a law, there would be enough pressure to make it a requirement for women when they leave their homes. He shrugged his shoulders and said, "Well women in Iran will tell you it's not so bad—you know that they just throw something on their heads and use makeup and go places, etc." True enough. But it wasn't like that at the beginning. It took them over two decades to be able to do that. In the eighties, women were hauled off the streets and detained or beaten for the way they dressed.

It's also not about covering the hair. I have many relatives and friends who wore a hijab before the war. It's the principle. It's having so little freedom that even your wardrobe is dictated. And wardrobe is just the tip of the iceberg. There are clerics and men who believe women shouldn't be able to work or that they shouldn't be allowed to do certain jobs or study in specific fields. Something that disturbed me about the election forms was that it indicated whether the voter was "male" or "female"—why should that matter? Could it be because in Shari'a, a women's vote or voice counts for half of that of a man? Will they implement that in the future?

Baghdad is once more shrouded in black. The buildings and even some of the houses have large black pieces of cloth hanging upon them, as if the whole city is mourning the election results. It's because of *Ashoura* or the ten days marking the beginning of the Islamic New Year but also marking the death of the Prophet's family 1,400 years ago in what is now known as Karbala. That means there are droves of religious Shia dressed in black from head to foot (sometimes with a touch of green or red) walking in the streets and beating themselves with special devices designed for this occasion.

We've been staying at home most of the time because it's not a good idea to leave the house during these ten days. It took us an hour and 20 minutes to get to my aunt's house yesterday because so many streets were closed with masses of men chanting and beating themselves. To say it is frightening is an understatement. Some of the men are even bleeding and they wear white to emphasize all the blood flowing down their backs and foreheads. It's painful to see small children wearing black clothes and carrying miniature chains that really don't hurt, but look so bizarre.

Quite frankly, it's disgusting. It's a quasi-political show of sadomasochism that has nothing to do with religion. In Islam it's unfavorable to hurt the human body. Moderate Shia also find it appalling and slightly embarrassing. E. teases the Shia cousin constantly, "So this your idea of a good time, ha?" But the cousin is just as revolted, although he can't really express it. We're so "free" now, it's not a good idea to publicly express your distaste to the whole bloody affair. I can, however, express it on my blog . . .

We've also heard of several more abductions and now assassinations. They say Badir's Brigade have come out with a new list of "wanted" . . . but dead, not alive. It's a list of mainly Sunni professors, former army generals, doctors, etc. Already there have been three assassinations in Saydiyeh, an area that is a mix of Sunnis and Shia. They say Badir's Brigade people broke into the house and gunned down the families. This assassination spree is, apparently, a celebration of the election results.

It's interesting to watch American politicians talk about how American troops are the one thing standing between Sunnis and Shia killing each other in the streets. It looks more and more these days like that's not true. Right now, during all these assassinations and abductions, the troops are just standing aside and letting Iraqis get at each other. Not only that, but the new army or the National Guard are just around to protect American troops and squelch any resistance.

There was hope of a secular Iraq, even after the occupation. That hope is fading fast. **posted by river @ 3:03 PM**

FINAL EMAIL CHANGE . . .

Ok—it's final. After trying several different email services, I've decided to use baghdad.burning@gmail.com

Please email me there from now on. Thank you. **posted by river @ 3:24 PM**

Tuesday, March 08, 2005

YOU WANT A RABBIT?

We are relieved the Italian journalist was set free. I, personally, was very happy. Iraqis are getting abducted these days by the dozen, but it still says something else about the country when foreigners are abducted.

Iraqis have a fierce sense of hospitality that can border on the obnox-
ious sometimes. When people come to our houses, we insist they have
something to drink and then we insist they stay for whatever meal is
coming—even if it's four hours away. We cringe when journalists and
aide workers are abducted because it gives us the sense that we're bad
hosts.

People are always wondering why they abduct journalists, and
other innocents. I think it's because the lines are all blurred right now.
It's difficult to tell who is who. Who is a journalist, for example, and who
is foreign intelligence? Who is a mercenary and who is an aide worker?
People are somewhat more reluctant to talk to foreigners than they were
at the beginning.

The irony of the situation lay in the fact that Sgrena was probably
safer with her abductors than she was with American troops. It didn't
come as a surprise to hear her car was fired at. Was it done on purpose?
It's hard to tell. I can't think why they would want to execute Giuliana
Sgrena and her entourage, but then on the other hand, I can't think how
it could have possibly happened that they managed to fire that many
rounds at a car carrying Italian intelligence officers and a journalist (usually they save those rounds for Iraqi families in cars).

There really is no good excuse for what happened. I've been rack
ing my brain trying to figure out what the Pentagon will say short of an
admission that it was either on purpose or that the soldiers who fired
at the car were drunk or high on something . . .

I have a feeling it will be the usual excuse, "The soldiers who almost
killed the journalist were really, really frightened. They've been under
lots of pressure." But see, Iraqis are frightened and under pressure too—
we don't go around accidentally killing people. We're expected to be very
level-headed and sane in the face of chaos.

I wager that this little incident will be shoved aside with one of those
silly Pentagon apologies that don't really sound like apologies, you
know: "It was an unfortunate incident, but Sgrena shouldn't have been
in Iraq in the first place. Journalists should stay safely in their own countries and listen for our daily military statements telling them democracy is flourishing and Iraqis are happy."

I don't understand why Americans are so shocked with this incident.
Where is the shock? That Sgrena's car was under fire? That Americans

killed an Italian security agent? After everything that occurred in Iraq—
Abu Ghraib, beatings, torture, people detained for months and months,
the stealing, the rape . . . is this latest so very shocking? Or is it shocking because the victims weren't Iraqi?

I'm really glad she's home safe but at the same time, the whole situation is somewhat painful. It hurts because thousands of Iraqis have
died at American checkpoints or face to face with a tank or Apache and
beyond the occasional subtitle on some obscure news channel, no one
knows about it and no one cares. It just hurts a little bit.

The event of the week occurred last Wednesday and I was surprised
it wasn't covered by Western press. It's not that big a deal, but it
enraged people in Baghdad and it can also give a better picture of what
has been going on with our *heroic* National Guard. There was an explosion on Wednesday in Baghdad and the wounded were all taken to
Yarmuk Hospital, one of the larger hospitals in Baghdad. The number
of wounded were around 30—most of them National Guard. In the hospital, it was chaos—patients wounded in this latest explosion, patients
from other explosions and various patients with gunshot wounds, etc.
The doctors were running around everywhere, trying to be in four different places at once.

Apparently, there weren't enough beds. Many of the wounded were
in the hallways and outside of the rooms. The stories vary. One doctor
told me that some of the National Guard began screaming at the doctors, telling them to ignore the civilians and tend to the wounds of the
Guard. A nurse said that the National Guard who weren't wounded began
pulling civilians out of the beds and replacing them with wounded
National Guard. The gist of it is generally the same; the doctors refused
the idea of not treating civilians and preferring the National Guard over
them and suddenly a fight broke out. The doctors threatened a strike
if the National Guard began pulling the civilians out of beds.

The National Guard decided the solution to the crisis would be the
following—they'd gather up some of the doctors and nurses and beat
them in front of the patients. So several doctors were rounded up and
attacked by several National Guard (someone said there was liberal use
of electric batons and the butts of some Kalashnikovs).

The doctors decided to go on strike.

It's difficult to consider National Guardsmen as heroes with the

image of them beating doctors in white gowns in one's head. It's difficult to see them as anything other than expendable Iraqis with their main
mission being securing areas and cities for Americans.

It seems that Da'awa Party's Jaffari is going to be the Prime Minister and Talbani is going to get the decorative position of president. It
has been looking like this since the elections. There is talk of giving our
token Sunni Ghazi Al-Yawir some high-profile position like National
Assembly spokesperson. The gesture is meant to appease the Sunni
masses but it isn't going to do that because it's not about Sunnis and
Shia. It's about occupation and Vichy governments. They all look the
same to us.

What it seems policy makers in America don't get, and what I suspect many Americans themselves *do* get, is that millions of Iraqis feel
completely detached from the current people in power. If you don't have
an alliance with one of the political parties (i.e. under their protection
or on their payroll) then it's difficult to feel any affinity with people like
Jaffari, Allawi, Talbani, etc. We watch them on television, tight-lipped
and shifty-eyed after a meeting where they quarreled about Kirkuk or
Shari'a in the constitution and it feels like what I imagine an out-of-body
experience should feel like.

In spite of elections, they still feel like puppets. But now, they are
high-tech puppets. They were upgraded from your ordinary string puppets to those life-like, battery-powered, talking puppets. It's almost like
we're doing that whole rotating president thing Bremer did in 2003 all
over again. The same faces are getting tedious. The old Iraqi saying sums
it up nicely, "*Tireed erneb—ukhuth erneb. Tireed ghazal—ukhuth
erneb.*" The translation for this is, "You want a rabbit? Take a rabbit.
You want a deer? Take a rabbit."

Except we didn't get any rabbits—we just got an assortment of
snakes, weasels, and hyenas.

Check out Imad Khadduri's blog—he has some great links about the
Italian journalist [http://abutamam.blogspot.com/2005_03_01_abuta-
mam_archive.html. Included among Khadduri's links is a link to the English translations of Giuliana Sgrena's writings on Iraq in *Il Manifesto*:
http://www.ilmanifesto.it/pag/sgrena/en]. **posted by river @ 2:34 PM**

CHALABI FOR THE NOBEL PEACE PRIZE . . .

We woke up this morning to a huge explosion. I was actually awake and just lying there, staring at the ceiling, trying to decide if today would be a good day to go shopping for some things we need in the house. Suddenly, there was a loud blast and the house shuddered momentarily. In a second I was standing in front of the window in my room, hands pressed to the cool glass. I couldn't really see anything, but the sky seemed overcast.

I rushed downstairs to find E. and my mother standing in the kitchen doorway, trying to see beyond the houses immediately in front of our own. "Where did it happen?" I asked E. He shrugged his shoulders indicating he couldn't tell either. We later learned it was a large garbage truck of explosives in front of Sadeer Hotel, a hotel famous for hosting foreign contractors—some of a dubious/mysterious reputation. It's said that the foreign security contractors stay at the hotel, like former South African mercenaries, etc. Since the hotel is quite far from our home, we assume it was a very large explosion. Immediately afterwards, black plumes of smoke began to drift into the sky.

I got an interesting email today telling me about an internet petition to nominate Sistani, of all people, for the Nobel Peace Prize. That had me laughing and a little bit incredulous. Why should Sistani get the Nobel Peace Prize? Because he urged his followers to vote for a list that wants to implement an Iranian-styled government in Iraq? Is that what the Nobel Peace Prize has come to?

Someone once told me that they thought Sistani was responsible for the fact that civil war didn't break out in Iraq. That's garbage. Sistani has no influence over Sunnis and he also has little influence over many Shia. Civil war hasn't broken out in Iraq because Iraqis are being tolerant and also because we're very tired. It's like we spent our lives in conflict with someone or another, and being in conflict with each other is not the most tempting option right now. Sistani is an Iranian cleric quietly pushing a frightening agenda and we're feeling the pressure of it every day.

If ANYONE should get the Nobel Peace Prize, it should be my

favorite Puppet—Ahmed Chalabi. No, really—stop laughing. Ahmed Chalabi is the one Iraqi politician we can all agree on. Iraqi political debates were never pretty. Lately, they've been worse than ever. I think, to a certain degree, we don't really know how to debate. Sometimes, a debate will begin over a subject both debating parties actually agree upon and then it will escalate into a full-blown yelling match. It never fails to happen with politics.

A debate will usually begin about two current parties or politicians—say Allawi and Jaffari. Someone will say something like, "Well it's too bad Allawi didn't win . . . Now we're stuck with that Da'awachi Jaffari . . ." Someone else will answer with, "Oh please—Allawi is completely American. We'll never have our independence if he gets power." A few more words will be exchanged in a "debating" tone of voice. The voices will get sharper and someone will drudge up accusations . . . In no time it turns into a full-scale political brawl with an underlying religious intonation. No one knows just how it happens—how that frightening thing that is an Iraqi political debate develops and escalates so quickly.

At some point there is silence. This is the point when both sides are convinced that the other one is completely inane and ridiculously intractable. It's sort of a huffy silence, with rolling eyes and lips drawn into thin slits of scorn.

I've learned the best way to mediate these arguments is to let them develop into what they will. Let the yellers yell, the shouters shout, and the name-calling and innuendos ensue. The important part is the end—how to allow the debating parties to part friends or relatives, or (at the very least) to make sure they do not part sworn enemies for life. It's simple, no matter what their stand is, all you have to do is get a couple of words in towards the end. The huffy silence at the end of the debate must be subtly taken advantage of and the following words murmured as if the thought just occurred that moment:

"You know who's really bad? Ahmed Chalabi. He's such a lowlife and villain."

Voila. Like magic the air clears, eyebrows are raised in agreement and all arguing parties suddenly unite to confirm this very valid opinion with nodding heads, somewhat strained laughter and charming anecdotes about his various press appearances and ridiculous sense of fashion. We're all friends again, and family once more. We're all lovey-dovey Iraqis who can agree nicely with each other. In short, we are at peace with each other and the world . . .

And that is why Ahmed Chalabi deserves the Nobel Peace Prize.
posted by river @ 9:01 PM

TWO YEARS . . .

We've completed two years since the beginning of the war. These last two years have felt like two decades, but I can remember the war itself like it was yesterday.

The sky was lit with flashes of red and white and the ground rocked with explosions on March 21, 2003. The bombing had actually begun on the dawn of the 20th of March, but it got really heavy on the 21st. I remember being caught upstairs when the heavier bombing first began. I was struggling to drag down a heavy cotton mattress from my room for an aunt who was spending a couple of weeks with us and I suddenly heard a faraway "whiiiiiiiiiiiiiz" that sounded like it might be getting closer.

I began to rush then—pulling and pushing at the heavy mattress; trying to half throw, half haul it down stairs. I got stuck halfway down the staircase and, at that point, the whizzing sound had grown so loud, it felt like it was coming out of my head. I shoved again at the mattress and called E.'s name to help lug the thing downstairs but E. was outside with my cousin, trying to see where the missiles were going. I repositioned and began to kick the heavy mattress, not caring how it got downstairs, just wanting to be on the ground floor when the missile hit.

The mattress finally budged and began to slip and slide down the remaining 10 steps, finally landing in a big pile at the end of the staircase. I followed it in a hurry, taking two steps at a time, expecting to feel a big "BOOM" at any moment. I tripped on the last step in the mad dash for the ground floor and ended up in a heap on the cotton mass on the ground. The explosion came the same moment—followed by a series of larger explosions that didn't sound like the ordinary missiles we had been experiencing the last 40 hours or so.

The house was chaotic that moment. The parents were running, dad trying to locate his battery-powered radio and mother making sure the stove was turned off. She was also yelling orders over her shoulder, commanding us to go into the "safe room" we had specially decorated with duct tape and soft cushions, or "bomb-proofed" as my cousin liked to say. The aunt that was staying with us was running around, shrilly trying to find her two granddaughters (who were already in the safe room with their mother). The cousin was rushing around turning off kerosene heaters and opening windows so that they wouldn't shatter with the impact. E. hurried in from outside, trying to keep his expression casual under the paleness of his face.

Through all of this, the bombing was getting louder and more frequent—the earth rumbling and shuddering with every explosion. E. was saying something about the sky but the whooshing sound coming from above was so loud, we couldn't hear what he was saying. "The sky is full of red and white lights . . ." He yelled, helping me rise shakily from the mattress. "You want to go outside and see?" I looked at him like he was crazy and made him help me drag the mattress into the living room. We rushed back into the safe room and the bombs were still falling loud and fast, one after the other. Sometimes they felt like they were falling right next door, and other times, it felt like they were falling a few blocks away. We knew they were further than that.

The faces in the safe room were white with tension. My cousin's wife sat in the corner, a daughter on either side, her arms around their shoulders, murmuring prayers softly. My cousin was pacing in front of the safe room door, looking grim and my father was trying to find a decent radio station on the small AM/FM radio he carried around wherever he went. My aunt was hyperventilating at this point and my mother sat next to her, trying to distract her with the voice of the guy on the radio talking about the rain of bombs on Baghdad.

A seemingly endless 40 minutes later, there was a slight lull in the bombing—it seemed to have gotten further away. I took advantage of the relative calm and went to find the telephone. The house was cold because the windows were open to keep them from shattering. I reached for the telephone, fully expecting to find it dead but I was amazed to find a dial tone. I began dialing numbers—friends and relatives. We contacted an aunt and an uncle in other parts of Baghdad and the voices on the other end were shaky and wary. "Are you OK? Is everyone OK?" was all I could ask on the phone. They were ok . . . but the bombing was heavy all over Baghdad. Shock and awe had begun.

Two years ago this week.

What followed was almost a month of heavy bombing. That chaotic night became the intro to endless chaotic days and long, sleepless nights. You get to a point during extended air raids where you lose track of the days. You lose track of time. The week stops being Friday, Saturday, Sunday, etc. The days stop being about hours. You begin to measure time with the number of bombs that fell, the number of minutes the terror lasted and the number of times you wake up in the middle of the night to the sound of gunfire and explosions.

We try to put it out of our heads, but it comes back anyway. We sit around sometimes, when there's no electricity, or when we're gathered for lunch or dinner and someone will say, "Remember two years ago when . . ." Remember when they bombed Mansur, a residential area . . . When they started burning the cars in the streets with Apaches . . . When they hit the airport with that bomb that lit up half of the city . . . When the American tanks started rolling into Baghdad . . . ?

Remember when the fear was still fresh—and the terror was relatively new—and it was possible to be shocked and awed in Iraq? **posted by river @ 5:36 PM**

April Through June 2005

In April the new National Assembly picks a Kurdish leader, Jalal Talbani, to be president. Ibraheim Jaffari, a Shia, is to be prime minister.

On May 1, the London *Sunday Times* publishes the Downing Street memo, which is actually the minutes of a secret meeting held on July 22, 2002. In the meeting, Prime Minister Tony Blair and top defense and foreign policy advisors discuss the growing likelihood of war in Iraq. It documents, more incontrovertibly than anything has before, the Bush administration's determination to overthrow Saddam Hussein, employing dubious claims about WMD and terrorism as an excuse, and planning little for the long-term effects of an invasion:

> . . . C reported on his recent talks in Washington. There was a perceptible shift in attitude. Military action was now seen as inevitable. Bush wanted to remove Saddam, through military action, justified by the conjunction of terrorism and WMD. But the intelligence and facts were being fixed around the policy. The NSC [National Security Council] had no patience with the UN route, and no enthusiasm for publishing material on the Iraqi regime's record. There was little discussion in Washington of the aftermath [of] military action. . . .

The Defence Secretary said that the US had already begun "spikes of activity" to put pressure on the regime. No decisions had been taken, but he thought the most likely timing in US minds for military action to begin was January, with the time-line beginning 30 days before the US Congressional elections. The Foreign Secretary said he would discuss this with Colin Powell this week. It seemed clear that Bush had made up his mind to take military action, even if the timing was not yet decided. But the case was thin. Saddam was not threatening his neighbours, and his WMD capability was less than that of Libya, North Korea, or Iran. We should work up a plan for an ultimatum to Saddam to allow back in the UN weapons inspectors. This would also help with the legal justification for the use of force. . . .

The memo receives relatively little coverage in the mainstream U.S. media. Ten days later, on May 11, Bush signs legislation providing some $76 billion for military operations in Iraq and Afghanistan.

In the streets of Iraq's cities and towns, violence continues to increase. May doubles April's total of Iraqi civilians killed in shootings and car bombings; the total for the month reaches 672.

On Memorial Day, Dick Cheney is on *Larry King Live*. King asks him: "Every day it seems we hear of more deaths in Iraq—Iraqis, Americans. Does that give you pause? Did you ever say to yourself, maybe we shouldn't have?" Cheney replies with his usual tough and upbeat rhetoric:

No. I'm absolutely convinced we did the right thing in Iraq. Obviously we wanted to get it over with as quickly as possible. We regret every loss of an American in combat any place in the world. One of the difficult things about the job the president has, for example, is he has to make those decisions about when to send young Americans in harm's way. And it was necessary to do in Afghanistan and it was also necessary to do in Iraq. But we're making major progress there. I mean we've got a new government stood up now. They had elections, free elections, really for the first time in centuries in January of this year.

They're going to be writing a constitution this summer. That will lead to elections under that constitution. Later this year, there'll be a brand new government in place, duly elected under a newly written constitution by the end of the year. At the same time, we're training Iraqis to take over the security requirements in Iraq.

In fact, the Iraqi police and security forces who are working with Coalition troops have become prime targets for insurgent attacks. The number killed each month is climbing, and by one estimate reaches 300 in June 2005.

At the same time, there is growing evidence that sectarian militias, some of which receive overt or tacit support from the Iraqi government, are being used to "fill in the gaps" left by the inadequate Iraqi police and army. Increasingly, these militia groups are facing accusations that include assassinations, prisoner abuse, and mistreatment of civilians.

Perhaps the most notorious of these groups is the elite Wolf Brigade, made up of about 2,000 mostly young, poor Shiites from Sadir City, under the command of former general Abu Walid. According to the *New York Times,* the government-funded unit, which has taken part in U.S.-backed counterinsurgency operations, has been accused of torturing prisoners and slaying six Sunni clerics. The group's fame draws in part from its role in "Terrorism in the Grip of Justice," a reality show on the government-run Al-Iraqiya television network, on which captured Iraqi insurgents are interrogated by Abu Walid and others (raising complaints from human rights organizations).

—James Ridgeway

AMERICAN MEDIA . . .

You wake up in the morning. Brush your teeth. Splash the sleep out of your eyes and head for the kitchen for a cup of coffee or tea and whatever is available for breakfast.

You wander to the living room and search for the remote control. It is in its usual place—stuck inexplicably between the sofa cushions. You turn on the television and stand there flipping from one channel to the other, looking for a news brief or something that will sum up what happened during those six hours you slept. You finally settle on the pleasant face on the screen—the big hair, bright power suit, capped teeth and colorful talons—blandly reading the news. The anchoress is Julie Chan. The program is CBS's *The Early Show* (Live from Fifth Avenue!).

Guess the nationality of the viewer above. Three guesses. American? No. Canadian? No. British? Japanese? Australian? No, no and no. The viewer is Iraqi . . . or Jordanian . . . or Lebanese . . . or Syrian . . . or Saudi . . . or Kuwaiti . . . or . . . but you get the picture.

Two years ago, the major part of the war in Iraq was all about bombarding us with smart bombs and high-tech missiles. Now there's a different sort of war—or perhaps it's just another phase of the same war. Now we're being assailed with American media. It's everywhere all at once.

It began with radio stations like Voice of America which we could access even before the war. After the war, there were other radio stations—ones with mechanical voices that told us to put down our weapons and remain inside our homes, ones that fed us American news in an Iraqi dialect and ones that just played music. With satellite access we are constantly listening to American music and watching American sitcoms and movies. To be fair—it's not just Iraq that is being targeted— it's the whole region and it's all being done very cleverly.

Al-Hurra, the purported channel of freedom, is the American gift to the Arab world. What they do is show us translated documentaries about certain historical events (American documentaries) or about movie stars (American stars) or vacation spots. Throughout this, there are Arab anchors giving us the news (which is like watching Fox in Arabic). It's news about the Arab world with the American twist.

Our new "national" channels are a joke. One of the most amusing, in a gruesome sort of way, is Al-Iraqiya. It's said to be American-sponsored but the attitude is decidedly pro-Iran, anti-Sunni. There's a program where they parade "terrorists" on screen for us to see in an attempt to show us that our National Guard are not only good at raiding homes and harassing people in the streets. The funny thing about the terrorists is that the majority of them have "Sunni" names like Omar and Othman, etc. They admit to doing things such as having sexual intercourse in mosques and raping women and the whole show is disgusting. Iraqis don't believe it because it's so obviously produced to support the American definition of the Iraqi, Sunni, Islamic fanatic that it is embarrassing. Couldn't the PSYOPS people come up with anything more subtle?

Then you have the whole MBC collection. MBC is actually financed by Saudi Arabia, but based in Dubai, as far as I know. They have several different channels. It started out with the original MBC, which was a mainly Arabic channel that was harmless enough. It showed some talk shows, debates and Egyptian movies with an occasional program on music or style.

Then we were introduced to MBC's Al-Arabia—a news channel

which was meant to be the Saudi antidote to Al-Jazeera. Simultaneously, we were accessing MBC's Channel 2, which is a channel that shows only English movies and programs. The programs varied from talk shows like *Oprah*, to sitcoms like *Friends*, *Third Rock from the Sun* and *Seinfeld*. Earlier this year, MBC did a mystifying thing. They announced that Channel 2 was going to be made a 24-hour movie channel which would show all sorts of movies—old Clint Eastwood cowboy movies, and newer movies like "A Beautiful Mind," etc. The programs and sitcoms would be transferred to the new MBC Channel 4.

Personally, I was pleased with the change at first. I'm not big on movies and it was nice to know our favorite sitcoms and programs would all be accessible on one channel without the annoyance of two-hour movies. I could turn on Channel 4 at any time and expect to find something interesting or humorous that would end within 30–60 minutes.

The first time I saw *60 Minutes* on MBC 4, it didn't occur to me that something was wrong. I can't remember what the discussion was, but I remember being vaguely interested and somewhat mystified at why we were getting *60 Minutes*. I soon found out that it wasn't just *60 Minutes* at night: It was *Good Morning, America* in the morning, *20/20* in the evening, *60 Minutes*, *48-Hours*, *Inside Edition*, *The Early Show* . . . it was a constant barrage of American media. The chipper voice in Arabic tells us, "So you can watch what *they* watch!" ^They^ apparently being millions of Americans.

The schedule on MBC's Channel 4 goes something like this:

9 a.m.—*CBS Evening News*
9:30 a.m.—*CBS The Early Show*
10:45 a.m.—*The Days of Our Lives*
11:20 a.m.—*Wheel of Fortune*
11:45 a.m.—*Jeopardy*
12:05 p.m.—A re-run of whatever was on the night before—*20/20*, *Inside Edition*, etc.

And the programming continues . . .

I've been enchanted with the shows these last few weeks. The thing that strikes me most is the fact that the news is so . . . clean. It's like hospital food. It's all organized and disinfected. Everything is partitioned and you can feel how it has been doled out carefully with extreme attention to the portions—2 minutes on women's rights in Afghanistan, 1 minute on training troops in Iraq and 20 minutes on Terri Schiavo! All the reportage is upbeat and somewhat cheerful, and the anchor person manages to look properly concerned and completely uncaring all at once.

About a month ago, we were treated to an interview on 20/20 with Sabrina Harman—the witch in some of the Abu Ghraib pictures. You know—the one smiling over faceless, naked Iraqis piled up to make a human pyramid. Elizabeth Vargus was doing the interview and the whole show was revolting. They were trying to portray Sabrina as an innocent who was caught up in military orders and fear of higher ranking officers. The show went on and on about how American troops never really got seminars on Geneva Conventions (like one needs to be taught humanity) and how poor Sabrina was being made a scapegoat. They showed the restaurant where she worked before the war and how everyone thought she was "such a nice person" who couldn't hurt a fly!

We sat there watching like we were a part of another world, in another galaxy. I've always sensed from the various websites that American mainstream news is far-removed from reality—I just didn't know how far. Everything is so tame and simplified. Everyone is so sincere.

Furthermore, I don't understand the world's fascination with reality shows. *Survivor*, *The Bachelor*, *Murder in Small Town X*, *Faking It*, *The Contender* . . . it's endless. Is life so boring that people need to watch the conjured up lives of others?

I have a suggestion of my own for a reality show. Take 15 Bush supporters and throw them in a house in the suburbs of, say, Fallujah for at least 14 days. We could watch them cope with the water problems, the lack of electricity, the check points, the raids, the Iraqi National Guard, the bombings, and—oh yeah—the "insurgents." We could watch their house bombed to the ground and their few belongings crushed under the weight of cement and brick or simply burned or riddled with bullets. We could see them try to rebuild their life with their bare hands (and the equivalent of $150) . . .

I'd not only watch *that* reality show, I'd tape every episode. **posted by river @ 1:08 AM**

Saturday, April 09, 2005

THE CRUEL MONTH . . .

Thousands were demonstrating today all over the country. Many areas in Baghdad were cut off today for security reasons and to accommodate the demonstrators, I suppose. There were some Sunni demonstrations but the large majority of demonstrators were actually Shia and followers of Al-Sadr. They came from all over Baghdad and met up in Firdaws Square—the supposed square of liberation. They were in the thousands. None of the news channels were actually covering it. Jazeera showed fragments of the protests in the afternoon but everyone else seemed to busy with some other news story. Thanks to E. for sending me this link. Check out the protest here. ["Massive 'End the Occupation' Protest in Baghdad Dwarfs the 'Saddam Toppled' Rally," Bellacio.org, April 9, 2005, http://bellaciao.org/en/article.php3?id_article=5723]

BBC and EuroNews were busily covering the wedding between Prince Charles and the dreadful Camilla. CNN was showing the Pope's funeral. No one bothered with the demonstrations in Baghdad, Mosul, Anbar and the south. There were hundreds of thousands of Shia screaming "No to America. No to terrorism. No to occupation. No to the devil. No to Israel." The numbers were amazing and a little bit frightening too.

Ever since Jalal Talbani was named president, there have been many angry Shia. It's useless explaining that the presidential chair is only symbolic—it doesn't mean anything. "*La izayid we la inaqis*," as we say in Iraq. "It doesn't increase anything, nor does it decrease anything." People have the sense that all the positions are "symbolic"—hence, why shouldn't the Shia get the head symbol? The disturbing thing is how the Kurds could agree to have someone with so much blood on his hands. Talbani is known for his dealings with Turkey, Britain, America and others and his feuds with Barazani have led to the deaths of thousands of Kurds.

The weather is warm now. We often turn on the ceiling fan (or panka) in an attempt to move around the muggy air. April is a month of fresh beginnings all over the world but in Iraq April is not the best of months. April is a month of muggy warmth and air thick with dust and sand—and now of occupation. We opened the month with a dust storm that left the furniture in our houses sand-colored with an opaque layer of dust. We breathed dust, ate dust and drank dust for a few days. The air is clearer now but everything is looking a little bit diminished and dirty. It suits the mood.

Two years and this is Occupation Day once more. One wonders what has changed in this last year. The same faces of April 2004, but now they have differing positions in April 2005. The chess pieces were moved around and adjusted and every one is getting tired of the game.

Who was it that said April was a cruel month? They knew what they were talking about . . . **posted by river @ 11:19 PM**

Monday, April 18, 2005

THE HOSTAGE CRISIS . . .

I'm sure many people have been following the story of the moment in Iraq: Dozens of Shia hostages taken by Sunni insurgents in a town called Medain? [http://news.bbc.co.uk/2/hi/middle_east/4452093.stm]

The first time we heard about it was a couple of days ago. I was watching the news subtitles on Arabiya [Al-Arabia] but the subtitle was vague. It went something like this, "Sunni guerrillas capture 60 hostages in Iraqi town and will kill them if all Shia do not leave the town." It said nothing about which town it was, who the guerrillas claimed to be representing and just how the whole incident happened.

We kept watching the channels and hoping for more information. I remember reading that subtitle and feeling my heart sink with worry. I kept checking other news channels and then finally decided to check the internet. There was another vague news article on Yahoo. This one had a few more details—the town was Medain, south of Baghdad and the person who had called in the hostage situation was some sort of high-profile Shia politician.

News channels were still being vague about it. The only two channels who were persistently talking about the hostage situation were Arabia and Iraqia [Iraqiya]—but the numbers had risen. It was now 150 Shia hostages in Medain and the Iraqi National Guard and the American army were taking their positions on the outskirts of the town, preparing for a raid.

Medain is a town of Sunnis and Shia who have lived together peacefully for as long as anyone can remember. The people in the town come from the local *Ashayir* or tribes. It's one of those places where everyone knows everyone else—even if only by name or family name. The tribes who dominate the town are a combination of Sunni and Shia. Any conflicts between the townspeople are more of the tribal or family type than they are religious.

The whole concept of a large number of Sunni guerrillas raiding the town and taking 60–150 of its members (including women and children) was bizarre, frightening and by the second day of the rumor, a little bit suspicious.

People in Baghdad didn't believe it. Most of them waved a hand dismissing the report and said, "They just want to raid Medain." It's a town that has been giving the Americans quite a bit of trouble this last year, a part of the Sunni Triangle. Many attacks were reported to have come from the area, but at the same time, it's not like Fallujah, Samarra, or Mosul—it's half Shia. It wouldn't be as easy or politically correct to raid.

Yesterday, there were actually Shia demonstrators from the town claiming that the rumors were false and the town was peaceful and there was no need for a raid or for door-to-door checks.

The last few days, Iraqi officials have been on television claiming that the whole hostage situation was "under control" and things were going to be sorted out, except that apparently, there's nothing to sort out. There have been no reports of hostages, even from the majority of Shia residents themselves. Someone mentioned that it was possible a couple of people had been abducted, but it had nothing to do with Sunni guerrillas chasing out Shia.

Now, Associated Press is claiming,

"The confusion over Madain [Medain] illustrated how quickly rumors spread in a country of deep ethnic and sectarian divides, where the threat of violence is all too real." [Khalid Mohammed, "Iraq Kidnap Reports May Be Exaggerated," AP, April 17, 2005, http://www.truthout.org/cgi-bin/artman/exec/view.cgi/37/10432.]

Uhm, no. Not really. See, this whole thing didn't start out as a rumor. Rumors come to you through actual people—the guy who brings you kerosene spreads rumors, that neighbor next door brings you rumors, the man you get your rations from spreads rumors. This came to us, very decidedly, from a news source. It first made its debut as breaking news and came from an "Iraqi Shia official who wished to remain unnamed." The official should have to answer to the rumor he handed over to the press.

And now . . .

"Shiite leaders and government officials had earlier estimated 35 to 100 people were taken hostage, but residents disputed the claim, with some saying they had seen no evidence any hostages were taken."

We know a lot of our new officials and spokespeople are blatantly lying and it's fine to lie about security, reconstruction and democracy— we've gotten used to it. In fact, we tell jokes about it and laugh about it at family gatherings or over the telephone. To lie about something as serious as Sunni-Shia hostage-taking is another story altogether. It's unacceptable and while Sunnis and Shia were hardly going to take up arms against each other over this latest debacle, it was still extremely worrisome and for people who wish to fuel sectarian violence, it was a perfect opportunity.

We have an Iraqi government that bans news channels and newspapers because they *insist* on reporting about such routine things as civilian casualties and raids, yet the Puppets barely flinch over media sources spreading a rumor as dangerous and provocative as this one.
posted by river @ 1:06 PM

GOOD NEWS AND BAD NEWS . . .

Bad news first: Brave, young Marla Ruzicka was killed in Baghdad while traveling along the Baghdad Airport road. Read more about her work and the lives she touched here: CIVIC Worldwide [The Campaign for Innocent Victims, an NGO founded in 2003 by the young Californian Marla Ruzicka (1976–2005): *"CIVIC gives a voice to victims of war. We believe civilian casualties and their families deserve to be recognized by nations and the public. We work to make sure their struggle is reflected in smart, compassionate policy"* (http://www.civicworldwide.org)]. Read more about her personally on Justin Alexander's site [http://justinalexander.net] and Raed's "Raed in the Middle."

The good news: Another shipment of emergency aid for Iraqi civilians has been sent out. Raed's family started and are organizing the whole thing. He has listed all the people who donated money and has taken endless pictures and scanned receipts—it's well documented on his blog. See it on his site [http://raedinthemiddle.blogspot.com]. Some of the amazing people behind this effort:

—Raed and Niki [http://raedandtheirani.blogspot.com]
—Khalid [http://secretsinbaghdad.blogspot.com]
—Majid [http://me-vs-myself.blogspot.com]
—Faiza [http://afamilyinbaghdad.blogspot.com]

posted by river @ 1:17 PM

Monday, May 02, 2005

SAVED BY THE CARROTS . . .

These last few days have been explosive—quite literally. It started about 4 days ago and it hasn't let up since. They say there were around 14 car bombs in Baghdad alone a couple of days ago   although we only heard 6 from our area. Cars are making me very nervous lately. All cars look suspicious—small ones and large ones. Old cars and new cars. Cars with drivers and cars parked in front of restaurants and shops. They all have a sinister look to them these days.

The worst day for us was the day before yesterday. We were sitting in the living room with an aunt and her 16-year-old son and listening patiently as she scolded the household for *still* having our rugs spread. In Iraq, people don't keep their carpeting all year round. We begin removing the carpeting around April and it doesn't come back until around October. We don't have wall to wall carpeting here like abroad.

Instead, we have lovely rugs that we usually spread in the middle of the room. The best kinds are made in Iran, specifically in Tabriz or Kashan. They are often large, heavy and intricately designed. Tabriz and Kashan rugs are very expensive and few families actually have them any more. Most people who do have Tabriz rugs in Baghdad got them through an inheritance.

We have ordinary Persian rugs (which we suspect aren't really Persian at all). They aren't expensive or even particularly impressive, but they give the living room that Eastern look many Iraqi houses seem to have—no matter how Western the furniture is. The patterns and colors are repeated all over the rugs in a sort of symmetrical fashion. If you really focus on them though, you can often see a story being told by the flowers, geometrical shapes and sometimes birds or butterflies. When we were younger, E. and I would sit and stare at them, trying to "read" the colors and designs—having them on the ground is almost like having a woolly blog for the floor.

So my aunt sat there, telling us we should have had the rugs cleaned and packed away long ago—like the beginning of April. And she was right. The proper thing would be to give the rugs a good cleaning and roll them up for storage in their corner in the hallway upstairs, to stand tall and firm for almost 7 months, like sentinels of the second floor. The reason we hadn't gotten around to doing this yet was quite simple—the water situation in our area didn't allow for washing the rugs in April and so we had procrastinated the rug situation, until one week became two weeks and two weeks melted into three . . . and now we were in the first days of May and the rugs faced us almost disapprovingly on the floor.

Within 20 minutes, the aunt decided she was going to stay and help us remove said rugs the next day. We would go upstairs to clean the roof of the house very thoroughly. We would drag the rugs to the roof the next day and one by one, beat them thoroughly to get out the excess dust, then wipe down the larger ones with my aunts secret rug-cleaning mix and wash the smaller ones and set them out to dry on the hot roof.

Her son couldn't spend the night however, and he decided to return home the same day. It was around maybe 1 p.m. when he walked out the door, planning to walk the two kilometers home. He listened to my aunt as she gave him instructions about heating lunch for his father, studying, washing fruit before eating it, picking up carrots on the way home, watching out for suspicious cars and people and calling as soon as he walked through the door so she could relax. He shook his head in the affirmative, waved goodbye and walked out the gate towards the main street.

Three minutes later, an explosion rocked the house. The windows rattled momentarily and a door slammed somewhere upstairs. I was clutching a corner of the living room rug where I had pulled it back to assure my aunt that there were no bugs living under it.

"Car bomb." E. said grimly, running outside to see where it had come from. I looked at my aunt apprehensively and she sat, pale, her hands shaking as she adjusted the head scarf she wore, preparing to go outside.

"F. just went out the door . . ." she said, breathlessly referring to her son. I dropped the handful of carpeting and ran outside to follow E. My heart was beating wildly as I tried to decide the direction of the explosion. I sensed my aunt not far behind me.

"Do you see him?" She called out weakly. I was in the middle of the street by then and some of the neighbors were standing around outside.

"Where did it come from?" I called across the street to one of the neighborhood children.

"The main street." He answered back, pointing in the direction my cousin had gone.

"Did it come from the main street?" My aunt cried out from the gate.

"No." I lied, searching for E. "No—it came from the other side." I was trying to decide whether I should go ahead and run out to the main street where it seemed more and more people were gathering, when I saw E. rounding the corner, an arm casually draped around my cousin who seemed to be talking excitedly. I turned to smile encouragingly at my aunt who was sagging with relief at the gate.

"He's fine." She said. "He's fine."

"I was near the explosion!" F. said excitedly as he neared the house. My aunt grabbed him by the shoulders and began inspecting him—his face, his neck, his arms.

"I'm fine mother . . ." he shrugged her off as she began a long prayer of thanks interspersed with irrational scolding about how he should be more careful.

"Did anyone get hurt?" I asked E., dreading the answer. E. nodded and held up three fingers.

"I think three people were killed and there are some waiting for the cars to take them to the hospital."

Back in the house, E. and I decided he'd go back and see if he could help. We gathered up some gauze, medical tape, antiseptic and a couple of bottles of cold water. I turned back to my cousin after E. had left. He was excited and tense, eyes wide with disbelief. His voice was shaking slightly as he spoke and his lower lip trembled.

"I was just going to cross the street but I remembered I should buy the carrots." He spoke rapidly, "So I stopped by that guy who sells vegetables and just as I was buying them—a big BOOM and a car exploded and the one next to it began to burn . . . If I hadn't stopped for the carrots . . ." The cousin began waving his arms around in the air and I leaned back to avoid one in the face.

My aunt gasped, stopping in the living room, "The carrots saved you!" She cried out, holding a hand to her heart. My cousin looked at her incredulously and the color slowly began to return to his face. "Carrots." He murmured, throwing himself down on the sofa and grabbing one of the cushions, "Carrots saved me."

E. came home an hour later, tired and disheveled. Two people had died—the third would probably survive—but at least a dozen others were wounded. Every time I look at my cousin, I wonder—gratefully—how it was that we were so lucky. **posted by river @ 11:59 PM**

Wednesday, May 18, 2005

THE DEAD AND THE UNDEAD . . .

. . . She stood in the crowded room as her drove of minions stood around her . . . A huddling mass trying to draw closer to her aura of evil. The lights flashed against her fangs as her cruel lips curled into a grimace. It was meant to be a smile but it wouldn't reach her cold, lifeless eyes . . . It was a leer—the leer of the undead before a feeding . . .

The above was not a scene from *Buffy the Vampire Slayer*—it was just Condi Rice in Iraq a day ago. At home, we fondly refer to her as The Vampire. She's such a contrast to Bush—he simply looks stupid. She, on the other hand, looks utterly evil.

The last two weeks have been violent. The number of explosions in Baghdad alone is frightening. There have also been several assassinations—bodies being found here and there. It's somewhat disturbing to know that corpses are turning up in the most unexpected places. Many people will tell you it's not wise to eat river fish anymore because they have been nourished on the human remains being dumped into the river. That thought alone has given me more than one sleepless night. It is almost as if Baghdad has turned into a giant graveyard.

The latest corpses were those of some Sunni and Shia clerics—several of them well-known. People are being patient and there is a general consensus that these killings are being done to provoke civil war. Also worrisome is the fact that we are hearing of people being rounded up by security forces (Iraqi) and then being found dead days later— apparently when the new Iraqi government recently decided to reinstate the death penalty, they had something else in mind.

But back to the explosions. One of the larger blasts was in an area called Ma'moun, which is a middle class area located in west Baghdad. It's a relatively calm residential area with shops that provide the basics and a bit more. It happened in the morning, as the shops were opening up for their daily business and it occurred right in front of a butcher's shop. Immediately after, we heard that a man living in a house in front of the blast site was hauled off by the Americans because it was said that after the bomb went off, he sniped an Iraqi National Guardsman.

I didn't think much about the story—nothing about it stood out: an explosion and a sniper—hardly an anomaly. The interesting news started circulating a couple of days later. People from the area claim that the man was taken away not because he shot anyone, but because he knew too much about the bomb. Rumor has it that he saw an American patrol passing through the area and pausing at the bomb site minutes before the explosion. Soon after they drove away, the bomb went off and chaos ensued. He ran out of his house screaming to the neighbors and bystanders that the Americans had either planted the bomb or seen the bomb and done nothing about it. He was promptly taken away.

. . .

The bombs are mysterious. Some of them explode in the midst of National Guard and near American troops or Iraqi police and others explode near mosques, churches, and shops or in the middle of sougs. One thing that surprises us about the news reports of these bombs is that they are inevitably linked to suicide bombers. The reality is that some of these bombs are not suicide bombs—they are car bombs that are either being remotely detonated or maybe time bombs. All we know is that the techniques differ and apparently so do the intentions. Some will tell you they are resistance. Some say Chalabi and his thugs are responsible for a number of them. Others blame Iran and the SCIRI militia Badir.

In any case, they are terrifying. If you're close enough, the first sound is that of an earsplitting blast and the sounds that follow are of a rain of glass, shrapnel and other sharp things. Then the wails begin— the shrill mechanical wails of an occasional ambulance combined with the wail of car alarms from neighboring vehicles . . . and finally the wail of people trying to sort out their dead and dying from the debris.

The day before yesterday, a bomb fell on Mustansiriya University— Khalid of Secrets in Baghdad blogs about it [http://secretsinbaghdad .blogspot.com/2005_05_01_secretsinbaghdad_archive.html].

We've been watching the protests about the *Newsweek* article with interest. [The article describes U.S. military officers desecrating the Quran as part of their humiliation techniques on Muslim prisoners at Guantanamo Bay.] I'm not surprised at the turnout at these protests—the thousands of Muslims angry at the desecration of the Quran. What did surprise me was the collective shock that seems to have struck the Islamic world like a slap in the face. How is this shocking? It's terrible and disturbing in the extreme—but how is it shocking? After what happened in Abu Ghraib and other Iraqi prisons how is this astonishing? American jailers in Afghanistan and Iraq have shown little respect for human life and dignity—why should they be expected to respect a holy book?

Juan Cole has some good links about the topic [http://www.juancole.com/2005/05/guantanamo-controversies-bible-and.html].

Now *Newsweek* has retracted the story—obviously under pressure from the White House. Is it true? Probably . . . We've seen enough blatant disregard and disrespect for Islam in Iraq the last two years to make this story sound very plausible. On a daily basis, mosques are raided, clerics are dragged away with bags over their heads . . . Several months ago the world witnessed the execution of an unarmed Iraqi prisoner inside a mosque. Is this latest so very surprising?

Detainees coming back after weeks or months in prison talk of being forced to eat pork, not being allowed to pray, being exposed to dogs, having Islam insulted and generally being treated like animals trapped in a small cage. At the end of the day, it's not about words or holy books or pork or dogs or any of that. It's about what these things symbolize on a personal level. It is infuriating to see objects that we hold sacred degraded and debased by foreigners who felt the need to travel thousands of kilometers to do this. That's not to say that all troops disrespect Islam—some of them seem to genuinely want to understand our beliefs. It does seem like the people in charge have decided to make degradation and humiliation a policy.

By doing such things, this war is taken to another level—it is no longer a war against terror or terrorists—it is, quite simply, a war against Islam and even secular Muslims are being forced to take sides. **posted by river @ 12:05 AM**

Sunday, May 29, 2005

SHIA LEADERS . . .

In Baghdad there's talk of the latest "Operation Lightning." It hasn't yet been implemented in our area but we've been hearing about it. So far all we've seen are a few additional checkpoints and a disappearing mobile network. Baghdad is actually split into two large regions—Karkh (west Baghdad) and Rasafa (east Baghdad) with the Tigris River separating them. Karkh, according to this plan, is going to be split into 15 smaller areas or subdistricts and Rasafa into 7 subdistricts. There are also going to be 675 checkpoints and all of the entrances to Baghdad are going to be guarded.

We are a little puzzled why Karkh should be split into 15 subdistricts and Rasafa only seven. Karkh is actually smaller in area than Rasafa and less populated. On the other hand, Karkh contains the Green Zone—so that could be a reason. People are also anxious about the 675 check points. It's difficult enough right now getting around Baghdad, more check points are going to make things trickier. The plan includes 40,000 Iraqi security forces and that is making people a little bit uneasy. Iraqi National Guard are not pleasant or upstanding citizens—to have thousands of them scattered about Baghdad stopping cars and possibly harassing civilians is worrying. We're also very worried about the possibility of raids on homes.

Someone (thank you N.C.) emailed me Thomas L. Friedman's article in the New York Times 10 days ago about Quran desecration titled "Outrage and Silence."

In the article he talks about how people in the Muslim world went out and demonstrated against Quran desecration but are silent about the deaths of hundreds of Iraqis in the last few weeks due to bombings and suicide attacks.

In one paragraph he says,

[Portions of Thomas L. Friedman's column of May 18, 2005, titled "Outrage and Silence," were quoted in Riverbend's blog. These quotations have been redacted in the text of this book because permission for this use was denied by the copyright holder. Those who wish to read Friedman's piece may do so on the web site of the *New York Times* at http://www.nytimes.com/2005/05/18/opinion/18friedman.html.]

First of all—it's not only Kurds or Shia who are dying due to car bombs. When a car detonates in the middle of a soug or near a mosque, it does not seek out only Shia or Kurdish people amongst the multitude. Bombs do not discriminate between the young and the old, male and female or ethnicities and religious sects—no matter what your government tells you about how smart they are. Furthermore, they are going off everywhere . . . not just in Shia or Kurdish provinces. They seem to be everywhere lately.

One thing I found particularly amusing about the article—and outrageous all at once—was in the following paragraph:

[Redacted]

Now, it is always amusing to see a Jewish American journalist speak in the name of Sunni Arabs. When Sunni Arabs, at this point, hesitate to speak in a representative way about other Sunni Arabs, it is nice to know Thomas L. Friedman feels he can sum up the feelings of the "Sunni Arab world" in so many words. His arrogance is exceptional.

It is outrageous because for many people, this isn't about Sunnis and Shia or Arabs and Kurds. It's about an occupation and about people feeling that they do not have real representation. We have a government that needs to hide behind kilometers of barbed wire and meters and meters of concrete—and it's not because they are Shia or Kurdish or Sunni Arab—it's because they blatantly supported, and continue to support, an occupation that has led to death and chaos.

The paragraph is contemptible because the idea of a "Shia leader" is not an utterly foreign one to Iraqis or other Arabs, no matter how novel Friedman tries to make it seem. How dare he compare it to having a black governor in Alabama in the 1920s? In 1958, after the July 14 Revolution which ended the Iraqi monarchy, the head of the Iraqi Sovereignty Council (which was equivalent to the position of president) was Mohammed Najib Al-Rubayi—a Shia from Kut. From 1958–1963, Abdul Karim Qassim, a Shia also from Kut in the south, was the Prime Minister of Iraq (i.e. the same position Jaffari is filling now). After Abdul Karim Qassim, in 1963, came yet another Shia by the name of Naji Talib as prime minster. Even during the last regime, there were two Shia prime ministers filling the position for several years—Sadoun Humadi and Mohammed Al-Zubaidi.

In other words, Sunni Arabs are not horrified at having a Shia leader (though we are very worried about the current Puppets' pro-Iran tendencies). Friedman seems to conveniently forget that while the New Iraq's president was a polygamous Arab Sunni—Ghazi Al-Yawir—the attacks were just as violent. Were it simply a matter of Sunnis vs. Shia or Arabs vs. Kurds, then Sunni Arabs would have turned out in droves to elect "*Al Baqara al dhahika*" ("the cow that laughs" or La Vache Qui Rit—it's an Iraqi joke) as Al-Yawir is known amongst Iraqis.

This sentence,

[Redacted]

. . .

. . . is just stupid. Friedman is referring to Sunni extremists without actually saying that. But he doesn't add that some Shia extremists also feel the same way about Sunnis. I'm sure in the "Christian World" there are certain Catholics who feel that way about Protestants, etc. Iraqis have intermarried and mixed as Sunnis and Shia for centuries. Many of the larger Iraqi tribes are a complex and intricate weave of Sunnis and Shia. We don't sit around pointing fingers at each other and trying to prove who is a Muslim and who isn't and who deserves compassion and who deserves brutalization.

Friedman says,

[Redacted]

The Arab world's spiritual and media leaders have their hands tied right now. Friedman better hope Islamic spiritual leaders don't get involved in this mess because the first thing they'd have to do is remind the Islamic world that according to the Quran, the Islamic world may not be under the guardianship or command of non-Muslims—and that wouldn't reflect nicely on an American occupation of Iraq.

Friedman wonders why thousands upon thousands protested against the desecration of the Quran and why they do not demonstrate against terrorism in Iraq. The civilian bombings in Iraq are being done by certain extremists, fanatics or militias. What happened in Guantanamo with the Quran and what happens in places like Abu Ghraib is being done systematically by an army—an army that is fighting a war—a war being funded by the American people. That is what makes it outrageous to the Muslim world.

In other words, what happens in Iraq is terrorism, while what happens to Iraqis and Afghanis and people of other nationalities under American or British custody is simply "counterinsurgency" and "policy." It makes me naseous to think of how outraged the whole world was when those American POW were shown on Iraqi television at the beginning of the war—clean, safe and respectfully spoken to. Even we were upset with the incident and wondered why they had to be paraded in front of the world like that. We actually had the decency to feel sorry for them.

Friedman focuses on the Sunni Arab world in his article but he fails to mention that the biggest demonstrations were not in the Arab world—

they happened in places like Pakistan and Afghanistan. He also fails to mention that in Iraq, the largest demonstration against the desecration of the Quran was actually organized, and attended by, Shia.

Luckily for Iraqis, and in spite of Thomas Friedman, the majority of Sunnis and Shia just want to live in peace as Muslims—not as Sunnis and Shia. **posted by river @ 3:43 PM**

Monday, May 30, 2005

OOPS . . .

Oh my.

Remember Muhsin Abdul Hameed? He's the head of the Iraqi Islamic Party in Iraq—a Sunni political party that was basically the only blatantly Sunni party taking part in post-occupation politics in Iraq. For those who have forgotten, Abdul Hameed was chosen as one of the rotating presidents back in 2003. Muhsin was actually, er, Mr. February 2004, if you will.

The last couple of days, we've been hearing about raids and detentions in various areas. One of these areas is Amriya. We've been hearing about random detentions of "suspects" who may be any male between the ages 15–65 and looting by Iraqi forces of houses. It's like the first months after the occupation when the American forces were conducting raids.

We woke up this morning to the interesting news that Muhsin Abdul Hameed had also been detained! A member of the former Iraqi Governing Council, a rotating puppet president, and *The Sunni.* He is The Sunni they hold up to all Sunnis as an example of cooperation and collaboration. Well, he's the religious Sunni. There is a tribal Sunni (supposedly to appease the Arab Sunni tribes) and that is Ghazi Al-Yawir and there is the religious Sunni—Muhsin Abdul Hameed.

The Americans are saying Muhsin was "detained and interviewed," which makes one think his car was gently pulled over and he was asked a few questions. What actually happened was that his house was raided early morning, doors broken down, windows shattered and he and his three sons had bags placed over their heads and were dragged away.

They showed the house, and his wife, today on Arabiya and the house was a disaster. The cabinets were broken, tables overturned, books and papers scattered, etc. An outraged Muhsin was on tv a few minutes ago talking about how the troops pushed him to the floor and how he had an American boot on his neck for twenty minutes.

Talbani was seemingly irritated. He wondered why no one asked him about the arrest before it occurred—as if he is personally consulted on every other raid and detention. The detention is disturbing. Now I am not personally fond of Muhsin Abdul Hameed—he looks somewhat like a dried potato, and he's a Puppet. It is disturbing, though, because if this was really a mistake, then just imagine how many other "mistakes" are being unfairly detained and possibly tortured in places like Abu Ghraib. Abdul Hameed is one of their own and even he wasn't safe from a raid, humiliation and detention. He was out the same day, but other Iraqis don't have the luxury of a huffy Talbani and outraged political party.

Was it meant to send a message to Sunnis? That's what some people are saying. Many people believe it was meant to tell Sunnis, "None of you are safe—even the ones who work with us." It's just difficult to believe this is one big misunderstanding or mistake.

On the other hand, watching the situation unfold was somewhat like watching one of those annoying reality tv shows where they take someone off of a farm, for example, and put them in New York and then watch how they cope—what was it called? "Faking It"? How will Muhsin feel about raids and detentions now that he's been on the other side of them?
posted by river @ 11:37 PM

Tuesday, June 21, 2005

GENERAL UPDATE . . .

The cousin, his wife S. and their two daughters have been houseguests these last three days. They drove up to the house a couple of days ago with several bags of laundry. "There hasn't been water in our area for three days . . ." The cousin's wife huffed as she dragged along a black plastic bag of dirty clothes. "The water came late last night and disappeared three hours later . . . what about you?" Our water had not been cut off completely, but it came and went during the day.

Water has been a big problem in many areas all over Baghdad. Houses without electric water pumps don't always have access to water. Today it was the same situation in most of the areas. They say the water came for a couple of hours and then disappeared again. We're filling up plastic containers and pots just to be on the safe side. It is not a good idea to be caught without water in the June heat in Iraq.

"I need to bathe the children and wash all these clothes," S. called to me as the older of the little girls and I hauled out their overnight bag. "And the sheets—you know nothing has been washed since last week's *ajaja* . . ." We call a dust storm an *ajaja* in Iraq. I don't think there's a proper translation for that word. Last week, a few large *ajajas* kept Baghdad in a sort of pale yellow haze. What happens when an *ajaja* settles on the city is that within a couple of hours, the air becomes heavy and thick with beige powdery sand. Visibility decreases during these dust storms and it often becomes difficult to drive or see out the window.

On such occasions, we rush about the house shutting windows tightly in a largely futile attempt to keep dust out of the house. For people with allergies or asthma—it's a nightmare. The only thing that alleviates the situation somewhat is air conditioning. The air feels a little less dusty when there's an air conditioner pumping cool air into the room.

One dust storm last week was so heavy, E. slept for a couple of hours during its peak and woke up with little beige-tipped lashes from the dust that had settled on his face while he was dozing. You can even taste the dust in the food sometimes. These storms can last anywhere from a few hours to several days.

After the *ajaja* is over and the air has cleared somewhat, we begin the cleaning process. By this time, the furniture is all covered with a light film of orangish dirt, the windows are grimy, and the garden, driveway and trees all look like they have recently emerged from a sea of dust. We spend the days after such storms washing, wiping, polishing and beating dust out of the house.

"I've been dying to wash the curtains and sheets since the *ajaja* . . ." S. breathed, pulling out dusty curtains from the plastic bag. She paused suddenly, a horrific idea occurring to her, "You have water, right? Right?" We had water, I assured her. I didn't mention, however, that there had been no electricity for the better part of the morning and the generator was providing only enough for the refrigerator, television and a few lights. The standard washing machine consumed too much water and electricity—we would have to use the little "National" washing tub, or "diaper machine" as my mother called it.

The pale yellow plastic washing tub is a simple device that is designed to hold a few liters of water to swish around said water with a few articles of clothing tossed in with some detergent. Next, the clothes have to be removed from the soapy water and rinsed separately in clean water, then hung to dry. While it conveniently uses less water than the standard washing machine, there is also a risk factor involved— a sock or undershirt is often sacrificed to the little plastic blade that swishes around the water and clothes.

We spent some of yesterday and a good portion of today washing clothes, rinsing them and speculating on how our ancestors fared without washing machines and water pumps.

The electrical situation differs from area to area. On some days, the electricity schedule is two hours of electricity, and then four hours of no electricity. On other days, it's four hours of electricity to four or six hours of no electricity. The problem is that the last couple of weeks, we don't have electricity in the mornings for some reason. Our local generator is off until almost 11 a.m., and the house generator allows for ceiling fans (or *pankas*), the refrigerator, television and a few other appliances. Air conditioners cannot be turned on and the heat is oppressive by 8 a.m. these days.

Detentions and assassinations, along with intermittent electricity, have also been contributing to sleepless nights. We're hearing about raids in many areas in the Karkh half of Baghdad in particular. On the television they talk about "terrorists" being arrested, but there are dozens of people being rounded up for no particular reason. Almost every Iraqi family can give the name of a friend or relative who is in one of the many American prisons for no particular reason. They aren't allowed to see lawyers or have visitors and stories of torture have become commonplace. Both Sunni and Shia clerics who are in opposition to the occupation are particularly prone to attacks by *Liwa il Theeb* or the special Iraqi forces Wolf Brigade. They are often tortured during interrogation and some of them are found dead.

There were also several explosions and road blocks today. It took the cousin an hour to get to work, which was only twenty minutes away before the war. Now, he has to navigate between closed streets, check points, and those delightful concrete barriers rising up everywhere. It is especially difficult to be caught in traffic and that happens a lot lately. Baghdad has been cut up into sections and several of them may be found to be off limits immediately after an explosion or before a Puppet meeting. The least pleasant situation is to be caught in midday traffic, on a crowded road, in the heat—waiting for the next bomb to go off.

What people find particularly frustrating is the fact that while Baghdad seems to be falling apart in so many ways with roads broken and pitted, buildings blasted and burnt out and residential areas often swimming in sewage, the Green Zone is flourishing.

The walls surrounding restricted areas housing Americans and Puppets have gotten higher—as if vying with the tallest of date palms for height. The concrete reinforcements and road blocks designed to slow and impede traffic are now a part of everyday scenery—the road, the trees, the shops, the earth, the sky . . . and the ugly concrete slabs sometimes wound insidiously with barbed wire.

The price of building materials has gone up unbelievably, in spite of the fact that major reconstruction has not yet begun. I assumed it was because so much of the concrete and other building materials was going to reinforce the restricted areas. A friend who recently got involved working with an Iraqi subcontractor who takes projects inside of the Green Zone explained that it was more than that. The Green Zone, he told us, is a city in itself. He came back awed, and more than a little bit upset. He talked of designs and plans being made for everything from the future U.S. Embassy and the housing complex that will surround it, to restaurants, shops, fitness centers, gasoline stations, constant electricity and water—a virtual country inside of a country with its own rules, regulations and government. Ladies and gentlemen, welcome to the Republic of the Green Zone, also known as the Green Republic.

"The Americans won't be out in less than ten years," is how the argument often begins with the friend who has entered the Green Republic. "How can you say that?" is usually my answer—and I begin to throw around numbers—2007, 2008 maximum . . . Could they possibly want to be here longer? Can they afford to be here longer? At this,

. . .

T. shakes his head—if you could see the bases they are planning to build—if you could see what already has been built—you'd know that they are going to be here for quite a while.

The Green Zone is a source of consternation and aggravation for the typical Iraqi. It makes us anxious because it symbolizes the heart of the occupation and if fortifications and barricades are any indicator—the occupation is going to be here for a long time. It is a provocation because no matter how anyone tries to explain or justify it, it is like a slap in the face. It tells us that while we are citizens in our own country, our comings and goings are restricted because portions of the country no longer belong to its people. They belong to the people living in the Green Republic. **posted by river @ 3:21 AM**

July Through September 2005

In July, Medact, a UK-based charity made up of health professionals, releases an update to an earlier report on the state of health care, living conditions, and infrastructure in Iraq, drawing much of its data from the most comprehensive survey that had been conducted since the war began. Medact cites a report from the Iraqi Ministry of Health, which says that 160 doctors were kidnapped in the first four months of 2005. It also quotes an Iraqi medical student:

> The security situation [has] reduc[ed] the hospital['s] capacity to serve the population . . . [D]octors fear to be attacked by the occupying forces and . . . many times cannot attend . . . due to road blocks or curfews, the fear does prevent people from going to the hospitals and people tend to spare the hospital visit [for] very serious . . . conditions . . . [A]mong the most affected people are the women (especially pregnant women), children and elderly.

Medact makes the further point that the security situation is eating up funds for reconstruction of the health care system and other civilian infrastructure:

> Although it is hard to find accurate figures, security expenses

are thought to consume a significant proportion of the budget of each private sector contract. One source estimates that 43% of U.S. reconstruction money has been spent on security. In its bilateral programme, the UK Department for International Development (DfID) has spent £17 million providing security for projects worth £32 million (35%).

Many aspects of Iraq's infrastructure remain severely compromised: Only 54 percent of Iraqi households have a stable water supply, and not all of this water is potable. Although most households are connected to the electrical grid, 78 percent face daily cut-offs or voltage problems. Modern sanitation facilities are lacking in 36 percent of households, and where they exist they do not always function [Medact, "Iraq Health Update—Summer 2005," July 26, 2005, http://www .reliefweb.int/rw/RWB.NSF/db900SID/RMOI-6EP9GR?OpenDocument].

At the beginning of August, Cindy Sheehan, whose son was killed in Iraq, sets up camp outside Bush's Texas ranch, where he is on one of his customary long vacations. The conservatives mock her, but Sheehan garners considerable media attention and growing public sympathy. Meanwhile, military recruitment rates continue to fall; National Guard recruitment, especially, is far below projected goals.

In an interview on ABC on September 9, former Secretary of State Colin Powell, who left office in January, says that he was led astray on Iraq by junior members of the intelligence community. These unnamed people fed him erroneous intelligence that went into his now-embarrassing speech at the United Nations, in which he charged Saddam had weapons of mass destruction.

CIA director George Tenet, Powell says, "believed what he was giving to me was accurate." But others, whom Powell describes as "not senior people . . . knew at that time that some of these sources were not good, and shouldn't be relied upon, and they didn't speak up. That devastated me." Powell sees this as a "blot" on his record, and feels "terrible" about the whole thing.

Powell says he is "always a reluctant warrior . . . but when the president decided that it was not tolerable for this regime to remain in violation of all these UN resolutions, I'm right there with him with the use of force. Loyalty is a trait that I value, and yes, I am loyal." Even as he makes his criticisms, Powell remains loyal to the administration that discarded him, absolving the White House and CIA leadership and blaming misinformation on rank-and-file intelligence officers.

In Baghdad, on September 7, a rumor of explosives on a bridge causes panic among a group of a million people taking part in a Shia religious procession. More than a thousand, many of them women and children, are killed. During September, 182 people are killed in various attacks in Baghdad alone.

In the wake of Hurricane Katrina, and with growing problems in Iraq, the president's approval rating falls below 40 percent, a career low.

—James Ridgeway

UNBELIEVABLE . . .

"Not only can they not find WMD in Iraq," I commented to E. as we lis-tened to the Bush speech, "But they have disappeared from his speech-es too!" I was listening to the voiceover on Arabiya, translating his speech to Arabic. He was recycling bits and pieces of various speech-es he used over two years.

E., a younger cousin, and I were sitting around in the living room, sprawled on the relatively cool tiled floor. The electricity had been out for 3 hours and we couldn't turn on the air conditioner with the gener-ator electricity we were getting. E. and I had made a bet earlier about what the theme of tonight's speech would be. E. guessed Bush would dig up the tired, old WMD theme from somewhere under the debris of idiocy and lies coming out of the White House. I told him he'd dredge up 9/11 yet again . . . tens of thousands of lives later, we would have to bear the burden of 9/11 . . . again.

I won the bet. The theme was, naturally, terrorism—the only men-tion of "weapon" or "weapons" was in reference to Libya. He actually used the word "terrorist" in the speech 23 times.

He was trying, throughout the speech, to paint a rosy picture of the situation. According to him, Iraq was flourishing under the occupation. In Bush's Iraq, there is reconstruction, there is freedom (in spite of an occupation) and there is democracy.

"He's describing a different country . . ." I commented to E. and the cousin.

"Yes," E. replied. "He's talking about the *other* Iraq . . . the one with the WMD."

"So what's the occasion? Why's the idiot giving a speech anyway?" The cousin asked, staring at the ceiling fan clicking away above. I reminded him it was the year anniversary marking the mythical handover of power to Allawi's Vichy government.

"Oh—Allawi . . . Is he still alive?" Came the indolent reply from the cousin. "I've lost track . . . was he before Al-Yawir or after Al-Yawir? Was he prime minister or did they make him president at some point?"

9/11 and the dubious connection with Iraq came up within less than a minute of the beginning of the speech. The cousin wondered whether anyone in America still believed Iraq had anything to do with September 11.

Bush said:

"The troops here and across the world are fighting a global war on terror. The war reached our shores on September 11, 2001."

Do people really still believe this? In spite of that fact that no WMD were found in Iraq, in spite of the fact that prior to the war, no American was ever killed in Iraq and now almost 2000 are dead on Iraqi soil? It's difficult to comprehend that rational people, after all of this, still actually accept the claims of a link between 9/11 and Iraq. Or that they could actually believe Iraq is less of a threat today than it was in 2003.

We did not have Al-Qaeda in Iraq prior to the war. We didn't know that sort of extremism. We didn't have beheadings or the abduction of foreigners or religious intolerance. We actually pitied America and Americans when the Twin Towers went down and when news began leaking out about it being Muslim fundamentalists—possibly Arabs—we were outraged.

Now 9/11 is getting old. Now, 100,000+ Iraqi lives and 1,700+ American lives later, it's becoming difficult to summon up the same sort of sympathy as before. How does the death of 3,000 Americans and the fall of two towers somehow justify the horrors in Iraq when not one of the people involved with the attack was Iraqi?

Bush said:

"Iraq is the latest battlefield in this war. . . . The commander in charge of coalition operations in Iraq, who is also senior commander at this base, General John Vines, put it well the other day. He said, 'We either deal with terrorism and this extremism abroad, or we deal with it when it comes to us.'"

He speaks of "abroad" as if it is a vague desert-land filled with heavily-bearded men and possibly camels. "Abroad" in his speech seems to indicate a land of inferior people—less deserving of peace, prosperity and even life.

Don't Americans know that this vast wasteland of terror and terrorists otherwise known as "abroad" was home to the first civilizations and is home now to some of the most sophisticated, educated people in the region?

Don't Americans realize that "abroad" is a country full of people—men, women and children who are dying hourly? "Abroad" is home for millions of us. It's the place we were raised and the place we hope to raise our children—your field of war and terror.

The war was brought to us here, and now we have to watch the country disintegrate before our very eyes. We watch as towns are bombed and gunned down and evacuated of their people. We watch as friends and loved ones are detained, or killed or pressured out of the country with fear and intimidation.

Bush said:

"We see the nature of the enemy in terrorists who exploded car bombs along a busy shopping street in Baghdad, including one outside a mosque. We see the nature of the enemy in terrorists who sent a suicide bomber to a teaching hospital in Mosul . . ."

Yes. And Bush is extremely concerned with the mosques. He might ask the occupation forces in Iraq to quit attacking mosques and detaining the worshipers inside—to stop raiding them and bombing them and using them as shelters for American snipers in places like Fallujah and Samarra. And the terrorists who sent a suicide bomber to a teaching hospital in Mosul? Maybe they got their cue from the American troops who attacked the only functioning hospital in Fallujah.

"We continued our efforts to help them rebuild their country. Rebuilding a country after three decades of tyranny is hard and rebuilding while a country is at war is even harder."

Three decades of tyranny isn't what bombed and burned buildings to the ground. It isn't three decades of tyranny that destroyed the infrastructure with such things as "Shock and Awe" and various other tactics. Though he fails to mention it, prior to the war, we didn't have sewage overflowing in the streets like we do now, and water cut off for days and days at a time. We certainly had more than the 8 hours of electricity daily. In several areas they aren't even getting that much.

"They are doing that by building the institutions of a free society, a society based on freedom of speech, freedom of assembly, freedom of religion and equal justice under law."

We're so free, we often find ourselves prisoners of our homes, with roads cut off indefinitely and complete areas made inaccessible. We are so free to assemble that people now fear having gatherings because a large number of friends or family members may attract too much attention and provoke a raid by American or Iraqi forces.

As to Iraqi forces . . . There was too much to quote on the new Iraqi forces. He failed to mention that many of their members were formerly part of militias, and that many of them contributed to the looting and burning that swept over Iraq after the war and continued for weeks.

"The new Iraqi security forces are proving their courage every day."

Indeed they are. The forte of the new Iraqi National Guard? Raids and mass detentions. They have been learning well from the coalition. They sweep into areas, kick down doors, steal money, valuables, harass the females in the household and detain the men. The Iraqi security forces are so effective that a few weeks ago, they managed to kill a high-ranking police major in Fallujah when he ran a red light, shooting him in the head as his car drove away.

He kept babbling about a "free Iraq" but he mentioned nothing about when the American forces might actually depart and the occupation would end, leaving a "free Iraq."

Why aren't the Americans setting a timetable for withdrawal? Iraqis are constantly wondering why nothing is being done to accelerate the end of the occupation.

Do the Americans continue to believe such speeches? I couldn't help but wonder.

"They'll believe anything," E. sighed. "No matter what sort of absurdity they are fed, they'll believe it. Think up the most outrageous lie . . . They have people who'll believe it."

The cousin sat up at this, his interest piqued. "The most outrageous lie? How about that Iraq was amassing aliens from Mareekh [Mars] and training them in the battle art of kung-fu to attack America in 2010!"

"They'd believe it." E. nodded in the affirmative. "Or that Iraq was developing a mutant breed of rabid, man-eating bunnies to unleash upon the Western world. They'd believe that too."

Mykeru has a fantastic post about the speech, as do Juan Cole (as usual), and TomDispatch.

http://www.mykeru.com, June 28, 2005
Respectable Murder and Pure Wind

Hoo boy, tonight George W. Bush delivered a major policy speech on the "War on Terror" at Fort Bragg.

And, really, I don't give a shit.

Because now every time I hear Bush or one of his apologists blathering away, I mentally superimpose a caption in the Fox News graphical style under their image containing one of George Orwell's more famous observations:

Political language . . . is designed to make lies sound truthful and murder respectable, and to give an appearance of solidity to pure wind.

> *Sure, this could be the one time Bush says something interesting, insightful, important and even, well, let's go for the big one here, truthful. In fact, by not really caring anymore what he says I might be missing out on the moment when George W. Bush blinks into the Teleprompter, hesitates and is suddenly awash in a blinding moment of self-revelation:*
>
> *"Um . . . err", he would say at this frat boy Siddhartha moment, "Uh, I just realized that I'm kind of an asshole . . . and I haven't really make anything of myself that wasn't handed to me . . . and I guess I got carried away trying to actually be somebody and . . . well, fuck, I sure did kill a whole lot of people who didn't really need killing."*
>
> *But, c'mon. That's not going to happen. There are just some people who aren't going to have that eyeball-rolling-inward moment and figure out that they are about as good a use of carbon as a #2 pencil. . . .*

posted by river @ 3:21 AM

Friday, July 15, 2005

PRAYERS FOR KHALID . . .

Raed of Raed in the Middle has some very bad news. His brother Khalid of the blog Tell Me a Secret has been abducted by the new Iraqi Mukhabarat.

We're all praying he'll be alright and that Allah/God gives his family the strength to make it through this.

Nid3eelek bil salameh wil rijoo3 ila il a7ibeh wil ahal wil 7'irooj min hathihi il mi7neh bi 7'air ya Khalid . . . **posted by river @ 12:01 PM**

Friday, September 09, 2005

BACK TO BLOGGING . . .

It has been a long blog vacation I've taken. There have been several reasons behind it but the main one has been that I simply have not felt like blogging.

Technically, it's the summer's end . . . But realistically, we have at least another month of stifling heat ahead of us. It's almost mid-September and the weather is still hot and dry in Baghdad. There are a few precious hours in the very early morning when the sun seems almost kind. If you wake early enough, you can catch a solid hour of light breezes and a certain summer coolness.

The electrical situation deteriorated this summer in Baghdad. We've gone from a solid 8–10 hours daily to around six. During the winter, we have generators in the area providing electricity when it goes off. In the summer, however, with the heat and the heavy electrical load from air-conditioners AND the fuel shortage, many generators have to be turned off for most of the day.

We're also having water difficulties, though people have grown accustomed to that. You can tell first thing in the morning that the water is cut off. I woke up this morning and knew it even before I had gotten out of bed. The house just sounds . . . dry. You strain your ears for the familiar house sounds and they aren't there—there's no drip-drip-drip from the faucet in the bathroom down the hall. There's no sound of dishes being washed in the kitchen downstairs. There's no sound of a toilet being flushed, and certainly no sound of a shower. The house is dry.

The dryness and heat are a stark contrast to the images we see on television of Mississippi and Louisiana. Daily, we watch the havoc Katrina left in its wake and try to determine which are more difficult to bear—man-made catastrophes like wars and occupations, or natural disasters like hurricanes and tsunamis.

Many areas in Baghdad seem almost shrouded in black these last two weeks—ever since the A'aima Bridge tragedy. There's a mosque a few kilometers away from our house and the last two years we've been accustomed to seeing the large black banners draped across its outer walls. On each banner are carefully painted words in elaborate Arabic fonts announcing the death of another Iraqi and notifying people that the male members of the family would be receiving condolences inside the mosque for the next few days.

Now, the dusty beige surface of the mosque wall is nearly invisible under the black of death announcements. The eye can barely take it all in. The most disquieting thing about the banners is that many of them no longer carry a single name—after the bridge stampede, the banners now announce the deaths of two, three, four members of the same family.

I've been reading and rereading the draft constitution. It's alarming. At times it feels like only a summary of what a constitution should be with articles that don't seem very well thought out—a cut and paste job if there ever was one. It doesn't seem complete and while in some places it comes across as too vague, in others it comes across as disturbingly elaborate. I'll have a whole blog about the draft constitution tomorrow—or at least what I've understood of it. **posted by river @ 1:48 AM**

Sunday, September 11, 2005

SEPTEMBER 11, 2005 . . .

"R.—come in here! *You have to see this!*" It was September 11, 2001 and I was in the kitchen rinsing some dishes from lunch. I paused at the urgency in my brother's voice but continued rinsing, thinking there was some vaguely important news item on Iraq's state controlled channel.

"I'm coming—a moment." I called back. The phone began to ring and I stopped to answer it on my way out of the kitchen.

"Alloo?" I answered.
L: "Are you watching tv???" L., my best friend, cried out with no preliminaries.
R: "Uh . . . no—but . . ."
L: "GO WATCH TV!"

The line went dead and I put down the phone, my heart beating wildly. I made my way to the living room, curious and nervous, wondering what it could be. Had someone died? Were they going to bomb us again? That was always a possibility. It never surprised anyone when the United States decided on an air strike. I wondered if, this time around, Bush had been caught with a presidential aide in the Oval Office.

I walked into the living room and E. was standing in the middle of it—eyes glued to the television, mouth slightly open, remote control clutched in his hand, and directed towards the television set.

"What is it?" I asked, looking at the screen. The images were chaotic. It was a big city, there was smoke or dust and people running across the screen, some screaming, others crying and the rest with astounded looks on their faces. They looked slightly like E., my brother, as he stood staring at the television, gaping. There was someone speaking in the background—in English—and there was a voiceover in Arabic. I can't remember what was being said; the images on the tv screen are all I remember. Confusion. Havoc.

And then they showed it again. The Twin Towers—New York . . . a small something came flying out of the side of the screen and it crashed into one of them. I gasped audibly and E. just shook his head, "That's nothing . . . wait . . ." I made my way towards the couch while keeping my eyes locked on the television. There was some more chaos, shocked expressions, another plane and the towers—they began to crumble. They began to fall. They disappeared into an enormous fog of smoke and dust.

I sucked in my breath and I couldn't exhale at that moment. I just sat there—paralyzed—watching the screen. A part of me was saying, "It's a joke. It's Hollywood." But it was just too real. The fear was too genuine. The incoherent voices in the background were too tinged with confusion and terror.

The silence in the living room was broken with the clatter of the remote control on the floor. It had slipped out of E.'s fingers and I jumped nervously, watching the batteries from the remote roll away on the ground.

"But . . . who? How? What was it? A plane? How???"

E. shook his head and looked at me in awe. We continued watching the television, looking for answers to dozens of questions. Within the hour we had learned that it wasn't some horrid mistake or miscalculation. It was intentional. It was a major act of terror.

Al-Qaeda was just a vague name back then. Iraqis were concerned with their own problems and fears. We were coping with the sanctions and the fact that life seemed to stand still every few years for an American air raid. We didn't have the problem of Muslim fundamentalists— that was a concern for neighbors like Saudi Arabia and Iran.

I remember almost immediately, Western media began conjecturing on which Islamic group it could have been. I remember hoping it wasn't Muslims or Arabs. I remember feeling that way not just because of the thousands of victims, but because I sensed that we'd suffer in Iraq. We'd be made to suffer for something we weren't responsible for.

E. looked at me wide-eyed that day and asked the inevitable question, "How long do you think before they bomb us?"

"But it wasn't us. It can't be us . . ." I rationalized.

"It doesn't matter. It's all they need."

And it was true. It began with Afghanistan and then it was Iraq. We began preparing for it almost immediately. The price of the dollar rose as people began stocking up on flour, rice, sugar and other commodities.

For several weeks it was all anyone could talk about. We discussed it in schools and universities. We talked about it in work places and restaurants. The attitudes differed. There was never joy or happiness, but in several cases there was a sort of grim satisfaction. Some Iraqis believed that America had brought this upon itself. This is what you get when you meddle in world affairs. This is what you get when you starve populations. This is what you get when you give unabashed support to occupying countries like Israel, and corrupt tyrants like the Saudi royals.

Most Iraqis, though, felt pity. The images for the next weeks of Americans running in terror, of the frantic searches under the rubble for relatives and friends left us shaking our heads in empathy. The destruction was all too familiar. The reports of Americans fearing the sound of airplanes had us nodding our heads with understanding and a sort of familiarity—you'd want to reach out to one of them and say, "It's ok—the fear eventually subsides. We know how it is—your government does this every few years."

It has been four years today. How does it feel four years later?

For the 3,000 victims in America, more than 100,000 have died in Iraq. Tens of thousands of others are being detained for interrogation and torture. Our homes have been raided, our cities are constantly being bombed and Iraq has fallen back decades, and for several years to come we will suffer under the influence of the extremism we didn't know prior to the war.

As I write this, Tel Afar, a small place north of Mosul, is being bombed. Dozens of people are going to be buried under their homes in the dead of the night. Their water and electricity have been cut off for days. It doesn't seem to matter much though because they don't live in a wonderful skyscraper in a glamorous city. They are, quite simply, farmers and herders not worth a second thought.

Four years later and the War on Terror (or is it the War of Terror?) has been won:

Score:
Al-Qaeda—3,000
America—100,000+

Congratulations. **posted by river @ 11:29 PM**

Saturday, September 17, 2005

DRAFT CONSTITUTION—PART I . . .

I've been reading and rereading the Iraqi draft constitution since the beginning of September. I decided to ignore the nagging voice in my head that kept repeating, *"A new constitution cannot be legitimate under an occupation!"* and also the one that was saying, *"It isn't legitimate because the government writing it up isn't legitimate."* I put those thoughts away and decided to try to view the whole situation as dispassionately as possible.

It was during the online search for the *real* draft constitution that the first problem with the document hit me. There are, as far as I can tell, three different versions. There are two different Arabic versions and the draft constitution translated to English in the *New York Times* a few weeks ago differs from them both. I wish I could understand the Kurdish version—I wonder if that is different too. The differences aren't huge—some missing clauses or articles. Then again, this is a constitution—not a blog . . . one would think precision is a must.

The constitution is basically in seven parts: Preamble, Chapter 1: Basic Principles, Chapter 2: Rights and Freedoms, Chapter 3: Federal Authorities, Chapter 4: Powers of the Federal Authorities, Chapter 5: Regional Authorities, and Chapter 6: Transitional and Final Guidelines.

I scanned the preamble once without bothering to reread it every time I saw a new version of the constitution. It is somewhat long and dark and reads more like a political statement than the opening lines of what should be a document that will go down in history. I later realized that this was a mistake. In the varying versions, the preamble differs in its opening lines, as freelance journalist Alexander Gainem notes in the following article:

> Furthermore, confusion has been added by the existence of two versions of the same draft, each with a different introduction in Arabic. The first begins, "We the peoples of Iraq . . ." while the second version starts off with "We the peoples of the valley of two rivers . . ." It is unclear which version will be submitted to the United Nations but there is stark distinction between the two versions. The latter would seem to indicate that people living in Iraq are not constitutionally obliged to call themselves Iraqi and this could potentially open the door for changing the name of the country at some point. ["Will Iraqis Have Access to the Constitution?" September 13, 2005: http://www.islamonline.net/English/In_Depth/Iraq_Aftermath/2005/09/article02.shtml]

Beginning with the first chapter, Basic Principles, there are several interesting articles. Article (2) seems to be the biggest concern for journalists and analysts abroad. It states:

Article (2):
1st—Islam is the official religion of the state and is a basic source of legislation, and no law that contradicts its fixed principles and rules may be passed.
2nd—No law can be passed that contradicts the principles of democracy, or the rights and basic freedoms outlined in this constitution.
3rd—The constitution respects the Islamic identity of the majority of the Iraqi people, and guarantees the full religious rights for all individuals and the freedom of creed and religious practices.

Now, I'm a practicing Muslim female. I believe in the principles and rules of Islam I practice—otherwise I wouldn't be practicing them. The problem is not with Islam, the problem is with the dozens of interpretations of Islamic rules and principles. Islam is like any other religion in that its holy book and various teachings may be interpreted in different ways. In Iraq we see this firsthand because we have ample example of varying Islamic interpretations from two neighbors—Iran and Saudi Arabia. Who will decide which religious rules and principles are the ones that shouldn't be contradicted by the constitution?

In the old constitution that was being used up until the war, the "Temporary Constitution" of 1970 which came into implementation on the 16th of July, 1970, the only reference to Islam is in Article (4) which simply states: "Islam is the religion of the state." There is nothing about its role in the constitution.

In one version of the constitution printed in some newspapers in August was another potentially problematic article in the first chapter. It was numbered Article (12). As far as I can tell, it isn't in the English version of the constitution—and has possibly been lifted from the final version. Article (12) states (and please excuse the translation):

Article (12):
The religious Marja'ia is respected for its spiritual role and it is a prominent religious symbol on the national and Islamic fronts; and the state cannot tamper with its private affairs.

Marja'ia in Arabic means "reference." Basically, this article discusses the "religious reference" which should mean, I suppose, any religious Marja'ia in Iraq. However, in Iraq, any time the word Marja'ia is used, it is in direct allusion to the Shia religious figures like Sistani and the other Marja'ia figures in Najaf and Karbala.

Why is it that the state can have no influence on the Marja'ia but there is no clause saying that, in return, the Marja'ia cannot tamper in matters of state or constitution? The Marja'ia has influence over the lives of millions of Iraqis (and millions of Muslims worldwide, for that matter). The laws of the Marja'ia for some supersede the laws of state. For example, if the Marja'ia declares the religiously acceptable marrying age to be 10 and the state declares the legal age to be 18, won't that be unconstitutional? The state cannot pass laws that do not agree with the basic principles and rules of Islam and for millions, the Marja'ia sets those rules.

The most interesting article in Chapter 1, however, was in the first draft of the constitution published on August 22 by some newspapers but it isn't in the final draft (at least it's not in the *New York Times*

English version). It is numbered Article (16), in the version of the draft constitution it appeared in:

Article (16):
1st—It is forbidden for Iraq to be used as a base or corridor for foreign troops.
2nd—It is forbidden to have foreign military bases in Iraq.
3rd—The National Assembly can, when necessary, and with a majority of two thirds of its members, allow what is mentioned in 1 and 2 of this article.

This one is amusing because in the first two parts of the article, foreign troops are forbidden and then in the third, they're kind of allowed . . . well sometimes—when the puppets deem it necessary (to keep them in power). What is worrisome about this article, on seeing the final version of the draft constitution, is its mysterious disappearance—in spite of the fact that it leaves a lot of leeway for American bases in Iraq. Now, in the final version of the constitution, there is nothing about not having foreign troops in the country or foreign bases, at the very least. The "now you see it" / "now you don't" magical effect of this article, especially, reinforces the feeling that this constitution is an "occupation constitution."

When we get to Chapter 2: Rights and Freedoms, the cutting and pasting really begins. Upon first reading it, many of the articles and clauses sounded very familiar. After a few, it hit me that some of them were taken almost word for word from the Temporary Constitution of 1970, implemented up until the war (this constitution having been based on the constitution before it).

Ironically, well over half of the section "Rights and Freedoms" was lifted from the 1970 Temporary Constitution, making the moral of the story: It's not the fancy words in the constitution, it's the government that will actually implement said words.

The rights of women in the new constitution are quite murky. In one version, printed in the *New Sabah* newspaper in August, there is a clause about the state guaranteeing the rights of women in their family, social and economic settings and equality between men and women in order to allow women to make substantial contributions to the state a*s long as it does not contradict the constitution!* This article is not in the final draft.

In the final draft of the constitution, women are mentioned as having the right to vote and run for government. The rest of the references to women are hardly flattering—women are mentioned in context with "children and the elderly." In the 1970 constitution, women aren't mentioned at all. References are made to "Iraqis" or "citizens"—this does not single out women as needing special attention or care because they are less capable people needing male guidance or surveillance.

Example:

Article (30):
1st—The state guarantees social and health insurance, the basics for a free and honorable life for the individual and the family—especially children and women—and works to protect them from illiteracy, fear and poverty and provides them with housing and the means to rehabilitate and take care of them. This shall be regulated by law.

Women's rights won't be apparent until the Personal Status Law is defined clearly. Former Iraqi Personal Status Law was the most advanced in the region. It secured advanced rights for Iraqi women. This, like everything else, is subject to change and the following article makes this very clear:

Article (39):
Iraqis are free in their adherence to their personal status according to their own religion, sect, belief and choice, and that will be organized by law.

Basically, Iraqis will be able to practice their own personal status laws according to religion and sect. This article, in itself, is a can of worms in the making and only a set of lawyers and a group of Muslim religious scholars will ever be able to explain the implications properly.

I'll blog more tomorrow about the issue of federalism, and the coming referendum—this post is already long enough. **posted by river @ 2:17 AM**

DRAFT CONSTITUTION—PART II

Warning: Loooong post.

The final version (Version 3.0) of the Iraqi draft constitution was finally submitted to the UN about ten days ago. It was published in English in the *New York Times* on the 15th of September.

I blogged about some of the articles in the first two chapters last week, so I'll jump right to Chapter Three: The Federal Authorities. The first notable difference between the final version of the constitution published in the *New York Times* and the Arabic version published in *Al-Sabah* [*New Sabah*] is in Article (47) under Chapter Three which sets down the general conditions for the "Council of Representatives." In the Arabic version, there 6 conditions, while in the English one there are only five.

The condition that isn't in the English version is the one mentioning that women should make up 25 percent of the members of the Council of Representatives.

Article (47):
4th—Voting laws aspire to achieve women's representation on the Council of Representatives of a ratio of not less than a quarter.

Previously, when rights groups complained that the draft did not go far enough in ensuring that women's rights were preserved and protected from an Iranian style theocracy, supporters of the draft would point to the above clause and say "see, women's rights ARE protected."

Upon reading the Arabic version of the constitution, that is not necessarily true—the key word in this phrasing is "aspire." This translates accordingly: it isn't mandatory to have 25 percent women on the council—it is an aspiration, like many of the noble aspirations set down on paper by our esteemed Puppet government.

Almost two years ago, the Governing Council (then headed by SCIRI Puppet Extraordinaire Abdul Aziz Al-Hakeem) came out with

Decree 137 to abolish the Personal Status Law. Women's rights groups rose up and demanded that Paul Bremer turn the decision around—which he did. We were made grateful that our secular laws were not abolished by the pro-occupation puppets!

With this draft constitution, Decree 137 has virtually been brought back to life and aspiring to have 25 percent of the Council of Representatives female isn't going to compensate for that—especially when the overwhelming majority of the above-mentioned women are from parties like Da'awa and SCIRI.

I'm wondering—where is the outrage of pro-occupation, pro-war women's rights advocates? Why the deafening silence, ladies?

According to Article (58) in the same section, the Council of Representatives will be responsible for the selection (through vote) of the president. *Why shouldn't presidential elections be through direct vote?*

On the issue of the President of the Republic, there is an interesting article in the Executive Authority section of the same chapter. Article (65) lists the conditions for the President of the Republic (which are the same for the Prime Minister):

Article (65):
The candidate for the president's post must:
1st—be Iraqi by birth from Iraqi parents.
2nd—be legally competent and have reached the age of 40.
3rd—have a good reputation and political experience and be known for his integrity, rectitude, justice and devotion to the homeland.
4th—not have been convicted of a crime that violates honor.

"Be Iraqi by birth from Iraqi parents" is significant in that it emphasizes that BOTH parents must be Iraqi (this is more pronounced in the Arabic version of the constitution with the use of grammar "*abouwayn iraqiayn*"). While this seems very natural it is noteworthy because it means that secular American darling Iyad Allawi is out of the picture as candidate for the presidency and the prime ministry. It is very well-known in Iraq that Allawi's mother is Lebanese from a prominent Lebanese family (and related to Chalabi's wife).

Saudi Arabia is speaking up lately against Iranian influence in Iraq. Many suspect it is because Saudi favorites like Ghazi Ajeel Al-Yawir and Allawi have been sidelined and Iran-influenced politicians like Jaffari and Hakim are now in power.

"Not have been convicted of a crime that violates honor" is also interesting. Does that mean it's ok to have been convicted of other types of crimes? Like Chalabi, for example—embezzlement—is that ok? Just what crimes violate honor and what crimes keep honor intact?

Federalism . . .

Chapter 5: Authorities of the Regions is troubling. I have no problem with the concept of federalism. We've been accustomed to an autonomous Kurdistan for decades. The current laws about federalism and regional policies in the draft constitution might better be titled the "Roadmap to Divide Iraq."

Article (115) is especially worrying. It states:

Article (115):
Every province or more has the right to establish a region based on a request for a referendum to be submitted in one of the following ways:
1st—A request from one-third of the members in each of the provincial councils in the provinces that wish to establish a region.
2nd—A request from one-tenth of the voters in each of the provinces that wish to establish a region.

This means that any two provinces can decide they'd like to become a "region" with laws and regulations differing from surrounding regions. Article (116) fortifies this right with:

Article (116):
The region writes a constitution for itself, defines the structure of the region's powers and its authorities as well as the mechanism of using these powers in a way that does not run contrary to the constitution.

So basically, each region will get their own constitution which must not run contrary to the draft constitution. Also, according to the language article (4), clause 5:

Article (4):
5th—Any region or province can take a local language as an
additional official language if a majority of the population
approves in a universal referendum. The abovementioned
region may take on its own "local" language.

Article (117) has a clause that authorizes "regional authorities" to:

Article (117):
5th—The regional government shall be in charge of all that's
required for administering the region, especially establishing
and regulating internal security forces for the region such as
police, security and guards for the region.

So here's a riddle: what do you call a region with its own constitution, its own government, its own regional guard and possibly its own
language? It's quite simple—you call it a country.
Article (137) of the Transitional Guidelines in Chapter 6 says:

Article (137):
The Transitional Administration Law for the Iraqi State and its
appendix are voided upon creation of the new government,
except for what appears in paragraph (a) of Article 53 and Article 58 of the Transitional Administration Law.

The above article refers to the Transitional Administration Law set
out by Paul Bremer during the very early days of the occupation. This
is one of the only clauses that shall remain:

Article 53 [Kurdistan Regional Government]
(A) The Kurdistan Regional Government is recognized as the
official government of the territories that were administered by
the that government on 19 March 2003 in the governorates of
Dohuk, Arbil, Sulaimaniya, Kirkuk, Diyala and Neneveh. The
term "Kurdistan Regional Government" shall refer to the Kurdistan National Assembly, the Kurdistan Council of Ministers,
and the regional judicial authority in the Kurdistan region.

. . .

This is outrageous because the areas administered by "that government" on the 19th of March, 2003 are highly disputed. Kirkuk, Diyala and Nenevah (Mosul) are certainly not parts of the autonomous Kurdish region, no matter what the Kurdistan Regional Government decided on the 19th of March, 2003—the very beginning of the war.

And Kurdistan is really the least of Iraq's worries. There is talk of possibly setting up an autonomous region in the south that will be run by pro-Iran extremists Da'awa and SCIRI. Should provinces like Karbala and Najaf decide to form a region in the south, America can congratulate itself on the creation of an extended Iran. Already, these provinces are running on their own rules and regulations, with their own militias.

Federalism is ok when a country is stable. It's fantastic when countries or troubled regions are attempting to unite. In present-day Iraq it promises to be catastrophic. It will literally divide the country and increase instability. This is especially true with the kind of federalism they want to practice in Iraq.

Federalism based on geography is acceptable, but federalism based on ethnicity and sect? Why not simply declare civil war and get it over with? **posted by river @ 11:44 PM**

OTHER LINKS . . .

Some other interesting Iraqi blog links—

Free Iraq (Imad Khadduri's blog) [http://abutamam.blogspot.com/], A Star from Mosul (another girl blog from Iraq—but this time from Mosul) [http://astarfrommosul.blogspot.com], Treasure of Baghdad (a guy blogger in Baghdad) [http://baghdadtreasure.blogspot.com], and an Iraqi blogger abroad, Truth About Iraqis [http://truth-about-iraqis.blogspot.com].
posted by river @ 11:53 PM

October Through December 2005

On October 7, International Atomic Energy Agency chief Mohamed El Baradei, who faced down the press hysteria over Saddam's supposed nuclear program, is awarded the Nobel Peace Prize. For years the United States had been fighting behind closed doors to get rid of Baradei, claiming he was soft on Iran as well as Iraq.

The following week, a report by a team of former intelligence officers concludes that the Bush Administration "apparently paid little or no attention" to the CIA predictions of chaos following a war in Iraq. The report, published by the Center for the Study of Intelligence, finds that while it was wrong on WMDs, prewar intelligence provided to the administration "accurately addressed such topics as how the war would develop and how Iraqi forces would or would not fight," and correctly "calculated the impact of the war on oil markets" and "forecast the reactions of the ethnic and tribal factions in Iraq."

In a CBS News poll on October 10, only 36 percent of those questioned say that the U.S. troops should "stay in Iraq for as long as it takes to make sure Iraq is a stable democracy," while 59 percent say troops should "leave as soon as possible."

The new Iraqi Constitution is approved by referendum on October 15. The Bush Administration declares this another victory for democracy—and by implication, a victory for the White House itself, and for its decision to go to war. Critics, however, say that the new Constitution is likely to further sectarian divisions. As Riverbend has noted, it creates a federal system with a dozen highly autonomous provinces in Shiite and Kurdish regions, further alienating the Sunni minority. It also declares Islam the state religion and a source for legislation, and makes reference to Shari'a law. In addition, as *The Nation* points out in a November 7 editorial, "the Constitution does not address the most explosive issue of all—the presence of foreign troops and foreign bases on Iraqi soil—and tacitly accepts many of the laws relating to the privatization of Iraqi industry imposed on the country by the Coalition Provisional Authority in the first days of the occupation. Occupation and the privatization of industry are anathema to most Iraqis."

In an October 19 speech, Colonel Lawrence Wilkerson, Powell's former chief of staff at the State Department, says that power in Washington had become so concentrated and the liaison between agencies so degraded that the government's ability to respond to truly threatening events is questionable. "Decisions that send men and women to die, decisions that have the potential to send men and women to die, decisions that confront situations like natural disasters and cause needless death or cause people to suffer misery that they shouldn't have to suffer, domestic and international decisions, should not be made in a secret way." He continues, "What I saw was a cabal between the Vice President of the United States, Richard Cheney, and the Secretary of Defense, Donald Rumsfeld," cutting out the foreign policy bureaucracy that brought expertise to decisions, and was responsible for carrying them out. Wilkerson says that the United States has "courted disaster in Iraq, in North Korea, in Iran, and generally with regard to domestic crises like Katrina," and predicts that in a future terrorist attack or major pandemic, "you are going to see the ineptitude of this government in a way that'll take you back to the Declaration of Independence."

At the end of October, the number of Americans killed in Iraq passes the 2,000 mark.

Ever since the offensive against Fallujah in November of 2004, rumors have been circulating that the United States used chemical agents. On November 8, the Italian satellite television station RAI airs a documentary containing evidence that U.S. forces used white phosphorous in the attack, killing and maiming insurgents and civilians alike. One former U.S. soldier tells the film's director, "I heard the order being issued to be careful because white phosphorus was being used on Fallujah. In military slang this is known as Willy Pete. Phosphorus burns bodies, melting the flesh right down to the bone. . . . I saw the burned bodies of women and children. The phosphorous explodes and forms a plume. Whoever is within a 150 meter radius has no hope." The film contains footage and still photographs of bodies showing damage consistent with white phosphorus. The U.S. military admits it used white phosphorus bombs—which it considers "incendiary devices" rather than chemical weapons—to illuminate battlefields in Fallujah and elsewhere, but denies ever using them in civilian areas.

For the first time, members of Congress from both parties are beginning to seriously question the progress of the war. On November 15, the Senate votes by an overwhelming margin to require the White House to report on its steps to disentangle the country from the war and draw down American troops.

On November 18, Pennsylvania's veteran Congressmember John Murtha, himself a Marine veteran with 37 years of service and deeply involved in military policymaking in the Congress, issues a public plea to get out of Iraq:

> The war in Iraq is not going as advertised. It is a flawed policy wrapped in illusion. The American public is way ahead of us. The United States and coalition troops have done all they can in Iraq, but it is time for a change in direction. Our military is suffering. The future of our country is at risk. We cannot continue on the present course. . . .
>
> The threat posed by terrorism is real, but we have other threats that cannot be ignored. We must be prepared to face all threats. The future of our military is at risk. Our military and their families are stretched thin. Many say that the Army is broken. Some of our troops are on their third deployment. Recruitment is down, even as our military has lowered its standards. Defense budgets are being cut. Personnel costs are skyrocketing, particularly in health care. Choices will have to be made. We cannot allow promises we have made to our military families in terms of service benefits, in terms of their health care, to be negotiated away. Procurement programs that ensure our

military dominance cannot be negotiated away. We must be prepared. The war in Iraq has caused huge shortfalls at our bases in the U.S.

Murtha's proposal: "To immediately redeploy U.S. troops consistent with the safety of U.S. forces. To create a quick reaction force in the region. To create an over-the-horizon presence of Marines. To diplomatically pursue security and stability in Iraq."

With Murtha's opposition setting off a firestorm, the White House tries to combat the bad press with a new PR offensive, this one a grandiose plan entitled *The National Strategy for Victory in Iraq*. It contains vague, lofty plans for the future, and resembles a politician's typical platform statement during an election rather than a concrete set of strategies and plans. It is rumored by some to have been written by Bush's political guru Karl Rove. The document flatly rejects setting a date for a pullout. Instead it reiterates Bush's words of 2003: "Rebuilding Iraq will require a sustained commitment from many nations, including our own: we will remain in Iraq as long as necessary, and not a day more."

On December 15, Iraqis elect members of the National Assembly. The United Iraqi Alliance, the Shiite coalition, wins a majority of seats. In an earlier time, following the Iranian revolution, the United States would have seen the rise of the Shiites as a lethal threat to national security. Now, however, the Bush government applauds the triumph of democracy and seems to skip over the Shiites. Behind the elections are plans for decentralizing the central Iraqi nation, and splitting up oil resources among regional entities—Kurds, Shiites, and Sunnis. The oil, the country's principal moneymaking commodity, is to be auctioned off to the big international companies through production sharing agreements. Essentially, Saddam's centralized oil apparatus is split into parts. The economic means to sustain a central state is gone. Whether this can be accomplished without civil war remains, at this stage, unclear.

Two days later Connecticut's conservative Democratic Senator Joe Lieberman says he sees light at the end of the tunnel. "The last two weeks have been critically important and I believe may be seen as a turning point in the war in Iraq and the war on terrorism."

Struggling to regain the high ground politically, the president makes a televised speech celebrating the elections in Iraq. He concedes that he was mistaken about WMDs, the pretense for going to war—but makes it clear that, once again, it really wasn't his fault: "Much of the intelligence turned out to be wrong." Nevertheless, he says, "It was right to remove Saddam Hussein from power."

An investigation by the *Los Angeles Times* reveals that the Lincoln Group, a Washington, D.C., public relations outfit, was hired by the Pentagon to plant dozens of pro-American stories in the Iraqi media. "Absolute truth [is] not an essential element of these stories," a military official coyly told the paper. Among the papers that publish the stories is one owned by associates of Ahmed Chalabi, the Bush's Administration's failed surrogate who was supposed to install a pro-U.S. government in Iraq.

When the project is exposed, the Pentagon makes no effort to end it. No less a personage than Donald Rumsfeld will step up to defend it. In a February speech before the Council of Foreign Relations he will say: "The U.S. military command, working closely with the Iraqi government and the U.S. embassy, has sought nontraditional means to provide accurate information to the Iraqi people in the face of an aggressive campaign of disinformation. Yet this has been portrayed as inappropriate." The widespread criticism of the project, he complains, "causes everything, all activity, all initiative, to stop, just frozen. Even worse, it leads to a chilling effect for those who are asked to serve in the military public affairs field."

—James Ridgeway

CONSTITUTION CONVERSATIONS . . .

I went to sit in the garden to peruse two different versions of the draft constitution. It was 7 p.m. and the electricity had just gone out for the sixth time that day. There was no generator because people usually allow their generators to rest during the evenings—the sun is on its way to setting so while it's still light outside, the heat is bearable.

In the yards of most Iraqi houses, there is often an old, rusting swing large enough for three adults (or five children). The swing is usually iron with white, peeling paint, and its seat is covered with dusty mats or cushions so that one doesn't rise from it with a grid-like pattern on one's backside from the crisscross of the thin iron bars.

Our summers and springs in Iraq revolve around those sofa-like swings or *marjuha*. As the summer comes to an end, Iraqis often have their evening tea outside in the garden, in the waning afternoon light, with plastic chairs gathered around the swing and a folding table in the center. At night, when the electricity goes out and the generator can't be turned on, we gather outside and sit on the swing, careful to keep bare legs and feet high enough to avoid insects lurking in the grass.

When adults want to have a confidential conversation far from

curious ears—you can find them out on the swing. During family gatherings, when the cousins want to hang out and gossip away from the prying
eyes of their parents, they'll be on the swing. Every family member has a
photo on the swing—and every child has at some point fallen off of it.

So four weeks ago, I went out to the swing carrying two different
versions of the draft constitution. Though the electricity had gone out,
it was still too early to light the kerosene lamps indoors. After beating
the dust out of the striped cushions and making myself comfortable, I
began with the Arabic version of the constitution.

I had been reading for five minutes when a rustling sound in one
of the trees caught my attention. It was coming from the *tooki* tree near
the wall separating our garden from our neighbor's driveway. The tree
is on our side of the wall, but more than half of its branches extend over
to Abu F.'s side.

I don't know the name for *tooki* in English, but it can best be
described as a berry-like fruit. It's either deep purple in color—border-
ing on black—or red or white. The fruit, when ripe, is both sweet and
sour all at once. Our *tooki* tree is the red *tooki* type and while the fruit
is lovely, it also stains everything it touches. Umm F. (Abu F.'s wife) constantly complains of it staining their driveway. Every once in a while, she
revolts against the tree and attacks it, armed with a large pair of rusting hedge clippers.

This thought occurred to me as I focused on the rustling leaves and
sure enough—a moment later—I saw the hedge clippers rise ominously from behind the wall clutched in a pair of hands. Snap, snap, crunch
. . . and a medium sized branch fell towards their driveway.

"Umm F.!!!" I called out exasperated from my seat on the swing,
"Again??? I thought we agreed last week you'd stop cutting the branches!!!"

The clippers paused in mid-air, like some exotic, mechanical bird
with its beak open. They lowered slowly and a head took their place.
Since the wall is about 180 cm high, I could tell Umm F. was standing on the pile of bricks she stacked adjacent to the wall. We had a similar pile of bricks under the tree, and we used our respective brick piles
when we needed to communicate with each other over the wall.

"My driveway is a mess!" she called back to me, "You know we
haven't had proper water for a week . . . how am I supposed to clean

it? This cursed *tooki* tree . . ." She waved her clippers in the air to emphasize her frustration.

"Well it wasn't cursed when you made *tooki* jam last month!" I got up and walked to the wall to face her. In one hand, I had the Arabic version of the draft constitution (Version 2.0) and in the other I was clutching the *New York Times* English version and fanning myself with it furiously.

"So Umm F., did you have a look at the constitution yet?" I asked casually, trying to change the subject.

"Well, Abu F. read me some of it from one of the newspapers last week or the week before . . ." came the disinterested reply. She raised the clippers and furtively snapped away at a couple of branches.

"And what do you think?" I was curious. I had my own ideas about the constitution back then but I wanted to hear hers.

"I don't care. They've written it and they'll ratify it—what does it matter what I think? Is it my father's constitution (*"Qabil distoor bayt abooyeh?"*)?"

I frowned and tried to hand her the Arabic version. "But you should read it. READ IT. Look—I even highlighted the good parts . . . the yellow is about Islam and the pink is about federalism and here in green—that's the stuff I didn't really understand." She looked at it suspiciously and then took it from me.

I watched as she split the pile of 20 papers in two—she began sweeping the top edge of the wall with one pile, and using the other pile like a dustpan, she started to gather the wilted, drying *tooki* scattered on the wall. "I don't have time or patience to read it. We're not getting water—the electricity has been terrible and Abu F. hasn't been able to get gasoline for three days . . . And you want me to read a constitution?"

"But what will you vote?" I asked, watching the papers as they became streaked with the crimson, blood-like *tooki* stains.

"You'll actually vote?" she scoffed. "It will be a joke like the elections . . . They want this constitution and the Americans want it—do you think it will make a difference if you vote against it?" She had finished clearing the top edge of the wall of the wilting *tooki* and she dumped it all on our side. She put the now dusty, *tooki*-stained sheets of paper back together and smiled as she handed them back, "In any case, let no one tell you it wasn't a useful constitution—look how clean the wall is now!

. . .

I'll vote for it!" And Umm F. and the hedge clippers disappeared.

It occurred to me then that not everyone was as fascinated with the constitution as I was, or as some of my acquaintances both abroad and inside of the country were. People are so preoccupied trying to stay alive and safe and just get to work and send their children off to school in the morning, that the constitution is a minor thing.

The trouble is that as the referendum gets nearer, interest seems to diminish. We see the billboards and the commercials on various channels all about the *distoor* and we hear the radio programs and the debates on channels like Arabiya and Jazeera, but there isn't real public involvement.

In August, there was more enthusiasm about the referendum. It was taken for granted that the Kurds, and Shia affiliated with SCIRI or Da'awa, would vote in the referendum. It was surprising, however, when the Association of Muslim Scholars (influential Sunni group) started what could almost be called a campaign encouraging Sunnis (and Shia) to vote against the constitution. The reasons they gave were that federalism, at this time and under the circumstances, would contribute to the division of Iraq, and also that the constitution encouraged secular and ethnic friction.

For a few weeks, there was actual interest on the part of Sunnis, especially in rural areas, to take part in the referendum. There were arguments about whether the referendum should be boycotted like the elections or whether it was the duty of Iraqis in general to vote it down.

And then the military operations on Sunni areas like Tel Afar, Ramadi, Qaim and Samarra began once again. The feeling has been that Sunni areas are being intentionally targeted prior to the referendum to keep Sunnis from voting. When your city is under fire, and you've been displaced with your family to some Red Crescent tent in the middle of the desert, the last thing you worry about is a constitution.

Sunnis are being openly threatened by Badir's Brigade people and the National Guard. Two days ago, in Ras il Hawash in the area of A'adhamiya in Baghdad, National Guard raided homes as an act of revenge because prior to the raid, they were attacked in A'adhamiya. People from the area complain that in every home they raided, windows were broken, doors kicked in, tables overturned, people abused and money and valuables looted.

In places like Tel Afar and Qaim, dozens of civilians have been killed or wounded and conveniently labeled "insurgents" so that people in the United States and United Kingdom can sleep better at night. Residents of Tel Afar who left the town returned to their homes to find many of them only rubble and to find family and friends dead or wounded. I read one report that said all civilians were evacuated before the military operation. That isn't true. Many residents didn't have cars or transport to leave the city and were forced to stay behind. Some weren't allowed out of it.

Now, as the U.S. troops attack a little village on the Syrian border, we hear reports that the civilians are heading towards Syria. Not Arab fighters, nor insurgents—ordinary men, women and children who feel that the Iraqi government cannot shelter them or give them refuge from the onslaught of occupation forces.

What is more disturbing is the fact that most of the people who do want to vote, will vote for or against the constitution based not on personal convictions, but on the fatwas and urgings of both Sunni and Shia clerics. The Association of Muslim Scholars is encouraging people to vote against it, and SCIRI and Da'awa are declaring a vote for the constitution every Muslim's duty. It's hardly shocking that Sistani is now approving it and encouraging his followers to vote for it. (If I were an Iranian cleric living in south Iraq, I'd vote for it too!)

It is utterly frustrating to talk to someone about the referendum— whether they are Sunni or Shia or Kurd—and know that even before they've read the constitution properly, they've decided what they are going to vote.

Women's rights aren't a primary concern for anyone, anymore. People actually laugh when someone brings up the topic. "Let's keep Iraq united first . . ." is often the response when I comment about the prospect of Iranian-style Shari'a.

Rights and freedoms have become minor concerns compared to the possibility of civil war, the reality of ethnic displacement and cleansing, and the daily certainty of bloodshed and death. **posted by river @ 2:58 AM**

THE REFERENDUM . . .

So the referendum is tomorrow—well, technically speaking, today.

We've been having more than the usual power outages. Government officials were saying "power problems," "overload," etc. for the last two days and then suddenly changed their minds today and claimed it was "sabotage." It's difficult to tell. All we know is that large parts of Baghdad are literally in the dark. We're currently on generator electricity. Water has been cut off for the last two days with the exception of an occasional dribble that lasts for ten to fifteen minutes from a faucet in the garden. We have a nice big pot under it to catch as much water as possible.

Private cars haven't been allowed to drive in the streets since Thursday—this will last until Sunday. It's been declared a "holiday" of sorts. Everyone is at home. In spite of these security measures, there were several explosions today.

The referendum promises to be somewhat confusing. People are saying it should be postponed. Now is not the right time. More changes were made a few days ago to the supposed "final" draft of the constitution—the one that was submitted to the UN. It was allegedly done to appease Sunnis.

The trouble is that it didn't address the actual problems Iraqis have with the constitution (Sunnis and Shia alike). The focus of negotiations by "Sunni representative" seemed to revolve around Iraq's Arab identity and de-Ba'athification. A clause has also been added which says that the constitution will be subject to change (Quelle surprise! Yet again!) with the new government after the next elections. That doesn't make me feel better because changes can work both ways: if the next "elected" government is, again, non-secular, pro-Iran, the amendments made to what is supposed to be a permanent constitution will be appalling.

Iraq's Arab identity, due to its Arab majority, won't be reduced just because it isn't stated over and over again in a constitution. It's as if the people negotiating the constitution chose to focus on the minute, leaving the more important issues aside. Issues like guaranteeing Iraq's unity and guaranteeing that it won't be turned into an Islamic state modeled on Iran.

The referendum is only hours away and the final version of the constitution still hasn't reached many people. Areas with a Sunni majority are complaining that there aren't polling stations for kilometers around—many of these people don't have cars and even if they did, what good would it do while there's a curfew until Sunday? Polling stations should be easily accessible in every area.

This is like déjà vu from January when people in Mosul and other Sunni areas complained that they didn't have centers to vote in or that their ballot boxes never made it to the counting stations. [Reuters.com, October 14, 2005, http://today.reuters .com/news/newsArticle.aspx?type=topNews&storyID=2005-10- 14T095211Z_01_SPI055701 _RTRUKOC_0_US-IRAQ.xml]

American media is trying to make it sound like Sunnis have suddenly been mollified with the changes made in a flurry of covert meetings these last few days, but the reality is that the only Sunni party openly supporting the constitution is the Iraqi Islamic Party which represents a very, very small percentage of Sunnis.

Most educated Iraqis want to vote against the constitution. This makes the fact that Iraqis abroad aren't being allowed to vote this time around worrisome. Why was it vital for them to vote for a temporary government back in January but it's not necessary for them to contribute to this referendum which will presumably decide a permanent constitution for generations and generations of Iraqis? Could it be that the current Iranian-inclined government knew that many Iraqis abroad didn't like the constitution because of federalism, women's rights, and the mention of no laws to be placed which contradict Islam?

Iraqis are going to be voting according to religious clerics and, in some areas, tribal sheikhs. They aren't going to be voting according to their convictions or their understanding of what is supposed to be a document that will set the stage for Iraqi laws and regulations. Juan Cole wrote about an example of this with Muqtada Al-Sadr's followers:

The young Shiite nationalist, Muqtada al-Sadr, advised his followers to consult the ruling of Ayatollah Kadhim al-Haeri (resident in Qom, Iran) concerning how to deal with the constitution.

He said that this was an issue that required independent juridical reasoning (ijtihad). [Informed Comment, October 14, 2005, http://www.juancole.com/2005/10/grand-ayatollahs-urge-yes-vote-sunni.html.

That's all we need—it's not enough that Zalmay Khalilzad is gushing over the constitution—all we need now is another cleric (stationed in Iran this time) to influence the masses.

Ok—it's almost dawn and I'm exhausted. I wasn't able to connect all day to post this. **posted by river @ 4:25 AM**

Sunday, November 06, 2005

MOVIES AND DREAMS . . .

My parents, like many Iraqis of their generation and educational background, discouraged too much tv. When E. and I were younger, they were vigilant about the type of shows and movies we were allowed to watch. They didn't like for us to be exposed to propaganda—Arab or Western—and any programs containing excessive violence, foul language or sexual content were prohibited. On the other hand, all types of books were encouraged. I grew up reading books by authors ranging from Jane Austen to John LeCarre, from Emily Bronte to Maxim Gorky to Simone de Beauvoir . . . nothing was ever off-limits.

Where movies and television were concerned, there were times when something would slip through their censorship—or rather, there were times when WE would slip through their censorship and watch something at a friend's house or at a relative's house, etc.

I believe everyone remembers a movie or two, seen during childhood, that remained ingrained in their memory for years. For me, there were two such events. One was a movie, the other was a recording or documentary—I can't remember which.

In my memory, neither of them have a name and neither of them have a place—I don't remember where I saw either one. The images, however, play themselves over in my head with the clarity of an original DVD being shown at the highest resolution.

The first one, I remember, was a movie about the Holocaust. It was fictional but obviously based on actual events. I saw that film sometime in the mid-eighties. The image that horrified me most was of a little girl, no more than six or seven years of age, being made to run by Nazi guards and try to scale a very high wall. She was told that if she could scale that wall, she would be free. As soon as she started running towards the wall, her little feet stumbling in the rush to cover the distance between her captors and freedom, the guards set free three large, ferocious, black dogs on her. I don't remember exactly what happened next, but I remember a symphony of terror—her screams, the barking dogs and laughing guards.

The second movie/film/actual footage had no actors—they were real people acting out atrocities. We were visiting Iraq and I was around 8 years old. I walked in on someone, somewhere, watching what I thought at first was news footage because of the picture quality. It showed what I later learned was an Iraqi POW in Iran. I watched as Iranian guards tied each arm of the helpless man to a different vehicle. I was young, but even I knew what was going to happen the next moment. I wanted to run away or close my eyes—but I couldn't move. I was rooted to the spot, almost as if I too had been chained there. A moment later, the cars began driving off in opposite directions—and the man was in agony as his arm was torn off at the socket.

I never forgot that video. Millions of Iraqis still remember it. Every time I hear the word *aseer*, which is Arabic for POW, that video plays itself in my head. For weeks, I'd see it in my mind before I fell asleep at night, and wake up to it in the morning. It haunted me and I'd wonder how long it took the man to die after that atrocity—I didn't even know human arms came off that way.

The horrors of what happened to the POWs in Iran lived with us even after the war. The rumors of torture—mental and physical—came back so often and were confirmed so much, that mothers would pray their sons were dead instead of taken prisoner in Iran—especially after that video that came out in either 1984 or 1986. Every Iraqi who had a missing relative from that war, saw them in the agonized face of that POW who lost his arm. SCIRI head Abdul Aziz Al-Hakeem and his dead brother Mohammed Baqir Al-Hakeem were both well-known interrogators and torturers of Iraqi POWs in Iran.

There isn't a single Iraqi family, I believe, that didn't lose a loved one, or several, to that war. There isn't a single family that didn't have horror stories to tell about the POW that came home. They were giving back our POWs up until 2003. In our family alone, we lost four men to that war—three were confirmed dead—one Shia and two Sunnis—and the fourth, S., has been missing since 1983.

When he left for the war, S. was 24 and engaged to be married within the year—the house was even furnished and the wedding date set. He never came back. His mother, my mother's cousin, finally gave up hope that he'd come back in 2003. With every new group of POWs returning from Iran, she'd make phone calls and beg for news of her darling S. Had anyone seen him? Had anyone heard of him? Was he dead? With every fresh disappointment, we'd tell her that in spite of the long years, it was possible he was still alive—there was hope he'd come back. In 2002, she confessed to my mother that she wished someone would come along and crush the hope once and for all—confirm he was dead. In her heart, a mother's heart, she knew he was dead—but she needed the confirmation because without it, giving up hope completely would be a form of betrayal.

The agony of the long war with Iran is what makes the current situation in Iraq so difficult to bear—especially this last year. The occupation has ceased to be American. It is American in face, and militarily, but in essence it has metamorphosed slowly but surely into an Iranian one.

It began, of course, with Badir's Brigade and the several Iran-based political parties which followed behind the American tanks in April 2003. It continues today with a skewed referendum, and a constitution that will guarantee a southern Iraqi state modeled on the Islamic Republic of Iran.

The referendum results were so disappointing and there have been so many stories of fraud and shady dealings (especially in Mosul), that there's already talk of boycotting the December elections. This was the Puppets' shining chance to show that there is that modicum of the democracy they claim the Iraqi people are enjoying under occupation—that chance was terribly botched up.

As for the December elections—Sistani has, up until now, coyly abstained from blatantly supporting any one specific political group. This will probably continue until late November/early December during which he will be persistently asked by his followers to please issue a fatwa about the elections. Eventually, he'll give his support to one of the parties and declare a vote for said party a divine obligation. I wager he'll support the United Iraqi Alliance—like last elections.

Interestingly enough, this time around the UIA will be composed of not just SCIRI and Da'awa—but also of the Sadrists (Jaysh il Mahdi)— Muqtada's followers! For those who followed the situation in Iraq last year, many will recognize Muqtada as the "firebrand cleric," the "radical" and "terrorist." Last year, there was even a warrant for Muqtada's arrest from the Ministry of Interior and supported by the Americans who repeatedly said they were either going to detain the "radical cleric" or kill him.

Well, today he's very much alive and involved in the "political process" American politicians and their puppets hail so energetically. Sadr and his followers have been responsible for activities such as terrorizing hairdressers, bombing liquor stores, and abductions of women not dressed properly, etc. because all these things are considered anti-Islamic (according to Iranian-style Islam). Read more about Sadr's militia here—who dares to say the Americans, Brits and Puppets don't have everything under control?!

Americans constantly tell me, "What do you think will happen if we pull out of Iraq—those same radicals you fear will take over." The reality is that most Iraqis don't like fundamentalists and only want stability—most Iraqis wouldn't stand for an Iran-influenced Iraq. The American military presence is working hand in hand with Badir, etc. because only together with Iran can they suppress anti-occupation Iraqis all over the country. If and when the Americans leave, their Puppets and militias will have to pack up and return to wherever they came from because without American protection and guidance they don't stand a chance.

We literally laugh when we hear the much subdued threats American politicians make towards Iran. The United States can no longer afford to threaten Iran because they know that should the followers of Sadr, Iranian cleric Sistani and Badir's Brigade people rise up against the Americans, they'd have to be out of Iraq within a month. Iran can do what it wants—enrich uranium? Of course! If Tehran declared tomorrow that it was currently in negotiations for a nuclear bomb, Bush would have to don his fake pilot suit again, gush enthusiastically about the War on Terror and then threaten Syria some more.

Congratulations, Americans—not only are the hardliner Iranian clerics running the show in Iran—they are also running the show in Iraq. This shift of power should have been obvious to the world when My-Loy-alty-to-the-Highest-Bidder-Chalabi sold his allegiance to Iran last year. American and British sons and daughters and husbands and wives are dying so that this coming December, Iraqis can go out and vote for Iran-influenced clerics to knock us back a good four hundred years.

What happened to the dream of a democratic Iraq?

Iraq has been the land of dreams for everyone except Iraqis—the Persian dream of a Shia-controlled Islamic state modeled upon Iran and inclusive of the holy shrines in Najaf, the pan-Arab nationalist dream of a united Arab region with Iraq acting as its protective eastern border, the American dream of controlling the region by installing permanent bases and a Puppet government in one of its wealthiest countries, the Kurdish dream of an independent Kurdish state financed by the oil wealth in Kirkuk . . .

The Puppets the Americans empowered are advocates of every dream except the Iraqi one: The dream of Iraqi Muslims, Christians, Arabs, Kurds and Turkmen . . . the dream of a united, stable, prosperous Iraq which has, over the last two years, gone up in the smoke of car bombs, military raids and a foreign occupation. **posted by river @ 12:47 AM**

Thursday, November 17, 2005

CONVENTIONAL TERROR . . .

It sat on my PC desktop for five days [Link to video: http://www .rainews24.rai.it/ran24/inchiesta/video/fallujah_ING.wmv].

The first day I read about it on the internet, on some site, my heart sank. White phosphorous in Fallujah. I knew nothing about white phos-phorous, of course, and a part of me didn't want to know the details. I tried downloading the film four times and was almost relieved when I got disconnected all four times.

E. had heard about the film too and one of his friends S. finally brought it by on CD. He and E. shut themselves up in the room with the computer to watch the brief documentary. E. came out half an hour later looking pale—his lips tightened in a straight line, which is the way he looks when he's pensive . . . thinking about something he'd rather not discuss.

"Hey—I want to see it too . . ." I half-heartedly called out after him, as he walked S. to the door.

"It's on the desktop—but you really don't want to see it," E. said.

I avoided the computer for five days because every time I switched it on, the file would catch my eye and call out to me . . . now plaintively—begging to be watched, now angrily—condemning my indifference.

Except that it was never indifference . . . it was a sort of dread that sat deep in my stomach, making me feel like I had swallowed a dozen small stones. I didn't want to see it because I knew it contained the images of the dead civilians I had in my head.

Few Iraqis ever doubted the American use of chemical weapons in Fallujah. We've been hearing the terrifying stories of people burnt to the bone for well over a year now. I just didn't want it confirmed.

I didn't want it confirmed because confirming the atrocities that occurred in Fallujah means verifying how really lost we are as Iraqis under American occupation and how incredibly useless the world is in general—the UN, Kofi Annan, humanitarian organizations, clerics, the Pope, journalists . . . you name it—we've lost faith in it.

I finally worked up enough courage to watch it and it has lived up to my worst fears. Watching it was almost an invasive experience, because I felt like someone had crawled into my mind and brought my nightmares to life. Image after image of men, women and children so burnt and scarred that the only way you could tell the males apart from the females, and the children apart from the adults, was by the clothes they are wearing . . . the clothes which were eerily intact—like each corpse had been burnt to the bone, and then dressed up lovingly in their everyday attire—the polka-dot nightgown with a lace collar . . . the baby girl in her cotton pajamas—little earrings dangling from little ears.

Some of them look like they died almost peacefully, in their sleep . . . others look like they suffered a great deal—skin burnt completely black and falling away from scorched bones.

I imagine what it must have been like for some of them. They were probably huddled in their houses—some of them—tens of thousands of them—couldn't leave the city. They didn't have transport or they simply didn't have a place to go. They sat in their homes, hoping that what people said about Americans was actually true—that in spite of their huge machines and endless weapons, they were human too.

And then the rain of bombs would begin . . . the wooooosh of the missiles as they fell and the sound of the explosion as it hit its target . . . and no matter how prepared you think you are for that explosion—it always makes you flinch. I imagine their children covering their ears and some of them crying, trying to cover up the mechanical sounds of war with their more human wails. I imagine that as the tanks got closer, and the planes got lower—the fear increased—and parents searched each other's faces for a solution, for a way out of the horror. Some of them probably decided to wait it out in their homes, and others must have been desperate to get out—fearing the rain of concrete and steel and thinking their chances were better in the open air, than confined in the homes that could at any moment turn into their tombs.

That's what we were told before the Americans came—it's safer to be outside of the house during an air strike than it is to be inside of the house. Inside of the house, a missile nearby would turn the windows into millions of little daggers and walls might come crashing down. In the garden, or even the street, you'd only have to worry about shrapnel and debris if the bomb was very close—but what were the chances of that?

That was before 2003 . . . and certainly before Fallujah.

That was before men, women and children left their homes only to be engulfed in a rain of fire.

Last year I blogged about Fallujah and said: "There is talk of the use of cluster bombs and other forbidden weaponry." [See November 10, 2004.]

I was immediately attacked with a barrage of emails from Americans telling me I was a liar and that there was no proof and that there was no way Americans would ever do something so appalling! I wonder how those same people justify this now. Are they shocked? Or do they tell themselves that Iraqis aren't people? Or are they simply in denial?

The Pentagon spokesman recently said:

"It's part of our conventional-weapons inventory and we use it like we use any other conventional weapon." ["US Defends use of White Phosphorus Against Iraqi Insurgents," Agence France Press, November 16, 2005, http://www.globalsecurity .org/org/news/2005/051116-us-phosphorus.htm]

This war has redefined "conventional." It has taken atrocity to another level. Everything we learned before has become obsolete. "Conventional" has become synonymous with horrifying. Conventional weapons are those that eat away the skin in a white blaze; conventional interrogation methods are like those practiced in Abu Ghraib and other occupation prisons . . .

Quite simply . . . conventional terror. **posted by river @ 1:32 AM**

Friday, November 18, 2005

HOUSE OF HORRORS . . .

The talk of the town is the torture house they recently found in Jadriya [John F. Burns, "Torture Alleged at Ministry Site Outside Baghdad, *New York Times*, November 16, 2005, http://www.nytimes.com/2005/ 11/16/international/middleeast/16iraq.html].

The whole world heard about the one in Jadriya, recently raided by the Americans. Jadriya was once one of the best areas in Baghdad. It's an area on the river and is special in that it's greener, and cleaner, than most areas. Baghdad's largest university, Baghdad University, is located in Jadriya (with a campus in another area). Jadriya had some of the best shops and restaurants—not to mention some of Baghdad's most elegant homes . . . and apparently, now, a torture house.

We hear constantly about these torture dungeons. Right after the war, certain areas became infamous for them. The world knows them as "torture houses" for the obvious reasons—they were once ordinary homes, and now they've become torture centers for suspects and innocents alike. The Iraqi government conveniently calls them "detention centers" and the Iraqi Ministry of Interior oversees and funds them.

One area which was well-known for its torture houses immediately after the war was Sadir City in Baghdad. Except they weren't called torture houses back then. The people who ran them called them *ma7akim* or "courts." They would bring "suspects" in for interrogation—often ordinary citizens—and beat and whip them for various confessions involving accusations and alleged crimes. A *Sayid* would then come in and sentence the culprit—the sentence would sometimes involve cutting off a hand or a foot and at other times it might be death. We heard this from an aunt's neighbor who was mistakenly taken in and beaten as a suspected former security agent. His family connections with influential Shia clerics in the area were the only things that got him out alive—bruised and broken—but alive.

These torture houses have existed since the beginning of the occupation. While it is generally known that SCIRI is behind them, other religious parties are not innocent. The Americans know they exist—why the sudden shock and outrage? This is hardly news for Americans in the Green Zone. The timing is quite interesting—it shouldn't matter that this raid came immediately after the whole white phosphorous story came out, but the Pentagon and American military have proven to be the ultimate masters of diversion.

Only last year in an area called Ghazaliya, one such house was discovered. It was on a smaller scale though. My cousin lives in Ghazaliya and he said that when the Americans got inside, they found several corpses and a man hanging from the ceiling on a makeshift noose. The neighbors had tried to get the Americans to check the house for months—no one bothered. They finally raided it because they got information from someone in the area that it was an insurgents' hiding place. I read once that in New York, if a woman is being raped, she should scream "fire" instead of "rape" because no one would come to save her if she was screaming "rape." That's the way it is with Iraqi torture houses—the only way they'll check it is if you tell them it's a terrorist cell.

And another thing—you know when they say "men dressed in Ministry of Interior uniforms" or "men in official cars claiming to be from the Ministry of Interior," etc. when describing some horror committed by the new Iraqi security forces in the news? Here's a thought: they aren't "claiming" and they aren't in costume—they actually ARE from the Ministry of Interior! One would think they'd do this covertly so as not to enrage Iraqis or humanitarian organizations, except that it doesn't matter to them because SCIRI and Da'awa aren't out to win hearts and minds. They have American favor—what more does one need in the New Iraq?

For over a year corpses have been turning up all over Baghdad. Corpses of people who are taken from their homes in the middle of the night (lately they've been more brazen—they just do everything in the light of day), and turn up dead somewhere. That isn't as disturbing as the reports about the bodies—the one I can't get out of my head is that many of the corpses are found with holes in the skull left by an electric drill.

I guess the lucky ones go to Abu Ghraib. . . .

And it's not only "suspected insurgents" who disappear—Iraqi security forces have been known to raid complete areas and detain any males from the ages of 12 to 60—especially in Sunni areas. Those "suspected terrorists" that are rounded up and taken away—you know where they disappear to now.

Interior Minister Bayan Jabr (SCIRI Thug-Made-Government-Official-In-Italian-Suits) is mollifying Iraqis with this little gem,

> . . . the group included Shiites as well as Sunnis . . . ["Iraqi interior minister calls torture allegations exaggerated," Associated Press, November 17, 2005, http://www.iht.com/articles/2005/11/17/africa/web.1117torture.php]

I'm sure we can all sleep better at night with the knowledge that SCIRI/Da'awa torturers don't discriminate according to religious sect—under the new constitution, American military guidance, and the blessings of the Pentagon—all Iraqis will be tortured equally. **posted by river @ 12:02 AM**

Friday, November 25, 2005

ASSASSINATIONS . . .

We woke up yesterday morning to this news: Sunni tribal leader and his sons shot dead.

> "Gunmen in Iraqi army uniforms shot dead an aging Sunni tribal leader and three of his sons in their beds on Wednesday,

relatives said . . ." [Paul Tait, "Sunni Leader and Sons Killed," Reuters, November 23, 2005, http://www.theepochtimes.com/news/5-11-23/34931.html]

Except when you read it on the internet, it's nothing like seeing scenes of it on television. They showed the corpses and the family members—an elderly woman wailing and clawing at her face and hair and screaming that soldiers from the Ministry of Interior had killed her sons. They shot them in front of their mother, wives and children . . . Even when they slaughter sheep, they take them away from the fold so that the other sheep aren't terrorized by the scene.

In war, you think the unthinkable. You imagine the unimaginable. When you can't get to sleep at night, your mind wanders to cover various possibilities. Trying to guess and determine the future of a war-torn nation is nearly impossible, so your mind focuses on the more tangible—friends . . . near and distant relations. I think that during these last two and a half years, every single Iraqi inside of Iraq has considered the possibility of losing one or more people in the family. I try to imagine losing the people I love most in the world—whether it's the possibility of having them buried under the rubble . . . or the possibility of having them brutally murdered by extremists . . . or blown to bits by a car bomb . . . or abducted for ransom . . . or brutally shot at a checkpoint. All disturbing possibilities.

I try to imagine what would happen to me, personally, should this occur. How long would it take for the need for revenge to settle in? How long would it take to be recruited by someone who looks for people who have nothing to lose? People who lost it all to one blow. What I think the world doesn't understand is that people don't become suicide bombers because—like the world is told—they get seventy or however many virgins in paradise. People become suicide bombers because it is a vengeful end to a life no longer worth living—a life probably violently stripped of its humanity by a local terrorist—or a foreign soldier.

I hate suicide bombers. I hate the way my heart beats chaotically every time I pass by a suspicious-looking car—and every car looks suspicious these days. I hate the way Sunni mosques and Shia mosques are being targeted right and left. I hate seeing the bodies pile up in hospitals, teeth clenched in pain, wailing men and women . . .

But I completely understand how people get there.

"One victim was holding his daughter. 'The gunmen told the girl to move then shot the father,' said a relative."

Would anyone be surprised if the abovementioned daughter grew up with a hate so vicious and a need for revenge so large, it dominated everything else in her life?

Or three days ago when American and Iraqi troops fired at a family traveling from one city to another, killing five members of the family.

"They are all children. They are not terrorists," shouted one relative. "Look at the children," he said as a morgue official carried a small dead child into a refrigeration room. [Faris al-Mehdawi, "U.S. Troops Fired on Baghdad Civilians: Reports," Reuters, November 21, 2005, http://www.commondreams .org/headlines05/1121-01.htm]

Who needs Al-Qaeda to recruit "terrorists" when you have Da'awa, SCIRI and an American occupation? The Iraqi Ministry of Interior is denying it all, of course. Just like they've been denying the whole Jadriya torture house incident and all of their other assassinations and killing sprees. They've gone so far as to claim that the Americans are lying about the Jadriya torture house.

In the last three weeks, at least six different prominent doctors/professors have been assassinated. Some of them were Shia and some of them were Sunni—some were former Ba'athists and others weren't. The only thing they have in common is the fact that each of them played a prominent role in Iraqi universities prior to the war: Dr. Haykal Al-Musawi, Dr. Ra'ad Al-Mawla (biologist), Dr. Sa'ad Al-Ansari, Dr. Mustafa Al-Heeti (pediatrician), Dr. Amir Al-Khazraji, and Dr. Mohammed Al-Jaza'eri (surgeon).

I don't know the details of all the slayings. I knew Dr. Ra'ad Al-Mawla—he was a former professor and department head in the science college of Baghdad University—Shia. He was a quiet man—a gentleman one could always approach with a problem. He was gunned down in his office, off campus. What a terrible loss.

Another professor killed earlier this month was the head of the pharmacy college. He had problems with Da'awa students earlier in the year. After Jaffari et al. won in the elections, their followers in the college wanted to have a celebration in the college. Sensing it would lead to trouble, he wouldn't allow any festivities besides the usual banners. He told them it was a college for studying and learning and to leave politics out of it. Some students threatened him—there were minor clashes in the college. He was killed around a week ago—maybe more.

Whoever is behind the assassinations, Iraq is quickly losing its educated people. More and more doctors and professors are moving to leave the country.

The problem with this situation is not just major brain drain—it's the fact that this diminishing educated class is also Iraq's secular class
. . . **posted by river @ 1:03 AM**

Thursday, December 01, 2005

NO VOICE . . .

I've lost my voice. That's not a metaphor for anything, by the way. I've managed to literally lose my voice. It's a bug that has been going around with the change of weather. It began three days ago—my voice was hoarse and I kept having to clear my throat. The next day it had completely disappeared! I didn't know it was gone until I had wandered downstairs and attempted a "good morning," which came out sounding like something from a psychological thriller.

Four things you should know about illnesses in Iraq. When you describe your malady to any Iraqi, there are some general guidelines you can take for granted:

Short of cancer and terminal illness, any Iraqi has had your malady before you, even in cases of cancer or other serious conditions— SOMEONE the abovementioned Iraqi knows *almost* personally has had the condition before you (the neighbor's sister's cousin's nephew) . . .

Every Iraqi you talk to knows the cure for whatever you're suffering from, and refusing to attempt abovementioned cure is both a personal insult to the well-intentioned curer and further affirmation of your foolhardiness which got you sick in the first place.

I've been no exception—everyone has had a cure for me to try.

My mother attempted various soup recipes. My father suggested gargling with a mixture of salt and water (which had me gagging). The cousin swore he cured his own voiceless state last week with a table-spoonful of olive oil three times daily and supervised my dosage (which made the salt and water mixture actually seem quite good). Umm Ala'a, from three houses down, claimed that my voice wouldn't return unless my whole neck was wrapped snugly in a wool scarf. Finally, the aunt concocted an interesting mixture of *baybun* (chamomile, which all Iraqis swear by), crushed dry mint leaves and lemon. This was all boiled together, strained and I was ordered to "INHALE" the steam rising from the greenish-yellow liquid and then drink the horrid stuff.

The only person who didn't have a cure for me was E. "Why would I want you to get your voice back?!" He asked incredulously.

So I've spent the last two days communicating with nods, elaborate hand gestures and hoarse whispers. It's interesting how friends and family react when they realize I'm voiceless—they either lower their own voices to just above a whisper, or they begin to speak unnaturally loud like I might have lost my hearing also.

And that's why blogging is a wonderful thing right now—it gives a voice to the temporarily voiceless.

I didn't get to see the Saddam trial—our electricity was out and the neighborhood generator was down. All I've been seeing these last two days are bits and pieces of it on various channels (they keep repeating the part where he scolds the judge).

The electricity schedule in what appears to be most areas in Baghdad is currently FIVE hours of no electricity for every one hour of electricity. It's very frustrating considering the fact that it's not really cool enough yet for excess electrical heater use—where is it all going? If the electrical situation is this bad now, what happens later when the populace starts needing more electricity?

I intend to spend the rest of the night reading about Bush's "strategy" for Iraq. I haven't seen it yet, but I expect it'll be a repetition of the nonsense he's been spewing for two and a half years now. Don't Americans get tired of hearing the same thing?

It's unbelievable that he's refused to set a timetable for withdrawal (is he having another "Bring it on . . ." moment?). It's almost as if some-one is paying him to intentionally sabotage American foreign policy. With every speech he seems to sink himself deeper into the mire. A timetable for complete withdrawal of American forces would be a positive step—it would give Iraqis hope that, eventually, sovereignty will return to Iraq.

As it is, people fear the Americans will be here for the next twen-ty years—unless they are bombed and attacked out of the country. Although many Iraqis support armed resistance in theory, I think that the average Iraqi simply wants to see them go back home in one piece—we feel sorry for them and especially sorry for their families at times. There are moments when you forget the personal affronts—the raids, the checkpoints, the fear of bombing, the detentions, etc. and you can see through it all to the actual person behind the weapons and body armor . . . On the other hand, you never forget that it's a foreign occu-pation and will meet with resistance like all foreign occupations.

Bush, Cheney, Rumsfeld and Rice can all swear that American troops will not pull out of the country no matter how many casualties they sustain, but history has proven otherwise . . . **posted by river @ 12:30 AM**

BAGHDAD BURNING LINKS . . .

Earlier this year, Baghdad Burning the blog was turned into Baghdad Burning—the book [http://www.feministpress.org]. The Feminist Press published the whole first year of blogs in book form and it was a huge honor. The book is available at both Amazon and Barnes & Noble. The British version was published by Marion Boyars Publishers [http://www.marionboyars.co.uk].

As if having the blog published as a book wasn't enough—the book itself won the third prize of the Lettre Ulysses Award for the Art of Reportage in October [http://www.lettre-ulysses-award.org/news/fourth-pe2005.html] . . . An amazing honor.

Also—Baghdad Burning in Japanese [http://www.geocities.jp/river-bendblog/]. . . and Baghdad Burning in Spanish [http://bagdadenlla-mas.blogspot.com/]. Many, many thanks to the people taking so much time to translate the blog! **posted by river @ 1:09 AM**

Monday. December 05. 2005

MOTHER OF ALL TRIALS . . .

I didn't get to see the beginning of the trial today. We were gathered in the kitchen after a brief rodent scare, trying to determine where the mouse had come from when I was attracted by the sound of yelling coming from the living room.

The cousin was standing in front of the television adjusting the volume and there was a lot of bellowing coming from the court. That was nearly the beginning—the defense lawyers were pulling out of the trial because apparently, Ramsey Clark wasn't allowed to speak in English—something to do with the sovereignty of the court or trial and the impropriety of speaking in a foreign language (slightly ironic considering the whole country is under foreign occupation). The lawyers were back later—although I didn't see that either.

I really began watching when they brought on the first witness, who was also the first plaintiff. He talked about the whole Dujail situation and his account was emotional and detailed. The details were intriguing considering he was only 15 years old at the time. The problem with his whole account is that so much of it is hearsay. He heard from someone that something happened to someone else, etc. Now, I'm not a lawyer but I'm a fan of *The Practice* and if watching Dylan McDermott has taught me anything, it's that hearsay is not acceptable evidence.

The second witness was more to the point but he was 10 when everything happened and that didn't help his case. In the end, when the judge asked him who he was making a complaint against, he said he wasn't making a complaint against anyone. Then he changed his mind and said he was complaining against one of the accused . . . Then he added his complaint was against anyone convicted of the crime . . . And finally it was a complaint against "All Ba'athists at the time."

Couldn't they find more credible witnesses? They were fifteen and ten at the time . . . it just doesn't make sense.

At one point, the defense lawyers wanted to leave the trial yet again because apparently some security guard or police officer was threatening them from afar—making threatening gestures, etc. The judge requested that he be pulled out of the court (the security person), but not before hell broke loose in the court. Saddam began yelling something, the defense lawyers were making accusations and Barazan got up and began shouting at the person we couldn't see.

The court was a mess. There was a lot of yelling, screaming, sermonizing, ranting, accusing, etc. I felt bad for the judge. He really seemed to be trying hard to control the situation, but everyone kept interrupting him, and giving him orders. He's polite and patient, he'd make a good divorce judge—but I don't think he's strong enough for the court. He just doesn't have the power to keep the court in its place.

It wasn't really like a trial. It reminded me of what we call a *fassil*, which is what tribal sheikhs arrange when two tribes are out of sorts with one another. The heads of the tribes are brought together along with the principal family members involved in the rift and after some yelling, accusations, and angry words they try to sort things out. That's what it felt like today. They kept interrupting each other and there was even some spitting at one point . . . It was both frustrating and embarrassing—and very unprofessional.

One thing that struck me about what the witnesses were saying—after the assassination attempt in Dujail, so much of what later unfolded is exactly what is happening now in parts of Iraq. They talked about how a complete orchard was demolished because the Mukhabarat thought people were hiding there and because they thought someone had tried to shoot Saddam from that area. That was like last year when the Americans razed orchards in Diyala because they believed insurgents were hiding there. Then they talked about the mass detentions—men, women and children—and it's almost as if they are describing present-day Ramadi or Fallujah. The descriptions of cramped detention spaces, and torture are almost exactly the testimonies of prisoners in Abu Ghraib, etc.

It makes one wonder when Bush, Rumsfeld, Cheney and the rest will have their day, as the accused, in court. **posted by river @ 8:25 PM**

Thursday, December 15, 2005

ELECTIONS . . .

Elections have been all we hear about for the last ten days at least.

The posters are everywhere in Baghdad. There are dozens of parties running for elections, but there are about four or five "lists" which
stand out from the rest:

> —**National Iraqi (731)**: Ayad Allawi's list, which now includes
> some other prominent puppets including Adnan Al-Pachachi,
> Ghazi Al-Yawir, Safiya Al-Suhail, etc. Ayad Allawi is a secular
> Shia, CIA-affiliated, ex-Ba'athist.
> —**Unified Iraqi Coalition List (555)**: Hakim, Jaffari and various
> other pro-Iran fundamentalists, in addition to Sadrists.
> —**Kurdistani Gathering (730)**: Barazani, Talbani and a few other
> parties.
> —**Iraqi Front for National Dialogue (667)**: Mainly Sunni, secular
> list—includes the Iraqi Christian Democratic Party and is
> headed by Salih Al-Mutlag.
> —**Iraqi Alliance Front (618)**: Mainly Sunni Islamic parties.

We've been flooded with election propaganda this last week. Every
Iraqi channel you turn to is showing one candidate or another. Allawi,
Hakim and a handful of others dominate the rest though. No one is bothering much with the other lists because quite frankly, no one hears of
them that often. Allawi's face is everywhere, as is Hakim's turbaned
head. It's disconcerting to scan a seemingly innocent wall and have a
row of identical Hakims smiling tightly down on you.

The last press conference I watched of Hakim was a few days ago.
He was warning his followers of electoral fraud, which is slightly ironic considering his group has been accused of all sorts of fraud this last
year. The audience was what caught my interest. The women were sitting on one side of the audience and the men were sitting on the other
side, the sexes separated by a narrow aisle. The women all wore black
abayas and headscarves. It could have been a scene out of Tehran.

Some of Allawi's campaign posters show himself and Safiya Al-

Suhail. I can only guess Safiya being used in his campaign posters is meant as a gesture to Iraqi women who have felt more oppressed this year than ever. The problem is that if there's one woman Iraqi females can't relate to—it's Safiya Suhail. She's the daughter of some tribal leader who was assassinated abroad in the eighties or seventies—I'm not sure. She was raised in Lebanon and when she's on TV she comes across as arrogant, huffy and awkward with her Iraqi accent tainted with the Lebanese dialect.

It's a poster war. One day, you see the posters of Allawi, featuring Safiya Suhail, the next day, Allawi's big face is covered with pictures of Hakim and Sistani. Allawi's supporters have been complaining that Hakim's supporters were sabotaging campaign posters.

Even SMS messages are all about voting lately. (Several rather vulgar jokes about list 555—I can't go into it on the blog, but Iraqis know what I'm talking about.)

Secular nationalists are leaning towards Salih Al-Mutlag (of list 667) who is seen as less of a puppet than the rest. After all, he is the only one heading one of the more popular electoral lists who wasn't blessed by the American army and Bremer when Iraq was invaded in 2003. He supports armed resistance (but not terrorism) and he has a group of prominent anti-occupation nationalists backing him. There's talk that after elections, his list will support Allawi to strengthen the secular movement.

The incident of the day yesterday was news of a tanker or truck that had been caught in the town of Wassit full of fake voting ballots from Iran. There is also news that voting centers haven't been properly equipped in several Sunni provinces. There was a skirmish between Iraqi National Guard and the electoral committee to preside over elections in Salah Al-Din.

More people are going to elect this time around—not because Iraqis suddenly believe in American-imposed democracy under occupation, but because the situation this last year has been intolerable. Hakim and Jaffari and their minions have managed to botch things up so badly, Allawi is actually looking acceptable in the eyes of many. I still can't stand him.

Allawi is still an American puppet. His campaign posters, and the horrors of the last year, haven't changed that. People haven't forgotten his culpability in the whole Fallujah debacle. For some Iraqis, however, he's preferable to Hakim and Jaffari after a year of detentions, abductions, assassinations and secret torture prisons.

There's a saying in Iraq which people are using right and left lately, and that I've used before in the blog, "*Ili ishuf il mout, yirdha bil iskhuna.*" He who sees death, is content with a fever. Allawi et al. seem to be the fever these days . . . **posted by river @ 4:41 AM**

January Through March 2006

Any suggestions that there will be a reduction in violence following the election are proved false in the two-day period of January 5 and 6, when more than 180 people die in a spate of attacks in Iraq. These include attacks on mourners at a funeral and outside a holy shrine and a double suicide bombing against Sunnis gathered at a police recruiting center.

The Pentagon releases a study confirming Murtha's worries, pointedly describing the decline in America's fighting strength. The military is described as a "thin green line" that is spread too thin, and cannot be maintained long enough to defeat the Iraqi insurgency, particularly with sharp drops in recruitment numbers.

Donald Rumsfeld, always the optimist, says he doesn't think the war will be a long one, although he, like all the other Bush officials, won't say when it might end.

Meanwhile, Bush wants more money. He asks for $120 billion in 2006 for Afghanistan and Iraq.

The attacks on Bush's policy towards Iraq are increasing. Paul Pillar, the CIA's national intelligence officer for the Near East and south Asia from 2000 to 2005, writes an article in *Foreign Affairs* magazine saying the government did not ask for intelligence analysis and went to war without any sort of strategic analysis. It wasn't until a year after the war that such a request was made, and then there was pressure to make intelligence fit with the government's policy. Pillar says the administration did not go to war because of any supposed ties to Al-Qaeda but "hitch[ed] the Iraq expedition to the 'war on terror' and the threat the American public feared most, thereby capitalizing on the country's militant post-9/11 mood."

On February 22, bombs destroy the Askari Mosque in Samarra, one of the holiest sites in Shia Islam. No one claims responsibility. By the end of the following day, the Sunni Association of Muslim Scholars says that 168 Sunni mosques have been attacked. Clerics, journalists, and other civilians, most of them Sunnis, are killed in widespread violence. Five days later, the Iraqi government reports that 379 have been killed and 458 wounded, despite a daytime curfew imposed in Baghdad and elsewhere. *The Washington Post*, on February 27, reports a much higher death toll of more than 1,300.

Several leading Shia clerics, including Ali Al-Sistani and Muqtada Al-Sadr, call for calm and instruct their followers to attack Sunnis. At the same time, there are reports that the incident is leading to a buildup of these clerics' private militias, and giving them leverage with the United States, which has clearly been powerless to quell the violence without their help.

Once again Bush carries the public relations battle forward. On March 19, the eve of the third anniversary of the invasion, he pledges to "finish the mission" with "complete victory." He does not predict when that victory will be won, but asks the public to stay the course. Soon thereafter he says that what happens in the future will have to be determined by future presidents, making it clear he believe the United States will be in Iraq until at least 2009.

A Zogby poll shows 72 percent of U.S. soldiers in Iraq think troops should be withdrawn.

In an interview with the BBC, U.S. Ambassador to Iraq Zalmay Khalilzad says that Iraq faces the possibility of civil war. He says that "polarization along sectarian lines" in increasing in the general population, in part due to the role of armed militias. He states that a civil war in Iraq could have a serious affect on the entire Middle East.

—James Ridgeway

2006 . . .

Here we are in the first days of 2006. What does the "6" symbolize? How about—6 hours of no electricity for every one hour of electricity? Or . . . 6 hours of waiting in line for gasoline that is three times as expensive as it was in 2005? Or an average of 6 explosions per day near our area alone?

The beginning of the new year isn't a promising one. Prices seem to have shot up on everything from fuels like kerosene and cooking gas, to tomatoes. A typical conversation with Abu Ammar our local fruit/vegetable vendor goes something like this:

> **R:** "Oh, nice lemons today Abu Ammar . . . give us a kilo."
> **Abu A:** "They are Syrian. You should see the tomatoes—if you think these are nice, take a look at those."
> **R:** "Hmmm . . . they do look good. Two kilos of those. How much will that be?"
> **Abu A:** "That will be 3,600 dinars."
> **R (feigning shock and awe):** "3,600 dinars! What? That is almost double what we paid a week ago . . . why?"

Abu A (feigning sorrow and regret): "*Habibti* . . . you know what my supplier has to go through to bring me these vegetables? The cost of gasoline has gone up! I swear on the life of my mother that I'm only profiting 50 dinars per kilo . . ."

R: "Your mother is dead, isn't she?"

Abu A: "Yes yes—but you know how valuable the dear woman was to me—may Allah have mercy on her—and on us all! The dogs in the government are going to kill us with these prices . . ."

R (sighing heavily): "You voted for the dogs last year Abu Ammar . . ."

Abu A: "Shhh . . . don't call them dogs—it's not proper. Anyway, it's not their fault—the Americans are making them do it . . . may Allah curse them and their children . . ."

R (with eyes rolling) and Abu A (in unison): " . . . and their children's children."

A few days ago, the cousin took me to buy a pack of recordable CDs. The price had gone up a whole dollar, which may seem a pittance to the average American or European, but it must be remembered that many Iraqis make as little as $100 a month and complete families are expected to survive on that.

"B. why has the price of these lousy CDs gone up so much???" I demanded from the shop owner who is also a friend. "Don't tell me your supplier has also pushed the prices up on you because of the gasoline shortage?" I asked sarcastically. No—supplies cost the same for him— he has not needed to stock up yet. But this is how he explained it: His car takes 60 liters of gasoline. It needs to be refueled every 2–3 days. The official price of gasoline was 50 Iraqi dinars before, so it cost him around 3,000 dinars to fill up his car, which was nearly two dollars. Now it costs 9,000 Iraqi dinars IF he fills it up at a gas station and not using black market gasoline which will cost him around 15,000 dinars—five times the former price—and this every two to three days. He also has to purchase extra gasoline for the shop generator which needs to be working almost constantly, now that electricity is about four hours daily. "Now how am I supposed to cover that increase in my costs if I don't sell CDs at a higher price?"

People buy black market gasoline because for many, waiting in line 5, 6, 7 . . . 10 hours isn't an option. We've worked out a sort of agreement amongst 4 or 5 houses in the neighborhood. According to a schedule (which is somewhat complicated and involves license plate numbers, number of children per family, etc.), one of us spends the day filling up the car and then the gasoline is distributed among the four or five involved neighbors.

The process of extracting the gasoline from the car itself once it is back at the house was a rather disgusting and unhealthy one up until nearly a year ago. A hose was inserted into the gasoline tank and one of the unlucky neighbors would suck on it until the first surge of gasoline came flowing out. Now, thanks to both local and Chinese ingenuity, we have miniature gasoline pumps to suck out the gasoline. "The man who invented these," my cousin once declared emotionally, holding the pump up like a trophy, "deserves a Nobel Prize in . . . something or another."

I know for most of the world, highly priced gasoline is a common concern. For Iraqis, it represents how the situation is deteriorating. Gasoline and kerosene were literally cheaper than bottled water prior to the war. It's incredibly frustrating that while the price of petrol is at a high, one of the world's leading oil-producing countries isn't producing enough to cover its own needs.

There is talk of major mismanagement and theft in the Oil Ministry. Chalabi took over several days ago and a friend who works in the ministry says the takeover is a joke. "You know how they used to check our handbags when we first walked into the ministry?" she asked the day after Chalabi crowned himself Oil Emperor, "Now WE check our handbags after we leave the ministry—you know—to see if Chalabi stole anything."

I guess the Iraqis who thought the United States was going to turn Iraq into another America weren't really far from the mark—we too now enjoy inane leaders, shady elections, a shaky economy, large-scale unemployment and soaring gas prices.

Goodbye 2005—the year of SCIRI, fraudulent elections, secret torture chambers, car bombs, white phosphorous, assassinations, sectarianism and fundamentalism . . . you will not be missed.

Let us see what 2006 has in store for us. **posted by river @ 11:32 PM**

Thursday, January 12, 2006

THANK YOU FOR THE MUSIC . . .

When I first heard about the abduction of *Christian Science Monitor* journalist Jill Carroll a week ago, I remember feeling regret. It was the same heavy feeling I get every time I hear of another journalist killed or abducted. The same heavy feeling that settles upon most Iraqis, I imagine, when they hear of acquaintances suffering under the current situation.

I read the news as a subtitle on tv. We haven't had an internet connection for several days so I couldn't really read about the details. All I knew was that a journalist had been abducted and that her Iraqi interpreter had been killed. He was shot in cold blood in Al-Adil district earlier this month, when they took Jill Carroll . . . They say he didn't die immediately. It is said he lived long enough to talk to police and then he died.

I found out very recently that the interpreter killed was a good friend—Alan, of Alan's Melody, and I've spent the last two days crying.

Everyone knew him as simply "Alan," or "Elin" as it is pronounced in Iraqi Arabic. Prior to the war, he owned a music shop in the best area in Baghdad, A'arasat. He sold some Arabic music and instrumental music, but he had his regular customers—those Westernized Iraqis who craved foreign music. For those of us who listened to rock, adult alternative, jazz, etc. he had very few rivals.

He sold bootleg CDs, tapes and DVDs. His shop wasn't just a music shop—it was a haven. Some of my happiest moments were while I was walking out of that shop carrying CDs and tapes, full of anticipation for the escape the music provided. He had just about everything from Abba to Marilyn Manson. He could provide anything. All you had to do was go to him with the words, "Alan—I heard a great song on the radio . . . you have to find it!" And he'd sit there, patiently, asking who sang it? You don't know? Ok—was it a man or a woman? Fine. Do you remember any of the words? Chances were that he'd already heard it and even knew some of the lyrics.

During the sanctions, Iraq was virtually cut off from the outside world. We had maybe four or five local tv stations and it was only during the later years that the internet became more popular. Alan was one of those links with the outside world. Walking into Alan's shop was like walking into a sort of transitional other world. Whenever you walked into the store, great music would be blaring from his speakers and he and Mohammed, the guy who worked in his shop, would be arguing over who was better, Joe Satriani or Steve Vai.

He would have the latest Billboard hits posted on a sheet of paper near the door and he'd have compiled a few of his own favorites on a "collection" CD. He also went out of his way to get recordings of the latest award shows—Grammys, AMAs, Oscars, etc. You could visit him twice and know that by the third time, he'd have memorized your favorites and found music you might be interested in.

He was an electrical engineer—but his passion was music. His dream was to be a music producer. He was always full of scorn for the usual boy bands—N'Sync, Backstreet Boys, etc.—but he was always trying to promote an Iraqi boy band he claimed he'd discovered, "Unknown to No One." "They're great—wallah they have potential." He'd say. E. would answer, "Alan, they're terrible." And Alan, with his usual Iraqi pride would lecture about how they were great, simply because they were Iraqi.

He was a Christian from Basrah and he had a lovely wife who adored him—F. We would tease him about how once he was married and had a family, he'd lose interest in music. It didn't happen. Conversations with Alan continued to revolve around Pink Floyd, Jimmy Hendrix, but they began to include F. his wife, M. his daughter and his little boy. My heart aches for his family—his wife and children . . .

You could walk into the shop and find no one behind the counter—everyone was in the other room, playing one version or another of FIFA soccer on the Play Station. He collected those old records, or "vinyls." The older they were, the better. While he promoted new musical technology, he always said that nothing could beat the sound of a vintage vinyl.

We went to Alan not just to buy music. It always turned into a social visit. He'd make you sit down, listen to his latest favorite CD and drink something. Then he'd tell you the latest gossip—he knew it all. He knew where all the parties were, who the best DJs were and who was getting married or divorced. He knew the local gossip and the international gossip, but it was never malicious with Alan. It was always the funny sort.

The most important thing about Alan was that he never let you down. Never. Whatever it was that you wanted, he'd try his hardest to get it. If you became his friend, that didn't just include music—he was ready to lend a helping hand to those in need, whether it was just to give advice, or listen after a complicated, difficult week.

After the war, the area he had his shop in deteriorated. There were car bombs and shootings and the Badir people took over some of the houses there. People went to A'arasat less and less because it was too dangerous. His shop was closed up more than it was open. He shut it up permanently after getting death threats and a hand grenade through his shop window. His car was carjacked at some point and he was shot at so he started driving around in his father's beaten-up old Toyota Cressida with a picture of Sistani on his back window, "To ward off the fanatics . . ." He winked and grinned.

E. and I would stop by his shop sometimes after the war, before he shut it down. We went in once and found that there was no electricity, and no generator. The shop was dimly lit with some sort of fuel lamp and Alan was sitting behind the counter, sorting through CDs. He was ecstatic to see us. There was no way we could listen to music so he and E. sang through some of their favorite songs, stumbling upon the lyrics and making things up along the way. Then we started listening to various ring tones and swapping the latest jokes of the day. Before we knew it, two hours had slipped by and the world outside was forgotten, an occasional explosion bringing us back to reality.

It hit me then that it wasn't the music that made Alan's shop a haven—somewhere to forget problems and worries—it was Alan himself.

He loved Pink Floyd:

Did you see the frightened ones?
Did you hear the falling bombs? . . .
"Goodbye Blue Sky"—Pink Floyd

Goodbye, Alan . . . **posted by river @ 10:05 PM**

Wednesday, January 18, 2006

A TRIBUTE TO IRAQI INGENUITY . . .

January 17, 2006 marks the 15th commemoration of the Gulf War in 1991 after Iraq occupied Kuwait (briefly) in 1990. (Or according to American terminology, after Iraq "liberated" Kuwait in 1990.)

For 42 days, Baghdad and other cities and towns were bombarded with nearly 140,000 tons of explosives, by international estimates. The bombing was relentless—schools, housing complexes, factories, bridges, electric power stations, ministries, sewage facilities, oil refineries, operators, and even bomb shelters (including the only baby formula factory in Iraq and the infamous Amirya Shelter bombing where almost 400 civilians were killed).

According to reports and statistics made by the "Iraqi Reconstruction Bureau" and the ministries involved in reconstruction, prior to the 2003 war/occupation, the following damage was done through 42 days of continuous bombing, and various acts of vandalism:

Schools and scholastic facilities—**3,960**
Universities, labs, dormitories—**40**
Health facilities (including hospitals, clinics, medical warehouses)—**421**
Telephone operators, communication towers, etc.—**475**
Bridges, buildings, housing complexes—**260**
Warehouses, shopping centers, grain silos—**251**
Churches and mosques—**159**
Dams, water pumping stations, agricultural facilities—**200**
Petroleum facilities (including refineries)—**145**
General services (shelters, sewage treatment plants, municipalities)—**830**
Factories, mines, industrial facilities—**120**

. . . And much, much more—including radio broadcasting towers, museums, orphanages, retirement homes, etc. While the larger damage—damage to dams, bridges, warehouses, ministries, food silos, etc.—was done by warplanes and missiles, the damage to smaller facilities was caused largely by vandalism in the south of the country and in areas like Kirkuk. In the south it was mainly the work of the *intifadah*," which was initiated by the *Tawabin* or "The Repentant" who infiltrated the south from Iran and found supporters inside of the country. (Many of the Tawabin are known today as Badir's Brigade.)

What happened in the south in 1991 is similar to what happened in Baghdad in 2003—burning, looting and attacks. The area fell into chaos after the Republican Guard was pulled out to different governorates for the duration of the war. Meanwhile, the United States was bombing the Iraqi army as it was pulling out of Kuwait and the Tawabin were killing off some of the Iraqi troops who had abandoned their tanks and artillery and were coming back on foot through the south. Many of those troops, and the civilians killed during the attacks, looting, and burning, were buried in some of the mass graves we conveniently blame solely on Saddam and the Republican Guard—but no one bothers to mention this anymore because it's easier to blame the dictator.

But I digress—the topic today is reconstruction. Immediately after the war, various ministries were brought together to do the reconstruction work. The focus was on the infrastructure—to bring back the refineries, electricity, water, bridges, and telecommunications.

The task was a daunting one because so many of Iraq's major infrastructure projects and buildings had been designed and built by foreign contractors from all over the world including French, German, Chinese and Japanese companies. The foreign expertise was unavailable after 1991 due to the war and embargo and Iraqi engineers and technicians found themselves facing the devastation of the Gulf War all alone with limited supplies.

Two years and approximately 8 billion Iraqi dinars later, nearly 90 percent of the damage had been repaired. It took an estimated 6,000 engineers (all Iraqi), 42,000 technicians, and 12,000 administrators, but bridges were soon up again, telephones were more or less functioning in most areas, refineries were working, water was running and electricity wasn't back 100 percent, but it was certainly better than it is today. Within the first two years over 100 small and large bridges had been reconstructed, 16 refineries, over 50 factories and industrial compounds, etc.

It wasn't perfect—it wasn't Halliburton . . . It wasn't KBR . . . but it was Iraqi. There was that sense of satisfaction and pride looking upon a building or bridge that was damaged during the war and seeing it up and running and looking better than it did before.

Now, nearly three years after this war, the buildings are still piles of debris. Electricity is terrible. Water is cut off for days at a time. Telephone lines come and go. Oil production isn't even at prewar levels . . . and Iraqis hear about the billions upon billions that come and go. A billion here for security . . . Five hundred million there for the infrastructure . . . Millions for voting . . . Iraq falling into deeper debt . . . Engineers without jobs simply because they are not a part of this political party or that religious group . . . And the country still in shambles.

One of the biggest, most complicated and most swiftly executed reconstruction projects was the Dawra Refinery in Baghdad. It is Iraq's oldest refinery and one of its largest. It was bombed several times during the Gulf War and oil production came to a halt. After the war, it is said that the Iraqi government negotiated with an Italian company to reconstruct it but the price requested by the company was extremely high. It was decided then that the reconstruction effort would be completely local and the work began almost immediately. Several months later, during the summer of 1991, when the Italian experts came back to assess the damage, they found that the refinery was functioning.

Below are some pictures that were sent to me by an engineer who was a part of the reconstruction effort and is currently jobless in Amman. The pictures are both painful and inspiring. Fifteen years later and it is difficult to see the damage that was wrought on the country . . . But the "after" pictures give me faith that Iraq will rise once more—in spite of occupiers and meddlers.

Note: I was tempted to stamp all the "after" pictures with "AMER-ICANS DID NOT RECONSTRUCT THIS" as I know that in a month some clueless Republican will send them back to me with the words, "Look at how we reconstructed your country!"

Alwiya Operator (public switchboard)

Before   After

Fayha Bridge in Basrah

Before   After

Special thanks to M. Hamed for the pictures and the info about the reconstruction effort. [For M. Hamed's images of the Dawa Refinery and to see these images in color, see Riverbend's blog at www.riverbend-blog.blogspot.com/2006_01_01_riverbendblog_archive.html] **posted by river @ 1:52 AM**

Thursday, February 02, 2006

ELECTION RESULTS . . .

Iraqi election results were officially announced nearly two weeks ago, but it was apparent from the day of elections which political parties would come out on top. I'm not even going to bother listing the different types of election fraud witnessed all over Iraq—it's a tedious subject and one we've been discussing for well over a month.

The fact that a Shia, Iran-influenced religious list came out on top is hardly surprising. I'm surprised, however, at Iraqis who seem to be astonished at the outcome. Didn't we, over the last three years, see this coming? Iranian-influenced clerics had a strong hold right from 2003. Their militias were almost instantly incorporated into the Ministry of Interior and the Ministry of Defense as soon a move was made to create new Iraqi security forces. Sistani has been promoting them from day one.

Why is it so very surprising that in times of calamity people turn to religion? It happens all over the world. During tsunamis, hurricanes, earthquakes, blockades, wars—people turn to deities . . . It's simple—when all else fails, there is always a higher power for most people.

After nearly three years of a failing occupation, I personally believe that many Iraqis voted for religious groups because it was counted as a vote against America and the occupation itself. No matter what American policy makers say to their own public—and no matter how many pictures Rumsfeld and Condi take with our fawning politicians—most Iraqis do not trust Americans. America as a whole is viewed as a devilish country that is, at best, full of self serving mischief towards lesser countries and, at worst, an implementer of sanctions, and a warmongering invader.

Even Iraqis who believe America is here to help (and they seem to have grown fewer in number these days), believe that it helps not out of love for Iraqis, but out of self-interest and greed.

Shia religious parties, like SCIRI and Da'awa, have decidedly changed their tone in the last year. During 2003, they were friends of America—they owed the United States their current power inside of the country. Today, as Iraqis are becoming more impatient with the American presence inside of Iraq, they are claiming that they will be the end of the "occupiers." They openly blame the Americans for the lack of security and general chaos. The message is quite different. In 2003, there was general talk of a secular Iraq; today, that no longer seems to be an option.

In 2003, Jaffari was claiming he didn't want to see Iraqi women losing their rights, etc. He never mentioned equal rights—but he did throw in a word here and there about how Iraqi women had a right to an education and even a job. I was changing channels a couple of weeks ago and I came across Jaffari speaking to students from Mustansiriya University—one of Iraq's largest universities, with campuses in several areas in Baghdad. I couldn't see the students—he might have been speaking with a group of penguins, for all I could tell. The camera was focused on him—his shifty eyes and low, mumbling voice.

On his right sat an Ayatollah with a black turban and black robes. He looked stern and he nodded with satisfaction as Jaffari spoke to the students (or penguins). His speech wasn't about science, technology or even development—it was a religious sermon about heaven and hell, good and evil.

I noticed two things immediately. The first was that he seemed to be speaking to only male students. There were no females in the audience. He spoke of their female "sisters" in absentia, as if they had absolutely no representation in the gathering. The second thing was that he seemed to be speaking to only Shia because he kept mentioning their "Sunni brothers," as if they too were absent. He sermonized about how the men should take care of the women and how Sunnis weren't bad at all. I waited to hear him speak about Iraqi unity, and the need to not make religious distinctions—those words never came.

In spite of all this, pro-war Republicans remain inanely hopeful. Ah well—so Ayatollahs won out this election—the next election will be better! But there is a problem . . .

The problem with religious parties and leaders in a country like Iraq, is that they control a following of fervent believers, not just political supporters. For followers of Da'awa and SCIRI, for example, it's not about the policy or the promises or the puppet in power. It's like the Pope for devout Catholics—you don't question the man in the chair because he is there by divine right, almost. You certainly don't question his policies.

Ayatollahs are like that. Muqtada Al-Sadr is ridiculous. He talks like his tongue is swollen up in his mouth and he always looks like he needs to bathe. He speaks with an intonation that indicates a fluency in Farsi and yet . . . he commands an army of followers because his grandfather was a huge religious figure. He could be the least educated, least enlightened man in the country and he'd still have people willing to lay down their lives at his command because of his family's religious history. (Lucky Americans—he announced a week ago that should Iran come under US attack, he and his followers would personally rise up to Iran's defense.)

At the end of the day, people who follow these figures tell themselves that even if the current leader isn't up to par, the goal and message remain the same—religion, God's word as law. When living in the midst of a war-torn country with a situation that is deteriorating and with death around every corner, you turn to God because Iyad Allawi couldn't get you electricity and security—he certainly isn't going to get you into heaven should you come face to face with a car bomb.

The trouble with having a religious party in power in a country as diverse as Iraq is that you automatically alienate everyone not of that particular sect or religion. Religion is personal—it is something you are virtually born into . . . it belongs to the heart, the mind, the spirit—and while it is welcome in day to day dealings, it shouldn't be politicized.

Theocracies (and we seem to be standing on the verge of an Iranian-influenced one), grow stronger with time because you cannot argue religion. Politicians are no longer politicians—they are Ayatollahs—they become modern-day envoys of God, to be worshipped, not simply respected. You cannot challenge them because, for their followers, that is a challenge to a belief—not a person or a political party.

You go from being a critic or "opposition" to simply being a heathen when you argue religious parties.

Americans write to me wondering, "But where are the educated Iraqis? Why didn't they vote for secular parties?" The educated Iraqis have been systematically silenced since 2003. They've been pressured and bullied outside of the country. They've been assassinated, detained, tortured and abducted. Many of them have lost faith in the possibility of a secular Iraq.

Then again . . . who is to say that many of the people who voted for religious parties aren't educated? I know some perfectly educated Iraqis who take criticism towards parties like Da'awa and SCIRI as a personal affront. This is because these parties are so cloaked and cocooned within their religious identity, that it is almost taken as an attack against Shia in general when one criticizes them. It's the same thing for many Sunnis when a political Sunni party comes under criticism.

That's the danger of mixing politics and religion—it becomes personal.

I try not to dwell on the results too much—the fact that Shia religious fundamentalists are currently in power—because when I do, I'm filled with this sort of chill that leaves in its wake a feeling of quiet terror. It's like when the electricity goes out suddenly and you're plunged into a deep, quiet, almost tangible darkness—you try not to focus too intently on the subtle noises and movements around you because the unseen possibilities will drive you mad . . . **posted by river @ 1:34 AM**

Saturday, February 11, 2006

THE RAID . . .

We were collected at my aunt's house for my cousin's birthday party a few days ago. J. just turned 16 and my aunt invited us for a late lunch and some cake. It was a very small gathering—three cousins—including myself—my parents, and J.'s best friend, who also happened to be a neighbor.

The lunch was quite good—my aunt is possibly one of the best cooks in Baghdad. She makes traditional Iraqi food and for J.'s birthday she had prepared all our favorites—dolma (rice and meat wrapped in grape leaves, onions, peppers, etc.), beryani rice, stuffed chicken, and some salads. The cake was ready-made and it was in the shape of a friendly-looking fish, J.'s father having forgotten she was an Aquarius and not a Pisces when he selected it, "I thought everyone born in February was a Pisces . . ." He explained when we pointed out his mistake.

When it was time to blow out the candles, the electricity was out and we stood around her in the dark and sang "Happy Birthday" in two different languages. She squeezed her eyes shut briefly to make a wish and then, with a single breath, she blew out the candles. She proceeded to open gifts—bear pajamas, boy band CDs, a sweater with some sparkly things on it, a red and beige book bag . . . Your typical gifts for a teenager.

The gift that made her happiest, however, was given by her father. After she'd opened up everything, he handed her a small, rather heavy, silvery package. She unwrapped it hastily and gasped with delight, "Baba—it's lovely!" She smiled as she held it up to the light of the gas lamp to show it off. It was a Swiss Army knife—complete with corkscrew, nail clippers, and a bottle opener.

"You can carry it around in your bag for protection when you go places!" he explained. She smiled and gingerly pulled out the blade, "And look—when the blade is clean, it works as a mirror!" We all oohed and aahed our admiration and T., another cousin, commented she'd get one when the Swiss Army began making them in pink.

I tried to remember what I got on my 16th birthday and I was sure it wasn't a knife of any sort.

By 8 p.m., my parents and J.'s neighbor were gone. They had left me and T., our 24-year-old female cousin, to spend a night. It was 2 a.m. and we had just gotten J.'s little brother into bed. He had eaten more than his share of cake and the sugar had made him wild for a couple of hours.

We were gathered in the living room and my aunt and her husband, Ammoo S. (*Ammoo* = uncle) were asleep. T., J. and I were speaking softly and looking for songs on the radio, having sworn not to sleep before the cake was all gone. T. was playing idly with her mobile phone, trying to send a message to a friend. "Hey—there's no coverage here . . . is it just my phone?" she asked. J. and I both took out our phones and checked, "Mine isn't working either . . ." I answered, shaking her head. They both turned to me and I told them that I couldn't get a signal either. J. suddenly looked alert and made a sort of "Uh-oh" sound as she remembered something. "R.—will you check the telephone next to you?" I picked up the ordinary telephone next to me and held my breath, waiting for a dial tone. Nothing.

"There's no dial tone . . . but there was one earlier today—I was online . . ."

J. frowned and turned down the radio. "The last time this happened," she said, "the area was raided." The room was suddenly silent and we strained our ears. Nothing. I could hear a generator a couple of streets away, and I also heard the distant barking of a dog—but there was nothing out of the ordinary.

T. suddenly sat up straight, "Do you hear that?" she asked, wide-eyed. At first I couldn't hear anything and then I caught it—it was the sound of cars or vehicles—moving slowly. "I can hear it!" I called back to T., standing up and moving towards the window. I looked out into the darkness and couldn't see anything beyond the dim glow of lamps behind windows here and there.

"You won't see anything from here—it's probably on the main road!" J. jumped up and went to shake her father awake. "Baba, baba—get up—I think the area is being raided," I heard J. call out as she approached her parents' room. Ammoo S. was awake in moments and we heard him wandering around for his slippers and robe asking what time it was.

Meanwhile, the sound of cars had gotten louder and I remembered that one could see some of the neighborhood from a window on the second floor. T. and I crept upstairs quietly. We heard Ammoo S. unlocking 5 different locks on the kitchen door. "What's he doing?" T. asked, "Shouldn't he keep the doors locked?" We were looking out the window and there was the glow of lights a few streets away. I couldn't see exactly where they came from, as several houses were blocking our view, but we could tell something extraordinary was going on in the neighborhood. The sound of vehicles was getting louder, and it was accompanied by the sound of clanging doors and lights that would flash every once in a while.

We clattered downstairs and found J. and the aunt bustling around in the dark. "What should we do?" T. asked, wringing her hands nervously. The only time I'd ever experienced a raid was back in 2003 at an uncle's house—and it was Americans. This was the first time I was to witness what we assumed would be an Iraqi raid.

My aunt was seething quietly, "This is the third time the bastards raid the area in 2 months . . . We'll never get any peace or quiet . . ." I stood at their bedroom door and watched as she made the bed. They lived in a mixed neighborhood—Sunnis, Shia and Christians. It was a relatively new neighborhood that began growing in the late eighties. Most of the neighbors have known each other for years. "We don't know what they're looking for . . . La Ilaha Ila Allah . . ."

I stood awkwardly, watching them make preparations. J. was already in her room changing—she called out for us to do the same, "They'll come in the house—you don't want to be wearing pajamas . . ."

"Why, will they have camera crews with them?" T. smiled wanly, attempting some humor. No, J. replied, her voice muffled as she put on a sweater, "Last time they made us wait outside in the cold." I listened for Ammoo S. and heard him outside, taking the big padlock off of the gate in the driveway. "Why are you unlocking everything J.?" I called out in the dark.

"The animals will break down the doors if they aren't open in three seconds and then they'll be all over the garden and house . . . last time they pushed the door open on poor Abu H. three houses down and broke his shoulder . . ." J. was fully changed, and over her jeans and sweater she was wearing her robe. It was cold.

My aunt had dressed too and she was making her way upstairs to carry down my three-year-old cousin B. "I don't want him waking up with all the noise and finding those bastards around him in the dark."

Twenty minutes later, we were all assembled in the living room. The house was dark except for the warm glow of the kerosene heater and a small lamp in the corner. We were all dressed and waiting nervously, wrapped in blankets. T. and I sat on the ground while my aunt and her husband sat on the couch, B. wrapped in a blanket between them. J. was sitting in an armchair across from them. It was nearly 4 a.m.

Meanwhile, the noises outside had gotten louder as the raid got closer. Every once in a while, you could hear voices calling out for people to open a door or the sharp banging of a rifle against a door.

Last time they had raided my aunt's area, they took away four men on their street alone. Two of them were students in their early twenties— one a law student, and the other an engineering student, and the third man was a grandfather in his early sixties. There was no accusation, no problem—they were simply ordered outside, loaded up into a white pick-up truck and driven away with a group of other men from the area. Their families haven't heard from them since and they visit the morgue almost daily in anticipation of finding them dead.

"There will be no problem," My aunt said sternly, looking at each of us, thin-lipped. "You will not say anything improper and they will come in, look around and go." Her eyes lingered on Ammoo S. He was silent. He had lit a cigarette and was inhaling deeply. J. said he'd begun smoking again a couple of months ago after having quit for ten years. "Are your papers ready?" she asked him, referring to his identi-fication papers which would be requested. He didn't answer, but nod-ded his head silently.

We waited. And waited . . . I began nodding off and my dreams were interspersed with troops and cars and hooded men. I woke to the sound of T. saying, "They're almost here . . ." And lifted my head, groggy with what I thought was at least three hours of sleep. I squinted down at my watch and noted it was not yet 5 a.m. "Haven't they gotten to us yet?" I asked.

Ammoo S. was pacing in the kitchen. I could hear him coming and going in his slippers, pausing every now and then in front of the window. My aunt was still on the couch—she sat with B. in her arms, rocking him gently and murmuring prayers. J. was doing a last-minute check, hiding valuables and gathering our handbags into the living room, "They took baba's mobile phone during the last raid—make sure your mobile phones are with you."

I could feel my heart pounding in my ears and I got closer to the kerosene heater in an attempt to dispel the cold that seemed to have permanently taken over my fingers and toes. T. was trembling, wrapped in her blanket. I waved her over to the heater but she shook her head and answered, "I . . . mmmm . . . n-n-not . . . c-c-cold . . ."

It came ten minutes later. A big clanging sound on the garden gate and voices yelling, "*Ifta7u* [OPEN UP]." I heard my uncle outside, calling out, "We're opening the gate, we're opening . . ." It was moments and they were inside the house. Suddenly, the house was filled with strange men, yelling out orders and stomping into rooms. It was chaotic. We could see flashing lights in the garden and lights coming from the hallways. I could hear Ammoo S. talking loudly outside, telling them his wife and the "children" were the only ones in the house. What were they looking for? Was there something wrong? he asked.

Suddenly, two of them were in the living room. We were all sitting on the sofa, near my aunt. My cousin B. was by then awake, eyes wide with fear. They were holding large lights or "torches" and one of them pointed a Kalashnikov at us. "Is there anyone here but you and them?" one of them barked at my aunt. "No—it's only us and my husband outside with you—you can check the house." T.'s hands went up to block the glaring light of the torch and one of the men yelled at her to put her hands down; they fell limply in her lap. I squinted in the strong light and as my sight adjusted, I noticed they were wearing masks, only their eyes and mouths showing. I glanced at my cousins and noted that T. was barely breathing. J. was sitting perfectly still, eyes focused on nothing in particular. I vaguely noted that her sweater was on backwards.

One of them stood with the Kalashnikov pointed at us, and the other one began opening cabinets and checking behind doors. We were silent. The only sounds came from my aunt, who was praying in a tremulous whisper and little B., who was sucking away at his thumb, eyes wide with fear. I could hear the rest of the troops walking around the house, opening closets, doors and cabinets.

I listened for Ammoo S., hoping to hear him outside but I could only distinguish the harsh voices of the troops. The minutes we sat in the living room seemed to last forever. I didn't know where to look exactly. My eyes kept wandering to the man with the weapon and yet I knew staring at him wasn't a good idea. I stared down at a newspaper at my feet and tried to read the upside-down headlines. I glanced at J. again—her heart was beating so hard, the small silver pendant that my mother had given her just that day was throbbing on her chest in time to her heartbeat.

Suddenly, someone called out something from outside and it was over. They began rushing to leave the house, almost as fast as they'd invaded it. Doors slamming, lights dimming. We were left in the dark once more, not daring to move from the sofa we were sitting on, listening as the men disappeared, leaving only a couple to stand at our gate.

"Where's baba?" J. asked, panicking for a moment before we heard his slippered feet in the driveway. "Did they take him?" Her voice was getting higher. Ammoo S. finally walked into the house, looking weary and drained. I could tell his face was pale even in the relative dark of the house. My aunt sat sobbing quietly in the living room, T. comforting her. "Houses are no longer sacred . . . We can't sleep . . . We can't live . . . If you can't be safe in your own house, where can you be safe? The animals . . . the bastards . . ."

We found out a few hours later that one of our neighbors, two houses down, had died. Abu Salih was a man in his seventies and as the Iraqi mercenaries raided his house, he had a heart-attack. His grandson couldn't get him to the hospital on time because the troops wouldn't let him leave the house until they'd finished with it. His grandson told us later that day that the Iraqis were checking the houses, but the American troops had the area surrounded and secured. It was a coordinated raid.

They took at least a dozen men from my aunt's area alone—their ages between 19 and 40. The street behind us doesn't have a single house with a male under the age of 50—lawyers, engineers, students, ordinary laborers—all hauled away by the "security forces" of the New Iraq. The only thing they share in common is the fact that they come from Sunni families (with the exception of two who I'm not sure about).

We spent the day putting clothes back into closets, taking stock of anything missing (a watch, a brass letter opener, and a walkman), and cleaning dirt and mud off of carpets. My aunt was fanatic about cleansing and disinfecting everything saying it was all "Dirty, dirty, dirty . . ." J. has sworn never to celebrate her birthday again.

It's almost funny—only a month ago, we were watching a commercial on some Arabic satellite channel—Arabiya perhaps. They were showing a commercial for Iraqi security forces and giving a list of numbers Iraqis were supposed to dial in the case of a terrorist attack . . . You call THIS number if you need the police to protect you from burglars or abductors . . . You call THAT number if you need the National Guard or special forces to protect you from terrorists . . . But . . .

Who do you call to protect you from the New Iraq's security forces?
posted by river @ 12:43 AM

Thursday, February 23, 2006

TENSIONS . . .

Things are not good in Baghdad.

There was an explosion this morning in a mosque in Samarra, a largely Sunni town. While the mosque is sacred to both Sunnis and Shia, it is considered one of the most important Shia visiting places in Iraq. Samarra is considered a sacred city by many Muslims and historians because it was made the capital of the Abassid Empire, after Baghdad, by the Abassid Caliph Al-Mu'tasim.

The name *Samarra* is actually derived from the phrase in Arabic "*Sarre men ra'a*" which translates to "A joy for all who see." This is what the city was named by Al-Mu'tasim when he laid the plans for a city that was to compete with the greatest cities of the time—it was to be a joy for all who saw it. It remained the capital of the Abassid Empire for nearly sixty years and even after the capital was Baghdad once again, Samarra flourished under the care of various Caliphs.

The mosque damaged with explosives today is the Askari Mosque, which is important because it is believed to be the burial place of two of the 12 Shia Imams—Ali Al-Hadi and Hassan Al-Askari (father and son) who lived and died in Samarra. Many Shia believe Al-Mahdi "*al muntadhar*" will also be resurrected or will reappear from this mosque.

I remember visiting the mosque several years ago—before the war. We visited Samarra to have a look at the famous *Malwiya* tower and someone suggested we also visit the Askari Mosque. I was reluctant as I wasn't dressed properly at the time—jeans and a t-shirt are not considered mosque garb. We stopped by a small shop in the city and purchased a few inexpensive black *abayas* for us women and drove to the mosque.

We got there just as the sun was setting and I remember pausing outside the mosque to admire the golden dome and the intricate minarets. It was shimmering in the sunset and there seemed to be a million colors—orange, gold, white—it was almost glowing. The view was incredible and the environment was so peaceful and calm. There was none of the bustle and noise usually surrounding religious sites—we had come at a perfect time. The inside of the mosque didn't disappoint either—elaborate Arabic script and more gold and this feeling of utter peace . . . I'm grateful we decided to visit it.

We woke up this morning to news that men wearing Iraqi security uniforms walked in and detonated explosives, damaging the mosque almost beyond repair. It's heart-breaking and terrifying. There has been gunfire all over Baghdad since morning. The streets near our neighborhood were eerily empty and calm but there was a tension that had us all sitting on edge. We heard about problems in areas like Baladiyat where there was some rioting and vandalism, etc. and several mosques in Baghdad were attacked. I think what has everyone most disturbed is the fact that the reaction was so swift, like it was just waiting to happen.

All morning we've been hearing/watching both Shia and Sunni religious figures speak out against the explosions and emphasise that this is what is wanted by the enemies of Iraq—this is what they would like to achieve—divide and conquer. Extreme Shia are blaming extreme Sunnis and Iraq seems to be falling apart at the seams under foreign occupiers and local fanatics.

No one went to work today as the streets were mostly closed. The situation isn't good at all. I don't think I remember things being this tense—everyone is just watching and waiting quietly. There's so much talk of civil war and yet, with the people I know—Sunnis and Shia alike—I can hardly believe it is a possibility. Educated, sophisticated Iraqis are horrified with the idea of turning against each other, and even not-so-educated Iraqis seem very aware that this is a small part of a bigger, more ominous plan . . .

Several mosques have been taken over by the Mahdi militia and the Badir people seem to be everywhere. Tomorrow no one is going to work or college or anywhere.

People are scared and watchful. We can only pray. **posted by river @ 1:21 AM**

M o n d a y ,   F e b r u a r y   2 7 ,   2 0 0 6

VOLATILE DAYS . . .

The last few days have been unsettlingly violent in spite of the curfew. We've been at home simply waiting it out and hoping for the best. The phone wasn't working and the electrical situation hasn't improved. We are at a point, however, where things like electricity, telephones and fuel seem like minor worries. Even complaining about them is a luxury Iraqis can't afford these days.

The sounds of shooting and explosions usually begin at dawn, at least that's when I first sense them, and they don't really subside until well into the night. There was a small gunfight on the main road near our area the day before yesterday, but with the exception of the local mosque being fired upon, and a corpse found at dawn three streets down, things have been relatively quiet.

Some of the neighbors have been discussing the possibility of the men setting up a neighborhood watch. We did this during the war and during the chaos immediately after the war. The problem this time is that the Iraqi security forces are as much to fear as the black-clad and hooded men attacking mosques, houses and each other.

It does not feel like civil war because Sunnis and Shia have been showing solidarity these last few days in a big way. I don't mean the clerics or the religious zealots or the politicians—but the average person. Our neighborhood is mixed and Sunnis and Shia alike have been outraged with the attacks on mosques and shrines. The telephones have been down, but we've agreed upon a very primitive communication arrangement. Should any house in the area come under siege, someone would fire in the air three times. If firing in the air isn't an option, then someone inside the house would have to try to communicate trouble from the rooftop.

The mosques also have a code when they're in trouble, i.e. under attack, the man who does the call for prayer calls out "*Allahu Akbar*" three times until people from the area can come help protect the mosque or someone gets involved.

Yesterday they were showing Sunni and Shia clerics praying together in a mosque and while it looked encouraging, I couldn't help but feel angry. Why don't they simply tell their militias to step down—to stop attacking mosques and *Husseiniyas*—to stop terrorizing people? It's so deceptive and empty on television—like a peaceful vision from another land. The Iraqi government is pretending dismay, but it's doing nothing to curb the violence and the bloodshed beyond a curfew. And where are the Americans in all of this? They are sitting back and letting things happen—sometimes flying a helicopter here or there—but generally not getting involved.

I'm reading, and hearing, about the possibility of civil war. The possibility. Yet I'm sitting here wondering if this is actually what civil war is like. Has it become a reality? Will we look back at this in one year, two years . . . ten . . . and say, "It began in February 2006 . . ."? It is like a nightmare in that you don't realize it's a nightmare while having it—only later, after waking up with your heart throbbing, and your eyes searching the dark for a pinpoint of light, do you realize it was a nightmare . . . **posted by river @ 2:27 AM**

AND THE OSCAR GOES TO . . .

It's Oscar time once again. We've been bombarded with Oscar propaganda for nearly a month now. MBC and One TV (a channel from the Emirates) have been promising us live Oscar coverage since January. It seems like all the interviews and programs for the last week at least have been about the Oscars—*Barbara Walters, Oprah, Inside Edition, Entertainment Tonight*—it's an endless stream of Oscar nominees and analysts.

Now I've seen the nominees—we see them every year—and I've come to a conclusion—Iraqis need an award show. While the Hollywood glitterati make good entertainers, our local super stars, Hakeem, Jaffari, Talbani, Allawi et al. make GREAT entertainers. This last year we've seen several dramas unfold and our political leaders have been riveting!

So . . . not to be outdone by Barbara Walters and Oprah Winfrey—we bring you the Baghdad Burning Oscar Special!! Except, for our award show I suggest we change the name of the little statuette from Oscar to something more local and familiar. (Oscar is too close in pronunciation to the Arabic word *iskar* which means "get drunk." Should we use "Oscar" I fear the award show would be hijacked by Sadr's religious militia, hence I would like to suggest the *Sayid* Awards!)

Ladies and gentlemen, without further ado, we bring you the nominees for the 2006 *Sayid* Awards!

Nominees for Best Actor:

Ibraheim Al-Jaffari in "Free Iraqi Elections" for his attempted portrayal of a non-sectarian, independent PM of a "legitimate" Iraqi government.

George W. Bush in "OIF: The War on Terror" The third sequel to the original "Operation Iraqi Freedom: Weapons of Mass Destruction" and "Operation Iraqi Freedom: Liberating Iraqis." Bush's nomination comes for his convincing portrayal as the world's first mentally challenged president.

Bayan Baqir Solagh in "Torture Houses," for his world-class acting as the shocked and indignant Iraqi Minister of Interior during the whole torture houses scandal.

Abdul Aziz Al-Hakeem in "Men in Black [Turbans]" as the deeply devout Mullah pretending to be independent of his masters in Iran.

Mihsan Abdul Hameed in "Fickle" for his compelling portrayal of a victimized pro-war, then suddenly anti-war, anti-occupation Sunni politician.

Nominee for Best Leading Actress:

Condi Rice in "Viva Iran!" as the vicious Secretary of State in the charade to stop Iran's nuclear power program (in spite of Iranian control in Iraq).

Nominees for Best Supporting Actor:

Jalal Talbani in "*Kaka* President" (*Kaka* = Kurdish word for "brother") for his attempt at playing the "legitimate" leader of the New Iraq (and although, technically, he's the star of the movie, we nominate him for best "supporting" actor as the PM managed to upstage him all year).

Dick Cheney in "OIF: The War on Terror" for his role as the devoted, fanatical VP and his relentless insistence that all goes well in Iraq.

Muqtada Al-Sadr in "Viva Iran!" as the young, charismatic, black-turbaned spiritual militia leader intent on protecting Iran from all harm and promoting tolerance between Sunnis and Shia (in spite of his Sadr militia, responsible for vandalism and attacks against Sunnis and secularists).

Scott McClellan in "OIF: The War on Terror" and "Denial," best known for his ability to keep a straight face while reading through White House press briefings.

Nominee for special effects:

Ahmed Al-Chalabi in "Disappearing Act" for his magnificent evaporation from the Iraqi political scene this year. Mr. Chalabi is quite the master of illusion and received a previous nomination for his disappearance from Jordan in "The Petra Bank Scandal."

Best production:

"OIF: The War on Terror" (originally called "My Daddy's War") produced by Washington neocons, including Rumsfeld, Wolfowitz, etc.

"Free Iraqi Elections" produced (and directed) by Abdul Aziz Al-Hakeem et al. and his army (quite literally) of supporters (the Badrists).

Best motion picture:

"OIF: The War on Terror" starring George W. Bush, Dick Cheney, and Condi Rice and others. A riveting drama set in Iraq. Rated "G" for "Gullibility" and "R" for "Republican."

"Disappearing Act" starring Ahmed Al-Chalabi, Adnan Al-Pachachi, and Ghazi Al-Yawir.

"Free Iraqi Elections"—A black comedy based on the far-fetched theory of free elections under foreign occupation starring Abdul Aziz Al-Hakeem, Ibraheim Al-Jaffari and Muqtada Al-Sadr.

"Kangaroo Court" starring Saddam Hussein, Barazan Hassen, and various judges, prosecutors and lawyers.

Many honorable mentions:

First and foremost, an honorable mention to Bush's speech writers. It must be the most difficult job in the world writing scripts to make George W. Bush sound/look not great, not even good—but passable. It must also be challenging having to write speeches using words with a maximum of two syllables.

An honorable mention to the Saudis for their support of Sunni extremists and Wahabis, the Iranians for their support of Shia extremist, and Americans for their support of chaos.

And so, as our Green Zone glitterati retire to their camps to celebrate their great victories, Iraqis wonder what wonderful, new cinematic opportunities await. There is much talk that a blockbuster is in the works—in the pre-production stage of this years most anticipated psychological thriller, "Iraqi Civil War." **posted by river @ 2:50 AM**

Saturday, March 18, 2006

THREE YEARS . . .

It has been three years since the beginning of the war that marked the end of Iraq's independence. Three years of occupation and bloodshed.

Spring should be about renewal and rebirth. For Iraqis, spring has been about reliving painful memories and preparing for future disasters. In many ways, this year is like 2003 prior to the war when we were stocking up on fuel, water, food and first aid supplies and medications. We're doing it again this year but now we don't discuss what we're stocking up for. Bombs and B-52's are so much easier to face than other possibilities.

I don't think anyone imagined three years ago that things could be quite this bad today. The last few weeks have been ridden with tension. I'm so tired of it all—we're all tired.

Three years and the electricity is worse than ever. The security situation has gone from bad to worse. The country feels like it's on the brink of chaos once more—but a pre-planned, pre-fabricated chaos being led by religious militias and zealots.

School, college and work have been on again, off again affairs. It seems for every two days of work/school, there are five days of sitting at home waiting for the situation to improve. Right now college and school are on hold because the *Arba3eeniya* or the "40th Day" is coming up—more black and green flags, mobs of men in black and *latmiyas*. We were told the children should try going back to school next Wednesday. I say "try" because prior to the much-awaited parliamentary meeting a couple of days ago, schools were out. After the Samarra mosque bombing, schools were out. The children have been at home this year more than they've been in school.

I'm especially worried about the Arba3eeniya this year. I'm worried we'll see more of what happened to the Askari mosque in Samarra. Most Iraqis seem to agree that the whole thing was set up by those who had most to gain by driving Iraqis apart.

I'm sitting here trying to think what makes this year, 2006, so much worse than 2005 or 2004. It's not the outward differences—things such as electricity, water, dilapidated buildings, broken streets and ugly concrete security walls. Those things are disturbing, but they are fixable. Iraqis have proved again and again that countries can be rebuilt. No—it's not the obvious that fills us with foreboding.

The real fear is the mentality of so many people lately—the rift that seems to have worked its way through the very heart of the country, dividing people. It's disheartening to talk to acquaintances—sophisticated, civilized people—and hear how Sunnis are like this, and Shia are like that . . . To watch people pick up their things to move to "Sunni neighborhoods" or "Shia neighborhoods." How did this happen?

I read constantly analyses mostly written by foreigners or Iraqis who've been abroad for decades talking about how there was always a divide between Sunnis and Shia in Iraq (which, ironically, only becomes apparent when you're not actually living amongst Iraqis they claim) . . . but how under a dictator, nobody saw it or nobody wanted to see it. That is simply not true—if there was a divide, it was between the fanatics on both ends. The extreme Shia and extreme Sunnis. Most people simply didn't go around making friends or socializing with neighbors based on their sect. People didn't care—you could ask that question, but everyone would look at you like you were silly and rude.

I remember as a child, during a visit, I was playing outside with one of the neighbor's children. Amal was exactly my age—we were even born in the same month, only three days apart. We were laughing at a silly joke and suddenly she turned and asked coyly, "Are you *Sanafir* or *Shanakil?*" I stood there, puzzled. *Sanafir* is the Arabic word for "Smurfs" and *Shanakil* is the Arabic word for "Snorks." I didn't understand why she was asking me if I was a Smurf or a Snork. Apparently, it was an indirect way to ask whether I was Sunni (*Sanafir*) or Shia (*Shanakil*).

"What???" I asked, half smiling. She laughed and asked me whether I prayed with my hands to my sides or folded against my stomach. I shrugged, not very interested and a little bit ashamed to admit that I still didn't really know how to pray properly, at the tender age of 10.

Later that evening, I sat at my aunt's house and remembered to ask my mother whether we were Smurfs or Snorks. She gave me the same blank look I had given Amal. "Mama—do we pray like THIS or like THIS?!" I got up and did both prayer positions. My mother's eyes cleared and she shook her head and rolled her eyes at my aunt, "Why are you asking? Who wants to know?" I explained how Amal, our Shanakil neighbor, had asked me earlier that day. "Well tell Amal we're not Shanakil and we're not Sanafir—we're Muslims—there's no difference."

It was years later before I learned that half the family were *Sanafir*, and the other half were Shanakil, but nobody cared. We didn't sit around during family reunions or family dinners and argue Sunni Islam or Shia Islam. The family didn't care about how this cousin prayed with his hands at his side and that one prayed with her hands folded across her stomach. Many Iraqis of my generation have that attitude. We were brought up to believe that people who discriminated in any way—positively or negatively—based on sect or ethnicity were backward, uneducated and uncivilized.

The thing most worrisome about the situation now, is that discrimination based on sect has become so commonplace. For the average educated Iraqi in Baghdad, there is still scorn for all the Sunni/Shia talk. Sadly though, people are being pushed into claiming to be this or that because political parties are promoting it with every speech and every newspaper—the whole "us"/"them." We read constantly about how "We Sunnis should unite with our Shia brothers . . ." or how "We Shia should forgive our Sunni brothers . . ." (note how us Sunni and Shia sisters don't really fit into either equation at this point). Politicians and religious figures seem to forget at the end of the day that we're all simply Iraqis.

And what role are the occupiers playing in all of this? It's very convenient for them, I believe. It's all very good if Iraqis are abducting and killing each other—then they can be the neutral foreign party trying to promote peace and understanding between people who, up until the occupation, were very peaceful and understanding.

Three years after the war, and we've managed to move backwards in a visible way, and in a not so visible way.

In the last weeks alone, thousands have died in senseless violence and the American and Iraqi army bomb Samarra as I write this. The sad thing isn't the air raid, which is one of hundreds of air raids we've seen in three years—it's the resignation in the people. They sit in their homes in Samarra because there's no where to go. Before, we'd get refugees in Baghdad and surrounding areas . . . Now, Baghdadis themselves are looking for ways out of the city . . . out of the country. The typical Iraqi dream has become to find some safe haven abroad.

Three years later and the nightmares of bombings and of shock and awe have evolved into another sort of nightmare. The difference between now and then was that three years ago, we were still worrying about material things—possessions, houses, cars, electricity, water, fuel . . . It's difficult to define what worries us most now. Even the most cynical war critics couldn't imagine the country being this bad three years after the war . . . "*Allah yistur min il rab3a*" (God protect us from the fourth year). **posted by river @ 3:28 AM**

Tuesday, March 28, 2006

UNCERTAINTY . . .

I sat late last night switching between Iraqi channels (the half dozen or so I sometimes try to watch). It's a late-night tradition for me when there's electricity—to see what the Iraqi channels are showing. Generally speaking, there still isn't a truly "neutral" Iraqi channel. The most popular ones are backed and funded by the different political parties currently vying for power. This became particularly apparent during the period directly before the elections.

I was trying to decide between a report on bird flu on one channel, a montage of bits and pieces from various *latmiyas* on another channel and an Egyptian soap opera on a third channel. I paused on the Sharqiya channel which many Iraqis consider to be a reasonably toned channel (and which during the elections showed its support for Allawi in particular). I was reading the little scrolling news headlines on the bottom of the page. The usual—mortar fire on an area in Baghdad, an American soldier killed here, another one wounded there . . . 12 Iraqi corpses found in an area in Baghdad, etc. Suddenly, one of them caught my attention and I sat up straight on the sofa, wondering if I had read it correctly.

E. was sitting at the other end of the living room, taking apart a radio he later wouldn't be able to put back together. I called him over with the words, "Come here and read this—I'm sure I misunderstood . . ." He stood in front of the television and watched the words about corpses and Americans and puppets scroll by and when the news item I was watching for appeared, I jumped up and pointed. E. and I read it in silence and E. looked as confused as I was feeling.

The line said:

الجيـش دوريـات لاوامر الانصيـاع عدم الـى المـواطنين تـدعو الـدفاع وزارة تلـك فـي العاملـة التحـالف قـوات برفقـة تكـن لـم اذا الليليـة والشـرطة المنطقـة

The translation:

The Ministry of Defense requests that civilians do not comply with the orders of the army or police on nightly patrols unless they are accompanied by coalition forces working in that area.

That's how messed up the country is at this point.

We switched to another channel, the "Baghdad" channel (allied with Muhsin Abdul Hameed and his group) and they had the same news item, but instead of the general "coalition forces" they had "American coalition forces." We checked two other channels. Iraqiya (pro-Da'awa) didn't mention it and Forat (pro-SCIRI) also didn't have it on their news ticker.

We discussed it today as it was repeated on another channel.

"So what does it mean?" My cousin's wife asked as we sat gathered at lunch.

"It means if they come at night and want to raid the house, we don't have to let them in." I answered.

"They're not exactly asking your permission," F. pointed out. "They break the door down and take people away—or have you forgotten?"

"Well according to the Ministry of Defense, we can shoot at them, right? It's trespassing—they can be considered burglars or abductors . . ." I replied.

The cousin shook his head, "If your family is inside the house— you're not going to shoot at them. They come in groups, remember? They come armed and in large groups—shooting at them or resisting them would endanger people inside of the house."

"Besides that, when they first attack, how can you be sure they DON'T have Americans with them?" E. asked.

We sat drinking tea, mulling over the possibilities. It confirmed what has been obvious to Iraqis since the beginning—the Iraqi security forces are actually militias allied to religious and political parties.

But it also brings to light other worrisome issues. The situation is so bad on the security front that the top two ministries in charge of protecting Iraqi civilians cannot trust each other. The Ministry of Defense can't even trust its own personnel, unless they are "accompanied by American coalition forces."

It really is difficult to understand what is happening lately. We hear about talks between Americans and Iran over security in Iraq, and then the American ambassador in Iraq accuses Iran of funding militias inside of the country. Today there are claims that Americans killed between 20 to 30 men from Sadr's militia in an attack on a *Husseiniya* yesterday. The Americans are claiming that responsibility for the attack should be placed on Iraqi security forces (the same security forces they are constantly commending).

All of this directly contradicts claims by Bush and other American politicians that Iraqi troops and security forces are in control of the situation. Or maybe they are in control—just not in a good way.

They've been finding corpses all over Baghdad for weeks now—and it's always the same: holes drilled in the head, multiple shots or strangulation, like the victims were hung. Execution, militia style. Many of the people were taken from their homes by security forces—police or special army brigades . . . Some of them were rounded up from mosques.

A few days ago we went to pick up one of my female cousins from college. Her college happens to be quite close to the local morgue. E., our cousin L., and I all sat in the car which, due to traffic, we parked slightly further away from the college to wait for our other cousin. I looked over at the commotion near the morgue.

There were dozens of people—mostly men—standing around in a bleak group. Some of them smoked cigarettes, others leaned on cars or pick-up trucks . . . Their expressions varied—grief, horror, resignation. On some faces, there was an anxious look of combined dread and anticipation. It's a very specific look, one you will find only outside the Baghdad morgue. The eyes are wide and bloodshot, as if searching for something, the brow is furrowed, the jaw is set and the mouth is a thin frown. It's a look that tells you they are walking into the morgue, where the bodies lay in rows, and that they pray they do not find what they are looking for.

The cousin sighed heavily and told us to open a couple of windows and lock the doors—he was going to check the morgue. A month before, his wife's uncle had been taken away from a mosque during prayer—they've yet to find him. Every two days, someone from the family goes to the morgue to see if his body has been brought in. "Pray I don't find him . . . or rather . . . I just—we hate the uncertainty." My cousin sighed heavily and got out of the car. I said a silent prayer as he crossed the street and disappeared into the crowd.

E. and I waited patiently for H., who was still inside the college and for L. who was in the morgue. The minutes stretched and E. and I sat silently—smalltalk seeming almost blasphemous under the circumstances. L. came out first. I watched him tensely and found myself chewing away at my lower lip, "Did he find him? *Inshalla* he didn't find him . . ." I said to no one in particular. As he got closer to the car, he shook his head. His face was immobile and grim, but behind the grim expression, we could see relief, "He's not there. *Hamdulilah* [Thank God]."

"*Hamdulilah*," E. and I repeated the words in unison.

We all looked back at the morgue. Most of the cars had simple, narrow wooden coffins on top of them, in anticipation of the son or daughter or brother. One frenzied woman in a black *abaya* was struggling to make her way inside, two relatives holding her back. A third man was reaching up to untie the coffin tied to the top of their car.

"See that woman—they found her son. I saw them identifying him. A bullet to the head." The woman continued to struggle, her legs suddenly buckling under her, her wails filling the afternoon, and although it was surprisingly warm that day, I pulled at my sleeves, trying to cover my suddenly cold fingers.

We continued to watch the various scenes of grief, anger, frustration and every once in a while, an almost tangible relief as someone left the morgue having not found what they dreaded most to find—eyes watery from the smell, the step slightly lighter than when they went in, having been given a temporary reprieve from the worry of claiming a loved one from the morgue . . . **posted by river @ 9:51 PM**

CREDITS

Cole, Juan. Excerpts from www.juancole.com. Copyright © 2004. By permission of the author.

"Eyewitness: Smoke and Corpses . . ." excerpts from *BBC News*, http://news.bbc.co.uk. November 11, 2004. Copyright © 2004.

Hamed, M. Personal photographs. Copyright © 2006.

Pink Floyd. "Goodbye Blue Sky." Copyright © 1979. Warner Chappell UK/Roger Walters.

The Feminist Press at the City University of New York is a nonprofit literary and educational institution dedicated to publishing work by and about women. Our existence is grounded in the knowledge that women's writing has often been absent or underrepresented on bookstore and library shelves and in educational curricula—and that such absences contribute, in turn, to the exclusion of women from the literary canon, from the historical record, and from the public discourse.

The Feminist Press was founded in 1970. In its early decades, the Feminist Press launched the contemporary rediscovery of "lost" American women writers, and went on to diversify its list by publishing significant works by American women writers of color. More recently, the Press's publishing program has focused on international women writers, who remain far less likely to be translated than male writers, and on nonfiction works that explore issues affecting the lives

Founded in an activist spirit, the **DATE DUE** initiatives that will bring its books and educational populations, including community colleges, public high schools dle schools, literacy and ESL programs, and prison education progr we move forward into the twenty-first century, we continue to expand work to respond to women's silences wherever they are found.

For a complete catalog of the Press's 250 books, please refer to our web site: www.feministpress.org.